The Emerging
Service Economy

SERVICES WORLD FORUM

SERVICES WORLD FORUM

The role of services in the world economy commands increasing attention among economists, business leaders and policy makers. Yet there exist at present no relevant body of theory, store of information, or independent forum for the exchange of ideas on these issues.

To fill this gap, a SERVICES WORLD FORUM has been established, the purpose of which is to facilitate the exchange of ideas among all those interested in the world services economy, *inter alia* by (1) facilitating intellectual dialogue among its members; (2) publishing a periodical compendium of information and analyses on services in the world economy; and (3) organizing conferences, symposia and similar meetings on services issues.

SERVICES WORLD FORUM is an independent educational and research association. Its purpose is to assist scholars, businessmen, policy-makers, the press and the public by providing objective analyses of national and international issues in services and to promote frank and open discussion of these issues. SERVICES WORLD FORUM is open to anyone wishing to contribute to the aims of the association.

The organs of the association are the Assembly consisting of all members and the Executive Committee.

The address of the association is: Mr. Orio Giarini, 18 chemin Rieu, 1208 Geneva, Switzerland.

Resources of the association consist of membership dues (presently fixed at S.F. 100.—), any untied gifts and bequests it may receive, and all other resources which can result from its activities.

The Emerging Service Economy

Edited by
ORIO GIARINI
FOR THE SERVICES WORLD FORUM, GENEVA

PERGAMON PRESS

OXFORD · NEW YORK · BEIJING · FRANKFURT
SÃO PAULO · SYDNEY · TOKYO · TORONTO

U.K.	Pergamon Press, Headington Hill Hall, Oxford OX3 0BW, England
U.S.A.	Pergamon Press, Maxwell House, Fairview Park, Elmsford, New York 10523, U.S.A.
PEOPLE'S REPUBLIC OF CHINA	Pergamon Press, Qianmen Hotel, Beijing, People's Republic of China
FEDERAL REPUBLIC OF GERMANY	Pergamon Press, Hammerweg 6, D-6242 Kronberg, Federal Republic of Germany
BRAZIL	Pergamon Editora, Rua Eça de Queiros, 346, CEP 04011, São Paulo, Brazil
AUSTRALIA	Pergamon Press Australia, P.O. Box 544, Potts Point, N.S.W. 2011, Australia
JAPAN	Pergamon Press, 8th Floor, Matsuoka Central Building, 1-7-1 Nishishinjuku, Shinjuku-ku, Tokyo 160, Japan
CANADA	Pergamon Press Canada, Suite 104, 150 Consumers Road, Willowdale, Ontario M2J 1P9, Canada

First edition 1987

Library of Congress Cataloging in Publication Data

The Emerging Service Economy.
Includes bibliographical references.
1. Service industries. I. Giarini, Orio.
II. Services World Forum (Association)
HD9980.5.E46 1987   338.4′6   86–25265

British Library Catologuing in Publication Data

Giarini, Orio
The emerging service economy.
1. Service industries
I. Title
338.4   HD9980.5
ISBN 0–08–034270–1

Printed in Great Britain by A. Wheaton & Co. Ltd., Exeter

Foreword

The Service Economy: new strategies for creating the Wealth of Nations

What economics is all about is the creation and distribution of wealth, and the Industrial Revolution — whatever its negative aspects — has been a period of major and historically unique achievements in this direction. The Service Economy is essentially concerned with developing strategies for the creation of wealth, at a time when the connotations of the Industrial Revolution are undergoing profound change.

In 1848, John Stuart Mill wrote in his *Principles of Political Economy* that the economic process was aimed exclusively at producing "utilities fixed and embodied in outward *objects* ".* Services were *per se* of little economic significance, as Adam Smith had already clearly stated in 1776.†

Consequently, the "service" (or "function") rendered by a tool did not need to be contemplated separately. Or, put more simply: an automobile provides a service of transport; but this utility (or economic value) can be considered as embodied in the object produced and actually exchanged in the market.

Similarly, economists will recall Engel's law which says that services (such as insurance) are only purchased once primary needs have been satisfied: they are — at best — goods of a secondary type.

Throughout the Industrial Revolution, the idea that economic utilities are exclusively "embodied in outward objects" has remained deeply rooted, and rightly so: the *priority* was to produce more goods and more tools to increase the wealth of nations. Today, it may be said that this

---

*John Stuart Mill, *Principles of Political Economy*, Routledge and Kegan, London, 1968 (reprint).

†"The labour of some of the most respectable orders . . . churchmen, lawyers, physicians . . . is unproductive of any value", in *The Wealth of Nations*, p. 430, Penguin Books, Middlesex, England, 1977.

assumption still dominates conventional economic thinking, although it has clearly become inadequate in an increasing number of cases.

The evidence is to be found in two fundamental issues: employment and technological development.

In all the world's "industrial" (and "industrializing") countries, service occupations have become dominant and employment in service activities is growing (in the United States it is even soaring). As Gershuny writes in his paper, the most striking development relates to services *within* the manufacturing sectors. This is a consequence, and only a slightly paradoxical one at that, of technological development.

In fact, we can no longer say today, as did John Stuart Mill, that the utility of a machine is embodied in the machine alone: a computer, for instance, before it can start to provide any utility, first needs the input of programmers and of a certain knowledge on the part of its users.

A simple hammer can be easily used and its mere existence can be said to embody the possibility of its utilization. Modern technologies, however, require the input of an increasing number of services in order to be of any use; moreover, since the 1930s, research and development have become quite distinct factors in the leap up to the invention, production and distribution of a new product. Probably the most conspicuous aspect of the Service Economy is the variety of services that have become essential production inputs, and which represent a quantitative and a qualitative jump from the previous Industrial Revolution. Services are not distinct from and should not be opposed to industrial products, as Dorothy Riddle clearly points out in her article. They are intricately integrated in and interrelated with the manufacturing productive processes. The reason why it is preferable to speak of a "Service Economy", rather than of an "Industrial" ("Post-industrial" or "Superindustrial") Economy, is that over 50% of production costs or over 50% of jobs involved are of a service nature. The problem is not just a question of definition; using the term "Service Economy" opens the way to a better insight into the way that wealth is created in today's economy. The studies by Juan Rada on Information Technology, and by Raymond Krommenacker on Space-Generated Services, are a clear case in point.

The Service Economy does, of course, also include certain more conventional service activities such as Tourism and Insurance, dealt with in the studies by Christine Richter and Anthony Baker. However, these services have acquired fundamentally new connotations and new economic significance in the contemporary Service Economy. Tourism is a complex activity bringing together the most varied and advanced technological innovations in areas ranging from booking, transportation and payment systems, to construction, entertainment and educational activities. Insurance is an increasingly important tool in managing the vulnerabilities of complex modern economic systems: insurability is often a criterion, or even a condition, for investment. As such, it is clearly a "production input".

The ultimate consequence of technological progress is the decisive contribution it can make to world interdependence: the Service Economy is a global "Worldeconomy". Its complexity, and the adaptability and flexibility of its tools, offers a tremendous opportunity to combine and stimulate the diversities of our planet Earth. Traditional industrial production, up to about 20 years ago, seemed to be moving towards increasingly dense concentration in an ever smaller number of selected centres. In the Service Economy, users increasingly form part of the "production" systems: they need to understand and operate complex systems applications, organize maintenance systems, and carry out repairs and recycling. They have become part of the production-utilization system which, in turn, needs their active contribution and participation. No longer are they, or can they be, "passive" consumers. No longer do they buy products where the utility or value is "embodied" in the object. Instead they have to make an effort to "extract" the utilization value from the products.

The Service Economy tends therefore to become a key factor in world trade development and world economic organization. It is only natural that this book should be opened by the article by Jagdish Bhagwati, accompanied by the contributions of a series of commentators, dealing, as it does, with the significance of services for economic development, the problems involved in international trade, and a number of fundamental questions about services and developing countries. John Richardson rounds off his analysis and offers the reader the insight of his European experience on this matter.

Finally, the last part of this first "Services Worldeconomy Series", besides containing basic information and a bibliography, makes a major contribution to the measurement of service activities — an arduous task which is likely to keep economists and statisticians busy for several years and which probably, in the end, will need to redefine the concept of economic value or — at least — some of its components.

As Alfred Marshall puts it in his *Principles of Economics*, "If the subject matter of a science passes through different stages of development, the laws which apply to one stage will seldom apply without modifications to others." This might well be the case for the "Service Economy".

ORIO GIARINI
President 1986
Services World Forum

Preface

This first issue of SERVICES WORLDECONOMY SERIES bears witness to the extraordinary vitality of contemporary economic thinking on an issue which has a long history of neglect by economists and policy-makers. Like Monsieur Jourdain in Molière's *Le Bourgeois Gentilhomme*, who discovered to his stupefaction and delight that he had been speaking prose all his life without knowing it, observers of the modern economic scene are suddenly discovering the omnipresence and the crucial rôle of services in all fields of production as well as in consumption. The reasons for this changeabout are not clear. Almost half a century ago, Allan Fischer and Colin Clark drew attention to the growing importance of services in their three-sector model of economic development, but no one paid much heed to these "residual" activities in the ensuing decades. It is perhaps the oil shock of 1973 which is at the origin of the new interest being shown in services, as it is of so many other changes in economic life. The stranglehold of oil producers could only be loosened by rapid advances in technology, and these in turn could only be obtained by a more systematic quest for efficiency and innovation in research, product engineering, management, finance, transport, distribution and consumption: all areas where progress depended on the applied knowledge and technical know-how of economic agents hitherto considered as more or less "unproductive" because they were not directly involved in making things.

Be that as it may, it has become increasingly apparent that without a better understanding of the dynamics and operating modes of services, either in national economies or internationally, it would not be possible to foresee the direction of changes in modern societies or to devise appropriate government policies to respond to such changes. Because the subject matter is still new, and only a handful of researchers working in relative isolation have devoted time and effort to studying it, a group of them has taken the initiative to establish a contact point in the guise of an independent, non-profit association called SERVICES WORLD FORUM, founded in October 1985. The FORUM is open to anyone in the world wishing to contribute to the objective analysis of national and international issues in services and to the promotion of frank and open dialogue on these issues. The aims of the FORUM are to gather and disseminate information on research on services and to organize seminars, symposia and similar gatherings on the subject. The SERVICES WORLD-

ECONOMY SERIES is the first published work resulting from the FORUM's activity. It will be followed by others.

In issuing this publication, the FORUM is also drawing public attention to a new concept, namely that of "worldeconomy". The paternity for this fusion of two ideas, one relating to human productive activity and the other to the geographical scope of this activity, is shared by at least two authors* and the FORUM has no claim to originality in this respect. However, its relevance to services is obvious in that they and the technology contained in them exercise considerable leverage on the process of creating a single global market for products of all kinds, hence a single integrated "worldeconomy". This outlook on present and future economic development adds a new dimension to the concept of interdependence, and it is to the analysis and discussion of this new dimension that the FORUM and the SERIES are devoted.

Our hope is that this SERIES will meet its target of encouraging the exchange of ideas on the subject of services, and that it will be found a useful tool by all those in the private sector and in government who are dealing with the issues in this area.

Jacques Nusbaumer
Vice-President 1986
SERVICES WORLD FORUM

---

*Immanuel Wallerstein may have been the first to introduce it in *Capitalism and the Worldeconomy, 1450–1640*, and Albert Bressand was probably the first to apply it to services in "Mastering the Worldeconomy", *Foreign Affairs*, Spring 1983.

Contents

PART 1
The Economics of Services

1

International Trade in Services and its Relevance for Economic Development*

JAGDISH BHAGWATI
Arthur Lehman Professor of Economics, Columbia University

Economics, as we all know to our regret if we are wedded to conventional wisdom and to our reward if we wish to write our next *magnum opus,* has a habit of being overtaken by reality. This is nowhere more true than in the area of services.

Until only a decade ago, economists tended to equate services with "nontraded goods". Doubtless, they were aware that occasionally a country's nationals bought foreign insurance policies or shipped goods in foreign bottoms. Indeed, if nothing else, their increased jetsetting to exotic lands to attend conferences and deliver lectures would have seemed to remind them of the possible tradeability of skilled services. A sophisticated economist should certainly have therefore noticed that the wholesale equating of services with nontraded goods was not quite consistent with reality.

But the weight of tradition continued to favour the older perception which might be best described as the "haircuts view" of services. Haircuts, universally considered as a service, typically cannot be had long distance, at least as of now. They have therefore been a classic example of how and why services are nontraded. Though, having procrastinated on getting a haircut this summer and gotten a cheaper one in consequence in India, I must say that even this example frays a little at the margin. But what this mainly proves is that few rules are totally unimpregnable. I must recall the embarrassing moment for Noam Chomsky, the celebrated linguist, who

---

*Xth Annual Lecture of the Geneva Association at the London School of Economics and at the Graduate Institute of International Studies, Geneva. This revised text of the lecture has benefited from comments by the invited discussants, Professors Henryk Kierzkowski, Victor Norman, Andre Sapir and Jean Waelbroeck, as also from suggestions made by Brian Hindley, Ronald Findlay, Sunil Gulati and Manuel Sebastiao.

3

asserted in a public lecture that, in every human language, two negatives make a positive but two positives do not make a negative only to have my good friend, the philosopher Sidney Morgenbesser, shout from the back of the room in rich Yiddish: "Yeah, yeah?"

Of course, today services are increasingly traded. International rules and regimes for overseeing and facilitating such trade have become increasingly the focal point of concern in international negotiations. Continuing equation of services with nontraded goods would appear therefore to be a travesty.

Nonetheless, it is useful, as a point of departure for my main theme today, to reflect more closely on why services have been traditionally regarded as synonymous with nontraded goods. Such an exercise serves to throw light on the reasons why trade in services, as distinct from goods, poses new and difficult problems. I shall take this opportunity also to digress at the outset on the empirical and theoretical puzzles and problems that preoccupied economists when they thought of services as nontraded goods, turning later to the shifting concerns that arise now that services are considered tradeable instead.

1. Characteristics of Services

In our classrooms, we typically write traditional utility functions as defined on the availability of "goods and services", conveying to the students that there is a difference between the two while, of course, proceeding to analyse the problems at hand as if there was none. The attempt at distinguishing between the two, along the lines of the Classical economists, who sought correspondingly to contrast "productive" and "unproductive" labour, has long disappeared from the modern scene. It has survived only in the national accounts of the socialist countries, which persist in excluding from national income the component of what we would call today "final demand" services.

On the other hand, our national income accounts, both in their sectoral composition of value-added as also in the sectoral breakdown of final expenditures in GDP, continue to draw upon the distinction between goods and services. The latter total, in focusing only on final expenditure, excludes the producer or intermediate services that enter the production process. Again, the IMF balance of payments procedures distinguish services as invisibles in the current account and proceed to differentiate factor services from non-factor services, and the former in turn from remittances which are instead categorized as transfers. The latter practice is in consonance with James Meade's prescription in his classic work on *The Balance of Payments*, based on the theory that what people (as distinct from foreign investment) produce abroad is part of the *foreign* national income and hence a remittance therefrom is a transfer, an assumption that sits wholly ill at ease with much modern international migration that consists simply of relocation without change in nationality.

How do services, so defined and measured in accounts which economists devise and constantly use, differ conceptually from goods? A glance at the sectors that are categorized as services is suggestive. Hotels and restaurants, education, medical services, communication, insurance, government, barber and beauty shops: these are among the common listings under the umbrella of services. What do they have in common that would legitimate the practice of setting them apart from "goods"?

Several attempts at defining the unique characteristics of services have been made. Among the least appealing is the criterion that services have a relatively low value of commodities embodied in them as intermediate inputs. Aside from the fact that this fails to provide an endogenous cut-off point in the continuum of goods and services, it is also a criterion that would exclude sectors such as retailing from categorization as services since the goods retailed must surely be treated as intermediates and are often a high proportion of retail sales.

I believe that Professor Hill, who has addressed the question splendidly in a classic paper in 1977, offers interesting observations on the matter. Thus, he remarks that:

> "The production of a service cannot generally be distinguished from that of a good by means of the technology used but by the fact that the producer unit operates directly on goods which already belong to the consumer of the service." (1977, p. 319)

> "Services are consumed as they are produced in the sense that the change in the condition of the consumer unit must occur simultaneously with the production of that

---

*Cf. Meade (1963): ". . . the clue to the logical and formal consistency of what we have done is to be found in the definition of the national income. Is the interest on A's capital invested in B part of A's or B's national income? And are the emigrants' remittances from B to A part of A's or of B's national income? There must be international consistency on this point. These items must be treated as either A's or B's income; they must not be treated as the income of both or of neither. We have treated the interest payment to A as an invisible export by A, because we shall treat the interest on this capital as part of A's national income and not as part of B's national income. If this is done, the receipt of a larger interest on A's foreign investment in B will represent an increase in A's national income; and the payment to A must be treated as a return for an export from A, since A's net visible and invisible exports to B are meant to represent all those payments by residents of B to residents of A which directly generate national income in A.

Emigrants' remittances from B to A we have, on the other hand, treated as part of B's national income and not as part of A's national income. That is to say, when an individual in B transfers $100 m. to an individual in A we have not represented that as a fall in B's and a rise in A's national income, but as a transfer out of a given national income in B to supplement the purchasing power obtained from a given national income in A. For this reason the transaction must be treated as a transfer and not an item of invisible trade; it does not directly generate income in A."

change by the producer: they are one, and the same change . . . the fact that services must be acquired by consumers as they are produced means that they cannot be put into stock *by producers.*" (1977, p. 337; italics inserted).

These descriptions or criteria immediately suggest exceptions. Thus, Peking Duck cooked, served and eaten in a Chinese restaurant is not altogether non-storable by producers: many of us have suffered from being served leftovers from the freezer at restaurants we do not care to visit again. Yet, by and large, it is true that restaurants do service us in the sense that Professor Hill describes: our use of the service occurs practically simultaneously with its provision by the producer of the service. Again, messages are now storable and indeed stored by "answering services", thus violating the letter again of the definition that suggests that services are non-storable because they are used as they are provided.

But I would say that the equation of services with nonstorability, resulting from the simultaneity of provision and use thereof, is a useful and generally sensible criterion. Its utility consists in the fact that, as I shall argue presently, this characteristic bears critically on the issues that the question of tradeability of services raises for theory and for trade policy.

The *other* characteristic of services which Professor Hill's discussion pinpoints is the fact that services occur *between* different economic agents. This, of course, immediately implies that the definition of services reflects economic organization or "market structure". The simple act of having Mr. Smith paint your goods in the assembly line by hiring him from another firm rather than by employing him directly will shift his contribution to national value added from being a good to being a service. This leads to the familiar "in-house out-house" conundrum that has plagued all analysts of questions such as the share of services in national income by sector of origin.

The popular conception that services are nontraded derives critically from the first of these two characteristics. If services must be used as they are produced, then a pertinent observation follows: there must be necessary *interaction* between the user and the provider of the service. A producer of goods, by contrast, can produce but store and generally transact with users at any subsequent time.

But this interaction, in turn, implies that we can contemplate two essential categories of services: *first*, those that necessarily require the physical proximity of the user and the provider; and *second*, those that do not, though such physical proximity may indeed be useful. I drew this important distinction sharply in my recent article in *The World Economy* (1984, p. 101):

"Basically one has to draw a distinction between services as embodied in the supplier of the services and requiring their physical presence where the user happens to be and services which can be disembodied from the supplier and provided without a physical presence being necessary."*

A. Physical Proximity Essential

The class of services where physical proximity is essential is again usefully thought of as consisting of three categories:

Category 1. *Mobile-Provider, Immobile-User:* There is an extraordinarily important class of services which *requires* that the provider go to the user, where the reverse mobility is simply impossible. When the M-6 was being built, and an Indian or South Korean construction firm was bidding for the contract, the designs and skilled inputs could perhaps be provided from home base. But the labour services simply could not have been provided except by moving Indian or South Korean labour to England where the motorway was to be built. Supplies of brute, Ricardian – style, basic labour services must be relocated where the user is, exactly as we have seen in the Middle-East during the 1970s and indeed the way your ancestors took mine to East Africa to build the railways there several decades ago.

Category 2. *Mobile-User, Immobile-Provider:* Next, there is another important class of services where the user must move to the provider because there is really no way to do it the other way around. Thus, open-heart surgery simply cannot be done in Zaire because, even though Dr. Cooley can go from Houston to Kinshasa, there is no way the necessary support and hospital care can be duplicated or even approximated. Again, President Houphonet Boigny cannot enjoy French cuisine in the elegance of Maxim's in Abidjan but must travel to Paris to so indulge himself. And I cannot shop in the English ambiance of Harrods except when I am in London. In this class of services, the location — specificity of the provider arises from the fact that the service provided is a vector of characteristics

---

*In my 1984 paper, I then proceeded to discuss the *latter* class of services which I had distinguished, discussing how the "disembodiment" effect can, in effect, frustrate the intention of immigration restrictions on skilled labour and also what implication followed for the comparative advantage of the developing countries in services. (Later in this Lecture, I christen this class of services as "long-distance" services.) On the other hand, Dr. Gary Sampson and Professor Richard Snape (1985), have drawn on this twofold distinction in my 1984 article to explore further the *former* class of services, where physical proximity of the provider and the user is involved, with an important taxonomy aimed at trade negotiations. By contrast, I offer here a simplified taxonomy where I focus more sharply on the aspect of the physical proximity being *required* for service transactions and, more importantly therefore, also on the conceptual implication concerning the traditional distinction between "factor-services" and "non-factor services". The latter, in turn, implies that we must model trade and factor-relocation across countries in critically related ways that are different from traditional trade-theoretic models: a task that my Columbia students, Sunil Gulati and Manuel Sebastiao, have already embarked upon.

where some key elements are simply not transferable geographically to the user's location, whereas in the preceding category this location specificity applied instead to the user of the service.

Category 3. *Mobile User and Mobile-Provider:* Finally, there is a range of services where mobility is symmetrically possible. Hair-cuts, tailored suits, lectures, *et al.* are in principle transmittable between user and provider in either's location, the only difference being the cost of so doing.

B.   Physical Proximity Inessential: The "Long-Distance" Services

But then there is also the second broad class of services where, while physical proximity between providers and users may be useful, it is not strictly speaking necessary.

There are basically what we should christen "long-distance" services, in the sense that transactions do not require the immediacy of geographical proximity. Traditional banking and insurance services fall into this category, I should imagine, because loans could be secured by mail or telephonic transactions, and insurance policies are indeed often so purchased. Again, retailing of the Sears-Roebuck stores variety, where one orders by catalogue, is an example which fits the "long-distance" pattern whereas retailing in my Harrods example is not.

I shall return to these distinctions below. But it is immediately evident, from reflecting on them, why services have tended to be internationally nontraded to date.

For the predominant class of services which require physical proximity, it is evident that the cost of the necessary mobility has often made it prohibitive for trade to occur, thus shifting such services into the ranks of nontraded activities internationally. And, in cases where such costs may not have been prohibitive, restrictions on the mobility of labour across countries have served to inhibit service transactions that required the provider to get to the user of the services. These restrictions have traditionally tended to apply to unskilled labour services rather more stringently than to skilled services. However, regulatory provisions by professional guilds, often indulging in what we call today directly-unproductive profit-seeking (DUP) behaviour aimed at earning rents from resulting protection, have also served to curtail such mobility by professionals from other nations, restricting therefore the provision of such services to the vastly narrower scale necessitated by the movement of the user to the producer instead.

I shall argue below that technical change, construed in a broad sense, is now changing this situation in ways that have tended to bring ever more services into the tradeable category, as when the need for physical proximity between user and producer is eliminated and the service can be rendered "long-distance". Immediately, however, let me turn to the issues that economists have addressed as they equated services by and large with nontraded goods.

2. Empirical Regularities and Service Characteristics

The revival of interest in services can be traced back at least to Friedrich List, who was interested in the evolution of growing economies through three stages culminating in the "commerce"-inclusive stage characterized by a significant share of the service sector in production and in consumption.[*] However, for the Anglo-Saxon economists in the mainstream of economic science, the economists who are commonly associated with the notion of stages are Allan Fisher and Colin Clark.

Writing from the 1930s through 1940s, these two pioneers proposed that it was fruitful to distinguish among the primary, secondary and tertiary sectors in the economy. But they did not agree on the precise definition of the tertiary sector, though Clark manifestly included with it what we would today call services. Colin Clark's practice was to include in this omnibus category "all forms of economic activity not included under primary and secondary",[†] thus defining the sector to include transport and communication, commerce and finance, professional workers and those engaged in public administration, entertainment and sport, personal and domestic service. [Construction was added to the group in some instances.][‡]

From these and subsequent writings, economists have inherited an interest in analysing several "stylized" facts and predictions concerning services as they interact with economic development. Principal among these have been two relationships: *first* the real (or relative) price of services as economies get richer; and *second,* the share of services in national income, by sector-of-origin and by final expenditure. Let me treat each, in turn, drawing on the analysis of the two key characteristics of services that I have discussed already.

---

[*]See the interesting historical discussion in Professor Henryk Kierzkowski's (1984) insightful, recent paper.
[†]This is cited in Allan G. B. Fisher (1939, p. 36); it is in turn extracted from Clark's 1938 Joseph Fisher Lecture.
[‡]By contrast, Fisher seems exceptionally confusing in his approach to the definition of the tertiary sector. Thus, he states in a remarkable passage (1939, p. 32) that " . . . tertiary production is concerned with every new or relatively new type of consumers' demand, the production and distribution of which is made possible by improvements in technical efficiency, which release resources hitherto required for primary or secondary production"! Then he adds, in a footnote, that "The production of radio sets, which was clearly a tertiary activity in, say, 1924, should perhaps today be regarded as secondary"! Then again, later (p. 33) he argues that services for final demand clearly belong to the tertiary sector but then wants to withdraw that epithet from services which are "merely ancillary to primary or secondary production", possibly excluding therefore "transport and retail trading"!

A. The Real Price of Services

Colin Clark had already argued in *The Conditions of Economic Progress* that his trend data showed a secular rise in the price of services relative to manufactures.

Since per capita incomes tend to rise with time, it would be natural to infer that growth of per capita income would also show, in cross-section data, that services were cheaper in the poor countries. I suspect that, if adjustment for quality was systematically made, the Colin Clark result would be only reinforced. For, manufactures have continually improved in quality: a fact which, when ignored, contributed to the erroneous inference at one time that the terms of trade of the primary-product-exporting developing countries had secularly declined. At the same time, the quality of many services has tended to decline over time. How many of you are aware, in 19th century London, there were twelve mail deliveries per day, including Saturday, and one delivery on Sunday? If you had the misfortune to live in New York, you would also have been witness to a decline in the mail service to the point where the regular 22 cents letter can take anywhere up to a week to reach Wall Street downtown from Columbia University uptown, the Special Delivery charge of $2.95 simply assures you that as and when your letter reaches downtown it will be promptly delivered, and an overnight Express Mail rate of $9.95 is now necessary to resurrect the next-day delivery that was routinely the practice at the lowest rate only a few years ago.

You may legitimately wonder that this is all casual empiricism and anecdotal economics. Though, let me remind you that the Law of Gravity and arguably also Relativity theory were born of casual empiricism. And, as for the value of anecdotal economics, I must recall the Oxford seminar run by the late Lord Balogh, my teacher, colleague and friend, where Professor Charles Kindleberger of MIT was lecturing only to have Balogh reject each of his empirical propositions by saying that it was not true for Algeria where he was advising President Ben Bella or for India where he had just been visiting Prime Minister Nehru. Frustrated, Kindleberger declared: no more anecdotal economics. Balogh sat quietly, biding his time until Kindleberger told a story. When Balogh jumped to his feet, expostulating that the story was anecdotal economics and hence inadmissable, Kindleberger swiftly retorted: "But Tommy, I read it in a book, that makes it scholarship!"

As it happens, careful and painstaking research, for which our profession is greatly indebted to Professors Irving Kravis, Alan Heston and Robert Summers, has provided systematic cross-sectional evidence supporting their proposition that increasing per capita income is associated with a rising real price of services. The source of this KHS finding is their monumental work on comparative price structures and their implications for international comparisons of national incomes. Extending to 34 countries, for 1975, and aggregated by six per capita GNP groups, their data show that the price of services, relative either to the GDP deflator or to commodity price, generally rises with per capita GDP: as indicated in Fig. 1.

This phenomenon has attracted the theorists among us, who have focussed on the nontradedness of services, to produce a variety of alternative explanations, all of which probably are pertinent simultaneously in varying degrees in explaining the empirical regularity at hand. I should like to distinguish among three principal explanations, all drawing on rather different ways of exploiting the theory of general equilibrium but each resting squarely on the fact that services are nontraded so that their prices do not tend to be equalized across countries through trade.

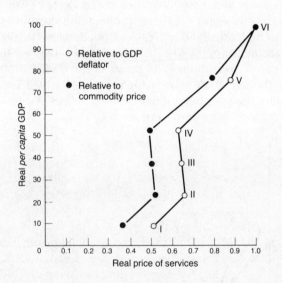

FIG. 1. Relative price of services and per capita GDP for six country groups, 1975

Explanation 1: International Productivity Differentials

One explanation, originally developed systematically by Professors Bela Balassa (1964) and Paul Samuelson (1964), and advocated by KHS (Kravis, Heston, Summers) subsequently, relies on the contention that wages reflect productivity in the traded goods sector; that rich countries have comparatively greater productivity in the traded sectors: that the traded goods prices being by and large equalized through trade the wages would be higher in the rich countries due to the higher productivity; and hence, with nontraded goods and services being characterized by much smaller productivity differentials if any, the unit cost of supplying services would be higher in the rich countries.

Although these distinguished economists worked essentially with single-factor Ricardian models to advance this explanation, it is easy to extend the argument to a less restrictive general-equilibrium model. Thus, consider Fig. 2 (a) where I illustrate the argument for a standard model with the following structure: 2 tradeables, 2 primary factors Capital (K) and Labour (L), and one service sector which is nontraded. [The argument I presently advance is immediately extended to the case where the 2×2 tradeable-cum-primary-factors structure is replaced by an $n \times n$ structure, and where the number of services is multiplied at will.] The suffixes R and P refer to the Rich and Poor countries respectively. With customary restrictions on constant-returns-to-scale production functions in all activities, the wage-rental price-line, ω, can be put tangent in Fig. 2 to the corresponding isoquants in the usual Lerner fashion, showing then in turn the associated goods price-ratio. With prices of the traded goods X and Y equalized fully through trade, the factor price-ratio ω will imply then in Fig. 2(a) a traded goods price-ratio which exchanges $\bar{X}_P$ for $\bar{Y}_P$ in the Poor country, each exchanging in turn for $\bar{S}_P$.

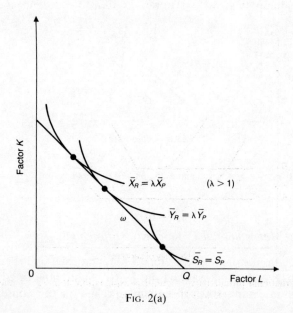

Fig. 2(a)

If then the Rich country is uniformly more productive in the two traded sector, this advantage being measured by scale factor $\lambda(>1)$, the same argument will imply that $\lambda \bar{X}_P$ will exchange for $\lambda \bar{Y}_P$ in the Rich country, each exchanging in turn for $\bar{S}_P$ ($= \bar{S}_R$ since there is no productivity differential between the Rich and the Poor countries in the service sector). It immediately follows that services will be λ-times more expensive in the Rich country.

Figure 2(b) retells you, in the more familiar Marshallian diagram in general equilibrium, focusing on the service sector equilibrium, what is happening. The supply curve for services $S(T_P) \mid_{\bar{E}}$ is for the Poor country, with its tradeable-goods technology (T) and endowments (E). It is perfectly elastic (as long as we remain within the diversification cone, defined by ω). When we shift to the Rich country, the supply curve remains flat but moves up to $S(T_R) \mid_{\bar{E}}$: tradeables are more productive but endowment is unchanged. The real *price* of services moves up from OA to OB. The *quantity* of services produced and transacted is all that demand determines. Figure 2(b) shows the demand curve shifting upward as income per capita rises. It also shows the quantity transacted in the Rich country increasing; but the quantity could well have fallen (absolutely) despite the increase in demand.

The Balassa-Samuelson-KHS explanation relies on two critical assumptions: *first,* that productivity rises less rapidly in services (and nontraded goods); and *second,* that it does not diffuse rapidly across countries. Both assumptions have something to be said for them. In regard to the postulate of stagnant productivity growth in the service industry, the recent evidence

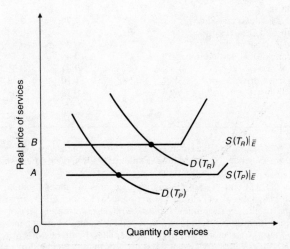

FIG. 2(b). International productivity differentials explanation: Balassa, Samuelson, Kravis-Heston-Summers

corroborates the casual impression that, while most services are characterized by stagnation, some are highly innovative, Thus, analysing data for the US economy for 1947–76 (Table 1), Professors Baumol, Blackman and Wolff (1985) have reported that, by various alternative measures, services indeed are generally unprogressive, a strong exception being communications and broadcasting and somewhat weaker ones being trade and (surprisingly) real estate.

TABLE 1. *Average Annual Rate of Productivity Growth by Sector, 1947–76*

Industry	GPO/L (1)	GDO/L (2)	ρ (3)	λ (4)
		Measure		
1. Agriculture	3.59	4.47	1.56	3.95
2. Mining	2.70	2.76	0.08	1.38
3. Construction	1.66	1.19	−0.34	1.49
4. Manufacturing-Durables	2.52	2.80	0.58	3.08
5. Manufacturing-Nondurables	3.21	3.23	0.41	2.56
6. Transportation and Warehousing	1.74	2.74	0.68	2.42
7. Communication and Broadcasting	5.42	5.50	3.99	5.21
8. Utilities	4.96	4.77	1.53	2.96
9. Trade		2.17	1.09	2.19
a. Wholesale Trade	2.37			
b. Retail Trade	1.99			
10. Finance and Insurance	0.50	0.31	−0.27	0.57
11. Real Estate	2.72	3.10	1.21	4.86
12. General Services	0.93			
a. Hotels, Personal and Repair (except auto)		1.37	−0.31	1.35
b. Business and Professional Services		1.70	0.83	2.30
c. Auto Repair and Services		1.45	−0.84	1.04
d. Movies and Amusements		0.99	−0.56	0.64
e. Medical, Educational and Nonprofit		−0.46	−1.14	−0.19
f. Household Workers		−0.21	−0.21	−0.21
13. Government Enterprises	−0.51	1.10	−0.52	0.99
14. Government Industry	0.31	−0.18	0.08	−0.18
Overall: *GDP*	2.16			
GNP		2.18	1.17	2.18

Source: Baumol, W. J., S. A. B. Blackman and E. N. Wolff, "Unbalanced Growth Revisited: Asymptotic Stagnancy and New Evidence", *American Economic Review,* September 1985, pp. 806–817, Table 1.

Notes: Measures (1), (2) and (4) are alternative measures of labour productivity change, involving calculations of annual (compounded) rates. GPO is gross product originating in the corresponding sector, with L representing persons employed; GDO is gross domestic output in constant dollars, an input-output concept, equalling the gross value of a sector's output or sales deflated by the sector's price deflator. λ is also a labour productivity measure but takes both direct and indirect labour inputs into account. ρ is the closest to a proper measure of productivity, being a *total*-factor-productivity measure. For details, see Baumol, Blackman and Wolff (1985).

Explanation 2: Factor Endowments

I have recently advanced (1984) however an alternative explanation that altogether eschews productivity differentials across countries and instead builds rigorously on the notion that factor endowments make labour cheaper in the poor country and that this makes services cheaper in turn since they are labour-intensive.

One advantage of this explanation is that it also can be shown to explain several other phenomena such as the Kuznets-Chenery-Syrquin finding for the period 1950–70 that the (labour) productivity of the service sector relative to the goods sector tends to be inversely related to the per capita income level of the country. It also has the advantage of symmetrically explaining why *some* services may, in fact, be more expensive in the poor countries: this may be simply because they are capital-intensive rather than labour-intensive. Thus, capital-intensity rather than nonprogressivity can explain why telephone communications are expensive in Poor compared to Rich countries. Indeed, if one adjusts for the quality of the service, they are wildly more expensive as a visit to Cairo or New Delhi from London or New York will underscore. In fact, I tell my students that one excellent way to tell apart the underdeveloped from the developed countries is by looking at their phone systems: in the underdeveloped countries, you go crazy making phone calls; in the developed countries, receiving them!

How does this explanation proceed analytically? Consider the same basic model as in Fig. 2(a). But now assume, as in Fig. 3(a) that the Rich and Poor countries have identical production functions in each sector: productivity differences are thus assumed to be non-existent. Let ω_R be the wage-rental ratio obtaining in the Rich country, implying that $\bar{X}_R$ exchanges for $\bar{Y}_R$ for $\bar{S}_R$.

If, however, the Poor country were to have this wage-rental ratio, its overall endowment ratio $(\bar{K}/\bar{L})_P$ for all employment would have to be spanned by OA and OC, with AOC (not drawn) constituting the McKenzie-Chipman diversification cone. But if, as in Fig. 3(a), $(\bar{K}/\bar{L})_P$ lies outside this diversification cone, ω_R is not feasible and the Poor country, being so abundantly endowed with labour, would have to have a *lower* wage-rental ratio such as ω_P. The consequence is that production of X is no longer possible at the goods price ratio $\bar{X}_R = \bar{Y}_R$ given from the Rich country, whereas $\bar{Y}_P$ ($=\bar{Y}_R$) will now exchange, *not* for $\bar{S}_P$ but for $\tilde{S}_P$, the choice of K/L ratios being OE and OD respectively in the Poor country. The new diversification cone defined by EOD, of course, spans $(\bar{K}/\bar{L})_P$. This immediately means that the relative price of services is cheaper in the Poor country, since $\tilde{S}_P > \bar{S}_P$.

Again, the factor-endowments explanation can be illuminated in the Marshallian diagram in Fig. 3(b). The supply curves are again totally

16   J. Bhagwati

elastic, but move up vertically for the Rich country with higher per capita
income due to higher capital relative to labour (E) while the productivity
or technology (T) is commonly shared. Further, this upward shift implies
that the real price of services is higher, though the quantity produced and
transacted will reflect the demand factor exactly as in the differential-
productivity explanation.

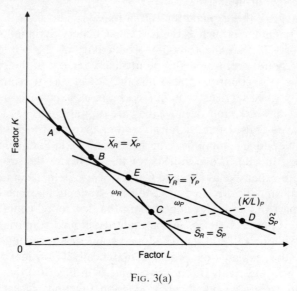

FIG. 3(a)

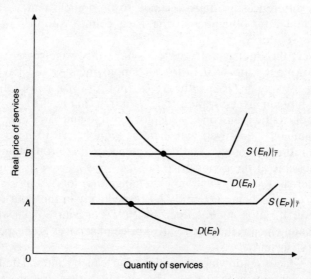

FIG. 3(b). Factor endowments explanation: Bhagwati, Kravis-Lipsey

Explanation 3:

An alternative argumentation has been presented recently by Professors Christopher Clague (1985) and Aravind Panagariya (1985), building on the specific-factors model. Let me present here just the essence of it. If the two traded sectors are modelled to use mobile labour but specific capitals, and the service sector is assumed to use only labour, it is immediately obvious that, for any given technology and endowments, the supply curve of services will be upward-sloping, unlike in the previous two models I just presented. Thus increased services can be produced only by drawing more labour away from the traded activities and, given diminishing returns due

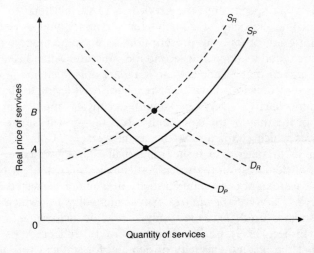

FIG. 4 Rising supply price: Clague, Panagariya

to the specific capitals there, release of labour for services can only take place at increasing marginal cost. If the Rich country then has more income per capita because it has more specific capital in the traded sectors or has neutral technical advantage there, the supply curve of the Rich country will be to the left of that for the Poor country. On the other hand, the Rich country should have, for normal goods, its demand curve for services shift to the right of that for the Poor country. As the dotted curves show, the Rich country will then have a higher real price for services.*

---

*Panagariya (1985) adds an interesting wrinkle to this model by allowing for economies of scale to operate in one of the traded sectors in this sector-specific model. In consequence, even if the Rich country is simply a *blown-up* version of the Poor country in its endowments (i.e. proportionately more of every factor) and has identical knowhow so that under constant-returns-to-scale and homothetic tastes, it could not have a higher per capita income, Panagariya can generate a higher service price plus a higher per capita income for the Rich country.

B. Service Share in National Income

All these formal explanations build, among other postulates, on the assumed basic property of services: that they tend to be nontraded. In turn, this conceptualization has a bearing on the other question of the shares of different sectors in national income that I distinguished earlier.

For, if services are largely nontraded, their income share would tend to be dominated by demand factors: the demand for nontraded items cannot *ipso facto* be satisfied by producing traded goods and exchanging them for the nontraded services that you wish to use. It follows that the thinking on shares has heavily reflected presuppositions concerning income elasticities of demand. More specifically, the service sector would tend to increase since the income elasticity of demand for services would exceed unity. Thus, equating prediction with prescription, as do some modern students of development and its impact on economic structure, Allan Fisher (1933, pp. 380–1) argued that "when certain standards of efficiency in primary and secondary production have been reached, it is desirable that Adam Smith's "unproductive" services should occupy a rapidly increasing proportion of the time of the community. It is the growing importance of these services which characterizes the tertiary stage." Colin Clark even went so far as to suggest to Fisher, in private correspondence, that "a precise line of demarcation [between goods and services] might be based upon the measurement of income elasticity of demand suggested in Allen and Bowley's *Family Expenditure*. Any commodity for which income elasticity, so measured, exceeded unity could be *defined* as a tertiary product"! (Fisher, 1939, p. 34; italics inserted). Indeed, it is safe to conclude that the income elasticity of demand for services was generally regarded as high.

Implicitly, however, this line of argument ignored the possibility that development could raise the real cost of supplying nontraded services, and thus reduce the output of services or at least their relative share in value added despite high income elasticities of demand for them. Thus, in all the three models I presented above the rising real price of nontraded services implies that, *ceteris paribus*, quantities transacted would fall if the demand curve was normally downward-sloping. As it happens, the economists who have followed Fisher and Clark have noted extreme intances of this effect: where specific services have been priced out by rising real prices thereof. Domestic servants are a prime example of this phenomenon; and I have often thought that the complaints of housewives that servants are getting harder to find and expensive to hire are one of the surest indexes of successful development! I might also add that life is further complicated for the Fisher-Clark thesis because it is not evident that all final-demand services would have high income elasticities of demand.

But the fact that there are also many *producer* services, which serve as intermediates, immediately suggests that the final-demand income elasticites are in any event an inadequate guide to what can happen to the sector-of-origin share of services in national income as distinct from their final-demand shares in national expenditure. Except for unpredictable compositional effects, one might expect that the sector-of-origin shares might be more stable because of possible Leontief-type fixed-requirement relationships between intermediates and outputs, whereas the final-demand composition at best might reflect more any possible Fisher-Clark effects.

Even this presupposition, however, is belied, and indeed turned on its head, by the statistics at hand. Professor Kravis has noted that rather his data suggest that, whereas there is no significant difference between the rich and the poor countries in their share of services in final expenditure, there is a significantly greater share of services by sector-of-origin in the rich than in the poor countries. Why?

The clue seems to be provided by the second key characteristic of services I distinguished earlier: namely, that they presuppose outhouse transactions between users and producers of the service. Imagine that, as development proceeds, services performed previously on an inhouse basis, and hence treated in goods production as part of value-added in goods, increasingly became provided instead by specialized firms on an outhouse basis and hence were now classified as services. This in itself would mean that a simple reorganization of the production process results in a greater share of services by sector-of-origin as development proceeds: an explanation that has not missed Professor Kravis's attention.

As it happens, this is precisely the kind of objection that Professors Peter Bauer and Basil Yamey, both now at our host institution, had raised in 1951 when they argued that Fisher, Clark *et al.* had been misled into thinking that the poor countries had fewer people in the service sector because much of the service sector activity which occurred outhouse in the rich countries was conducted inhouse by producers and hence not accounted for as services. Focusing on the proposition in both Clark and Fisher that higher per capita income was associated with relatively greater numbers in the tertiary sector, they wrote (1951, p. 753):

"Over a considerable period of development many activities, especially trading, porterage and domestic service, would not be regarded as separate occupations either by official enumerators or by the subjects themselves . . . As specializations becomes more definite and pronounced and as these activities are carried out by specialists, the performers and their performance are more easily identified and recognised and their quantitative extent looms larger, possibly much larger in occupational statistics, even though in total the volume of these activities may be unchanged or even reduced."

The *caveat* that changing shares in services may reflect largely organizational changes rather than objective shifts in occupational and production structure needs to be reinforced by reminding ourselves that service data are bedevilled by several other factors which may bear differentially on countries at different stages of development. Three deserve attention.

(1) A difficult and deeper issue is raised if we reflect on the Bauer-Yamey observation that economic development, or secular economic change more generally, can itself shift specific services in and out of the household. Thus, if electrical repairs get expensive, households will tend to allocate their own time to in-household repairs on a do-it-yourself basis. And if a service gets cheaper to buy, as when influx of cheaper foreign labour occurs legally or illegally, housewives would have an added incentive to work outside rather than on household chores inside. What happens then is that unless the corresponding household work is computed as part of national income you get, not a shift in given value-added between goods and services as you go from in*household* to out*household* mode of production but instead, a shift in the computed value-added itself. Questions raised since the earliest days of national income accounting, concerning imputation procedures for nonmarket transactions, and debated recently in connection with feminist demands to include women's contribution in the household in national accounts,* thus bear directly also on the question of the share of services in national income.

(2) Next, the illegal, underground, "black", "second" or "parallel" economy may well be more important in the developing countries where controls tend to proliferate so that the invisible hand is hardly ever seen. Insofar as such activities tend to belong disproportionately to the service sector — construction, repairmen, and domestic servants typically come to mind — and are not picked up in the official statistics, the data on service-sector share in the developing countries would be downward-biased.

(3) Again, the developing countries typically have a relatively larger share of what is now formally described as the "informal" sector but has, in my judgement, no formal definition that is satisfactory analytically. This is generally the urban sector where small-scale entrepreneurship flourishes, with self-employed artisans and repair shops, teastalls, car washing services and numerous such activities characterized therefore by job and employment characteristics that approximate in some fashion the "secondary" labour sector in Professor Michael Piore's celebrated dual-labour markets thesis. Insofar again as this sector escapes systematic documentation by the

---

*See Professor Padma Desai's (1975) useful analysis of this question for the first International Women's Year Conference by UN in Mexico, and the early references cited therein on questions pertaining to imputation in national income accounting.

statistical organizations of the developing countries *and* is disproportionately intensive in services, as seems to be the case from recent
studies, the service share in national income of the poor countries would be
understated.

All this only underscores the fact that services are an omnibus category,
subsumed under one umbrella by principles that I outlined earlier. These
principles still permit enormous diversity in the relationship of different
services to direct final demand, intermediate demand, accounting-
conventions, evasion-proneness and other characteristics that bear on
questions such as their observed share in national income. It seems useful
therefore to depart from a highly-aggregated approach and to consider
subsets of services that are grouped by criteria that are more consonant
with the question being addressed and with the empirical regularity being
searched and then sought to be explained. More robust structural
regularities, reflecting the share of these narrower groups of services in
national income, could certainly emerge; and it is conceivable that the
aggregate tendency of services to show a positive relationship between per
capita GDP and service share in GDP by sector-of-origin may conceal
important segments of services where the relationship is the opposite or
non-existent.

3. The Splintering Process

This kaleidoscope of services and goods is in fact a shifting one as
technical change, in a broad sense embracing organizational innovations as
well, occurs. Technical change leads to what I have christened recently as
the "splintering process" where goods splinter from services and services,
in turn, from goods.

Then again, technical change has also served increasingly to transform
services, as part of what I have described (1984) as a "disembodiment"
phenomenon, from the category where physical proximity between users
and providers was necessary to the "long-distance" category I distinguished
above: with direct implications of course for the tradeability of services.
Again, services, even where physical proximity remains essential, have
increasingly shifted into the tradeable category by making essential but
hitherto *de facto* impossible provider-mobility a distinct economic possibility thanks to organizational innovations resulting from fortuitous changes
in the world economy.

I shall presently return to these implications for the increased tradeability of services and their consequences in turn for the question as to how we
ought to approach the current question of the appropriate framework for
governing trade in services. First however let me turn to the shifting-

kaleidoscope argument, for it helps also to illuminate, in my view, why many services are stagnant and some are not.

Services splinter off from goods, as I have already noted, mainly through being shifted from the inhouse to the outhouse mode. This often happens as economics of scale make it advantageous, as enough demand develops with development, to set up specialized firms supplying these services. I would hypothesize that, *properly measured,* services that materialize this way would tend to show more progressivity: as indeed the Baumol-Blackman-Wolff calculations suggest for the broad category entitled *Business and Professional Services.* There has been recent evidence of reversion in some instances in the United States to inhouse professional services: but I suspect that a fraction of it must reflect the need to have inhouse professionals, much like terminals, to receive and process the outhouse inputs.

It also occurs to me that the process of "service-destruction", as against service-splintering, which arises when stagnant services get increasingly expensive *a la* the Balassa-Samuelson-KHS argumentation and then retreat into the household as unrecorded do-it-yourself amateur activities, will tend to take out of reckoning the stagnant components in services and thus "bias" upwards the measured progressivity of these service sectors.

But when we contemplate the reverse splintering process where goods spring from services, the effect is likely to be exactly the opposite: and for an interestingly exotic reason. In many services where technical change is rapid, I would contend that the change itself often proceeds to splinter off new goods to supply (in a Lancastrian vector-of-characteristics sense) similar needs. In the process, the service sector in question is left behind, in statistical records, as an unprogressive sector, with the technical progressivity being subsumed instead under the goods sector where the new goods are statistically assigned.

I can do no better than quote from my 1984 essay to illustrate what I have in mind:

> "When the gramophone was invented, there was in fact a tremendously sharp technical change in the service activity called "musical services'. But what happened in the classification of goods and services? Gramophones and records are 'goods' and the technical change simply resulted in a new industry which goes into the goods sector. Thus we have been left with the *ex post* observation that the 'musical services' industry is technically unprogressive and also highly labour intensive in general. If technical progress in traditional services industries, such as music, lecturing et cetera (mostly final-use services), indeed takes the form where the service is 'disembodied' from the physical presence of the provider and embodies those services in goods which can then be bought in the market place, then we have a splintering process where technical change simply creates new goods that tend to displace the services from which they grew and where technical change therefore leaves behind, in the services sector, the labour-intensive and 'unprogressive' component of the pre-technical-change sector."

The disembodiment effect that characterizes technical change creating goods from services is accordingly responsible for a class of services where progressivity is generally considered to be low. We then have this paradox: that technical progress in these sectors itself creates the outcome that, given the way these sectors are defined, they wind up technically stagnant!"

While, appropriately measured, progressivity in the service sectors that experience such goods-creating technical change will indeed show stagnation, I might warn that the crude and wholly inappropriate *labour*-productivity measures, all too often used to infer progressivity or lack thereof, could in principle go either way in these service sectors. You can convince yourself of this "paradoxical" possibility by simply constructing an outcome where the wage-rental ratio rises with the technical-change-led emergence of the new good, the (old) service sector is labour-intensive, its capital-labour ratio and hence labour-productivity as well rise in consequence, and may do so even differentially relative to other sectors.

4. Increased Tradeability of Services: Long-distancing Phenomenon and Innovations in Provider Mobility

(1) The "disembodiment" phenomenon I have discussed above in the form of services splintering into goods extends alternatively to services becoming, not goods, but *long-distance* services so that the physical presence of the provider of the services is no longer necessary for the transaction with the user.* Two consequences then follow.

(i) The technical progressivity *will* then continue to be recorded in the service sector, unlike in the case where the disembodiment led to embodiment instead in goods.

(ii) Moreover, nontradeability resulting from artificial or natural barriers to bringing the provider in physical proximity to the user will yield to tradeability and may indeed lead to trade.

The enormous speed with which technological change has progressed in the communications and information sectors, commonly grouped under the "telematics" rubric, has shifted an ever-increasing number of activities to the long-distance category where they may be executed "over the wire" and hence become more readily tradeable and traded in consequence. Banking transactions from computer terminals at home, engineering services communicated by satellite and medical diagnosis by video

---

*Thus, instead of Pavarotti singing on the gramophone record, he sings over satellite TV. The former is disembodiment *via* embodiment into goods, the latter is disembodiment *via* long-distance service. In both cases, the physical presence of the provider in proximity to the user is eliminated.

transmission are evident examples. My favourite illustration has been President Reagan's bringing Dresser Industries' Paris branch to a halt over President Mitterrand's recalcitrance over the Soviet gas pipeline affair by simply turning off the transmission of critical engineering and related information flows from Dresser Industries headquarters in Dallas. But this will not hold a candle to the story I read recently which carried pictures of a young lady standing in her lingerie in front of a mirror and trying on dresses over the wire in a fashion store hundreds of miles away!

(2) But if tradeability of services has increased through "long-distancing" trends in provision of services, it has also increased for the very different reasons that, where physical proximity continues to be necessary but has been traditionally difficult or impossible to achieve across countries, "organizational" innovations have appeared recently which have made such proximity feasible and even economical.

Thus, in the class of services where, as with my M–6 example, the provider of services had to travel to where the motorway had to be built, it has been rare in modern times for unskilled labour services to be so provided. Both lack of *supply* by organized construction firms and of demand due to restrictions ill-adapted to accommodating such supply in any event have generally prevented such services from being internationally transacted.

However, this is no longer true as numerous construction firms have materialized in the post-OPEC 1970s to take, not just skilled but also entire teams of unskilled labour, to the labour-scarce Middle East economies feverishly engaged in spending oil revenues. This "innovation" in organization, fortuitously resulting from the OPEC-led change in the world economy, has made it possible now for us to contemplate a transition of unskilled labour services, and hence of the category of services where the provider must necessarily move to the user, from its hitherto nontraded status to the tradeable category.

Several instances, as when entire medical facilities for instances were provided inclusive of nonimmigrant doctors and administrators who would come into Saudi Arabia and Kuwait on fixed-term contracts, underscore the vastly increased opening up of this form of relocation of the provider of services to where the user is in the *skilled*-labour categories as well.

(3) Paradoxically, however, the major thrust towards negotiations for a framework governing trade in services has come, not from the beneficiaries of the two phenomena I just outlined as increasing tradeability of services. Rather, it has come from sectors such as banking where traditional long-distancing practices and reasonable ongoing tradeability are considered to be no longer adequate because of technical change that, in revolutionizing the nature of banking services, has made extremely profitable the possibility of physical proximity by the provider where the user is.

Demands for the "right to establish" or its euphemestic equivalent, the "right of presence", reminiscent of Commodore Parry's demand on the Tokugawa Japan and Secretary Connolly's demands on today's Japan, have thus appeared from potential beneficiaries such as the American Express Company.

The contrast with the preceding case of unskilled and several skilled labour services is interesting. These latter have always required provider-mobility — either as a physical necessity as with unskilled services or as a virtual necessity with skilled services which require complementary facilities simply impossible to duplicate in the user location. Organizational innovations have rendered such provider-mobility internationally increasingly feasible and therefore restrictions on it, as I shall contend below, must be viewed as necessarily restrictive of trade in services. On the other hand, the same degree of *necessity* does not, in my judgement, characterise the services that seek the "right to establish" presently.

This asymmetry of need on the one hand and desirability on the other hand between these two classes of services seeking provider-mobility should suggest that the beneficiaries in the *former* than in the latter class should have taken the center stage. Ironically, the articulate lobbies have emerged for the *latter* group instead, while there are no matching spokesmen for the former! This irony also has an added twist since the latter group is overwhelmingly in the developed, and the former is preponderantly in the developing countries.

5. Developed and Developing Country Interests: Conflict or Convergence?

There are several reasons in fact why the United States has played the catalytic role in the ongoing exploration for an international framework to regulate and facilitate trade in services. These also explain why the focus of the US role has tended to be on certain kinds of services and why the developing countries have found themselves in an adversary role on this.

The US focus, given its pluralistic politics, has naturally reflected the lobbying pressures from those service sectors in the US that seek greater access, and right to establish, in other countries. This was evident from the considerable pressures that were brought to bear on the participants at the November, 1982 GATT Inter-Ministerial where, as Sir Roy Denman has remarked, the hardsell from the US multinational banks in particular was manifest and almost counterproductive.

But it is not just the lobbying pressure. There is also a substantial element of economic philosophy or ideology, reflecting the conviction that the liberal trading order is desirable, which drives the United States leadership towards the extension of the rule of law in trade to the service sectors. The United States efforts can therefore be interpreted, quite properly in my judgement, as part of its leadership role that Professor Charles Kindleberger believes is central to providing the "collectives good" that an international trade regime represents. If you are skeptical of this benign interpretation, I would remind you that Peel's repeal of the Corn Laws, which constituted the first triumph of the free traders, was not just a result of the relative strength of Cobden over his opposing lobby. In the end, Peel confessed, he was simply convinced of the virtues of free trade. As Disraeli accused him, when he crucified him in Parliament, Peel had unscrupulously let political economy triumph over loyalty to his party!

There has also been an acute sense in the United States that *national* interest, and not just the narrow interest of the lobbies or the general interest of the world at large, dictates that services be brought into the trading order. This is a result of the increasing perception that the US comparative advantage has shifted to service transactions. And that it is simply "unfair" to have US markets open to goods while foreign markets are closed to US services. Given the rise of the doctrine of "aggressive reciprocity", and of the increased demands for "a level playing field" unmindful of the fact that some live up on the mountain and others down in the valley, this has translated into an aggressive posture by the US on the question of trade in services and has also shaped the central thrust of these demands in terms of the concepts embraced for legitimacy and the sectors chosen for emphasis.

The lack of enthusiasm of the developing countries in general for these initiatives and pressures — though there are notable exceptions such as Singapore whose outward orientation extends also to offshore banking, giving them a greater stake in the extension of the trade regime to services — has stayed fairly robust since 1982. Their latest willingness at Geneva to play along can only be put down to circumspection prompted by the sense that, compared to 1982, more developed countries had joined US ranks, notably the United Kingdom where the pro-manufactures and anti-services views of Professor Nicholas Kaldor and his Cambridge pupils seem less fashionable now than some years ago.* Again, the protectionist threat in the United States has grown extremely acute, after years of neglect of the budget and trade deficits, so that the choice has seemed increasingly to narrow down politically to having the US open up new markets abroad or closing old ones at home, and hence also to talking about services or having the US door closed to goods.

What have been the worries of the developing countries? And what do we need to bring them more fairly and enthusiastically into the regime-

---

*See my commentary (1984) on the Kaldor views. There is also a splendid critique by Lady Hall (1968).

making game on services? I would group their concerns into three broad categories:

first, that comparative advantage in services belongs to the developed countries and therefore the returns to extension of orderly trade rules to services enabling service transactions to expand will accrue to the developed rather that to the developing countries;

second, that focusing on services will turn attention away from making progress on keeping trade in goods reasonably free, thus harming the developing countries whose comparative advantage lies in goods trade instead; and

third, that the services which will expand under such a new regime will be in areas where infrastructure buildup, externalities and political sensitivity are important; the rule-oriented GATT-type regime, where quantities may come out where they will, is inapplicable in consequence.

Let me address these issues in turn.

(1) The fear that comparative advantage in services belongs to the developed countries, and implied rejection therefore of the initiatives to open up trade in them, are understandable but misplaced.

Economists will immediately assert that, by and large, dismantling of trade barriers should be welfare-improving mutually. Of course one knows, thanks to the theory of second-best which was conceived at LSE (London School of Economics) itself, that perverse effects can always follow for both parties to trade if barriers are dismantled only partially. But, unless one is clever but not wise, or (in Sir Dennis Robertson's classic description of a younger and brilliant colleague) is "silly-clever", these are exceptions that are best confined to the classroom in the present instance.

Thus, in the context of services, it has been customary for economists, as also negotiators from the developed countries, to emphasize the virtues of freer trade in services and its advantage to the developing countries even if they are importers of services. In particular, the argument has been advanced that giving their own producers and exporters greater access to cheaper and more efficient banking and insurance services from the developed countries will imply better export and economic performance for the developing countries. And that they are only hurting themselves by protecting their banking and insurance sectors, much as protecting intermediates such as imported steel would hurt the export of tractors and diesel engines and hence the economy in turn.

Unfortunately, in the game of trade, these arguments are rarely compelling. Where economists see mutual gain, politics tends often to see zero-sum outcomes. Typically, the other's gain is seen as possibly one's loss. If therefore service liberalization will expand others' exports, the gains accrue to *them,* not to oneself.

Again, the developing countries tend to see the economic arguments advanced by developed-country spokesmen in favour of service trade as self-serving when for decades these very service sectors were heavily regulated domestically and protected against external competition (and, in the case of the US, even against inter-state competition down to this day). While one may not buy the imperial theory of free trade in the 19th century, it would be naive to ignore the fact that many countries have tended to embrace free trade only when they felt they were strong and ahead.

All of this suggests that, to bring the developing countries into the service negotiations, it will be necessary to encourage them, as indeed one can, to see that they too have advantage in *some* services: that this particular extension of trading rules, complex as it is, has something for everyone in this political-economy sense. In order to do this, we also have to move away from the biased focus that has been provided in the discussions to date on those services where the developed countries have substantial advantage, and to bring into the agenda those services where the developing countries have something to export.

(2) Before I utilize my earlier themes to elaborate on how this can be done, let me turn to the fear that the focus on services would reduce the energies spent on goods. The recent GATT Expert-Group Report (1985, p. 46) addresses this concern by stating:

> ". . . we are also convinced that there will be no progress on services without substantial progress on trade in goods. There is no future for an effort to involve GATT in services while neglecting its central and essential responsibilities. An attempt to extend a rule-based approach to new areas of economic relations while permitting the rules for trade in goods to continue to decay would lack credibility."

But it is precisely lack of faith in this built-in safeguard against neglect of goods if services are let in past the door that worries the developing countries; and the GATT experts offer no convincing reason to them to do otherwise.

A variant on this services *versus* goods theme is that the developed countries will want to swap concessions on services (where they will benefit) against concessions on goods (where the developing countries will benefit). And that the concessions offered on goods will mostly consist of rolling back the *de facto* violations of GATT such as Voluntary Export Restrictions against them, including the MFA (Multi Fibers Agreement) which while arranged under GATT auspices is widely regarded by developing countries as, at best, a bastard progeny that should never have been delivered. In short, since services are a new area not contemplated as subject to GATT protocol, the developing countries will get a raw bargain: an unrequited concession masquerading as a *quid pro quo* trade agreement.

This contention of the developing countries, in my view, has merit. On the other hand, it runs into the contrary viewpoint, advanced by some developed-country proponents, that the developing countries have been hiding behind Part IV and have undertaken few GATT obligations on goods in consequence,* and that it is time now for them to "begin paying" through graduated suspension of Part IV provisions and also through other areas, especially services. In short, "free lunch" is over, and the ongoing, GATT-sanctioned unrequitted transfer to the developing countries must stop!

To recapitulate these two conflicting perceptions in terms of Table 2, the developing countries' viewpoint is that current protection under item (3) is quasi-illegal and item (4) has no merit since Part IV, like Article XXIV, is a well-recognized exception to corresponding GATT obligations, so that the developed-countries' demand for item (2) is simply gratuitous and unfair, whereas the developed countries see item (3) as the *quid pro quo* for developing countries granting item (2) and agreeing to item (4).

It is evident that little multilateral progress on services can be made if they are caught in the middle of these irreconcilable overall-bargaining perspectives. My view therefore is that we broaden the scope of (2), and as I argue below in a manner that appropriate conceptualisation of the question requires in any event, so that it goes on *both* sides of Table 2, generating a *quid pro quo,* no matter how unequal, *within the service sector itself.*

(3) This need is further compounded by the fact that the lobbies-led focus has inevitably been on service sectors where the developed countries *ipso facto* appear to have advantage. Besides, these particular sectors

TABLE 2. *Benefit-Perceptions on Different Trade-Negotiating Proposals*

Proposals perceived as resulting in	
Benefit to developing countries	Benefit to developed countries
Add Agriculture (1) to GATT (or similar action) Standstills and (3) Rollbacks on Existing Protection (including MFA)	*Add* Services to (2) GATT (or similar Agency) *Remove* Part IV (4) benefits (on graduated basis)

*I include here the entire question of discriminatory, special and preferential treatment of developing countries (including the NICs).

happen to raise acutely rather difficult questions concerning infrastructure, externalities, and hence also political control of sensitive areas of economic activity.

While, as many have recently noted,* there is a tendency to exaggerate the untoward effects, the problem remains that perceptions are not easily changed by analysis and logic. In my judgement, it is not inconceivable that substantial progress can be made in both banking and insurance, for example, towards permitting foreign companies to operate under rules of "national treatment," without compromising infrastructure control. However, the political obstacles may still be insurmountable when the developing countries want to have only state-owned firms in these sectors and therefore entry by foreign firms is off-bounds, similar to the situation in the defence sector in many countries. In that event, political preferences become dominant, as when the United States denies "national treatment" even to foreign residents in regard to ownership in its media sector.

This question has arisen even more sharply in the area of telematics which is seen, as in France, as critical to the evolution of society at several levels in view of the importance of the Information Revolution. For India and Brazil, among the more influential developing countries, domestic control over this key, broad sector does not appear to be an item that should be brought under a GATT-type "rule of law" regime. "Who gets what", rather that "what rules do you play by", become the relevant question, much as in the question of disarmament negotiations.

Compounding yet further the difficulties that some developing countries envisage is the question of the "right to establish" that some of these sectors have raised, as I noted earlier. For, that raises in turn questions relating to direct foreign investment; and, in many developing countries, that is a politically more sensitive area than trade.

If then the developing countries are to be brought on board as willing and energetic participants instead of being dragged screaming into the service-trade negotiations, we need to recognize frontally these problems. A two-front assault is necessary.

First, the comparative advantage of the developing countries in service trade itself must be explored and the negotiations must clearly embrace the areas where such comparative advantage lies and not just those where the developed countries have advantage. *Second,* the negotiating forums and modalities must reflect the constraints imposed by the special characteristics of such services, rather than constituting a simple extension of existing

---

*Of particular interest and importance is the recent article by Professors Brian Hindley and Alasdair Smith (1984), which analyses in depth the contentions concerning infant-industry type externalities, problems arising from need to regulate *et al.*, and generally concludes that these worries are unduly exaggerated.

frameworks and institutions such as the GATT which have evolved primarily in relation to trade in goods.

Comparative Advantage of Developing Countries in Services. It is probably true that the developing countries will not have comparative advantage in services such as banking and insurance. Even here, however, I am not entirely sure since, as with trade in similar goods, there may well be opportunities for trade in similar services. Indeed services are even more likely to depart from the identical-product mould and to lead therefore to the possibility of mutual trade between developed and developing countries. Thus, for example, it is not uncommon to find travellers who prefer to fly Singapore or Japan Airlines because they offer more effusive onboard treatment than on Pan Am or TWA: each reflecting the personal-service culture of the country of the airline! The developing countries may therefore well be too pessimistic about such trade being *all* one-way to them rather than from them.

Again, I think that some of the developing countries ought to develop considerable comparative advantage in the newly-emerging "long-distance" services as time passes by. If I may quote from my recent paper (1984) again:

> ". . . it is possible to argue that the more advanced developing countries, the newly industrializing countries, which are abundantly endowed with skills, may well find a new comparative advantage opening up in the over-the-wire transmission of their skilled services! This has already happened with respect to software. It could happen, *a la* Dresser engineering services, with data being transmitted to users in overseas locations for engineering, medical and a host of other skilled services. Thus the newly industrializing countries may well find that there is something for them, too, in the GATT being extended to trade in services — provided that the extension is truly to services of all kinds."

But, for a really substantial class of services where a number of developing countries can confidently expect to have comparative advantage, we must turn to the category of provider-mobility where labour is relocated for the purpose of providing services to users abroad. South Korea, India, the Philippines, Egypt, Bangladesh, Pakistan and a growing number of developing countries are already waiting to redo in the developed countries what they have been allowed to do in the Middle East. Indeed, I am informed that South Korea has already applied to the European Economic Community for formal permission to enable its firms to enter the EEC in this fashion. More will certainly follow suit. With numerous qualified professionals also available in some of these developing countries, and unable to get past the immigration controls for permanent residence in the developed countries, there is also increasing prospect of such demands for provision of medical facilities, legal firms etc. where the professionals may enter, not as permanent residents, but to execute specific medium-term jobs and assignments in the developed countries.*

I believe that it is inappropriate to reject such "temporary relocation of factors to execute service transactions" as inadmissible simply because it is a "factor-service" transaction in current conceptualisation. What I have argued above is that such factor relocation is *necessary* to permit the service transaction in these cases, so that the very nature of these services requires that restrictions on such temporary relocation of the provider must be removed if we are examining the question of service trade with an appropriate conceptual framework. We need to discard the notion that, *for the purpose at hand,* the distinction between factor-services and non-factor services is meaningful. Rather, we need to take what I would christen as the *"provider-relocation-requiring"* services out of the factor-service category and put them squarely into the net and treat them as on a par with non-factor service trade for the question of analysing the framework of rules for trade in services.

If we do not do that, we are not merely ignoring the essential nature of certain services and rendering therefore transactions or trade in them unfeasible. We are also doing that in a manner which systematically stacks against the developing countries the emerging discussion of the rules to be designed for service trade!

Negotiations: where and how? The agenda that emerges from this analysis then forcefully indicates the difficulties that attend the question of expanding the goods-trade GATT-type framework to services.

Goods trade, by and large, does not get us entangled into questions of externalities, infrastructure, and especially the need to allow for provider-relocation across borders with its own attendant difficulties which are so evident that I have not thought it necessary to spell them out explicitly. On the other hand, services, by and large, do raise these questions. Besides, different services raise each of these questions in differing degree. Moreover, they benefit the developing and the developed countries, in the narrow but politically relevant sense, differently.

All of this immediately suggests that:

first, the negotiations on services ought to be comprehensive in scope, with simultaneity in these negotiations on several services ensuring that tradeoffs can occur between different sectors and hence progress assured on the entire subject matter;

second, seeking common rules extending to all international service transactions is doomed to failure; however, such rules can indeed be

---

*Progress is already being made in some cases, such as the legal profession. On the general question of trade in professional services, and the problems and prospects therein, see the contributions by Barton, Bhagwati, Feketekuty, Cone and Rossi in THE LEGAL FORUM, a new Journal of the Chicago University Law School: forthcoming in Fall 1986.

sought *within* each service sector, while we must recognize that the rule-led GATT-type approach will have to be compromised to permit negotiated quantity-outcomes, at least for developing countries, in many sectors; and

third, the GATT experience with negotiating NTB (Non Tariff Barriers) codes in the Tokyo Round provides one key component of the requisite expertise in providing the umbrella for service transactions negotiations: for, in case of NTBs, commonality of rules was again unobtainable between different NTB practices concerning goods trade but nonetheless progress was made on rules within broad groups of NTB instruments.

I would therefore urge the developing countries to join the developed countries in service negotiations under GATT auspices, ensure that the negotiations are comprehensive in scope and extend to services of interest to themselves, and that adequate quantity-outcome safeguards are negotiated where, after careful analysis, they are deemed neccssary and reasonable in specific sectors.* Equally, I should stress that the developed countries must recognize the interests of the developing countries and broaden the scope of the proposed negotiations away from near-exclusive focus on services of interest largely to themselves.[†]

Otherwise, there is real danger, as the GATT Expert-Group Report correctly emphasizes, of bilateral and regional fragmentation of the trading world in the area of service trade. Such an outcome would surely be tragic when it is evident that we must move to bring services systematically and increasingly into the discipline of the world trading order.

References

BALASSA, B., (1964), "The Purchasing-power Parity Doctrine: a Reappraisal", *Journal of Political Economy*, Vol. 72 December, pp. 584–96.

BAUER, PETER and BASIL YAMEY, 1951, "Economic Progress and Occupational Distribution", *Economic Journal*, December.

BAUMOL, WILLIAM, SUE, BLACKMAN, and EDWARD WOLFF, (1985) "Unbalanced Growth Revisited: Asymptotic Stagnancy and New Evidence", *American Economic Review*, Vol. 75, pp. 806–817.

BHAGWATI, JAGDISH N., (1984) "Splintering and Disembodiment of Services and Developing Nations", *The World Economy*, June.

BHAGWATI, JAGDISH N., (1984) "Why are Services Cheaper in the Poor Countries?" *Economic Journal*, June.

BHAGWATI, JAGDISH N., (1985a) "Opening up Trade in Services: US Should Heed Third World Demands", *The New York Times*, November 10.

BHAGWATI, JAGDISH N., (1985b) "GATT and Trade in Services: How We Can Resolve the North-South Debate", *The Financial Times* (London), November 27.

BHAGWATI, JAGDISH N., (1985c) "Trade in Services: How to Change Indian Strategy", *The Economic Times* (India), December 2.

---

*This was the main theme of my *Op. Ed.* piece in *The Economic Times*, addressed to Indian policymakers and public opinion; cf. Bhagwati (1985c).

[†]This, on the other hand, was the main contention of my *Op. Ed.* articles in *The New York Times* (1985a) and *The Financial Times* (1985b).

CLAGUE, CHRISTOPHER, (1985) "A Model of Real National Price Levels", *Southern Economic Journal*, Vol. 51.

CLARK, COLIN, (1951) *The Conditions of Economic Progress*, MacMillan & Company: London, 2nd Edition.

DESAI, PADMA, (1975) "Participation of Women in the Economies of Developing and Developed Countries, Ways of Recognizing their Contribution to National Income, and Strategies for Ensuring their Economic Independence in Developing Countries", Paper prepared for the International Women's Year Conference, United Nations, Mexico, June; *mimeographed*.

FISHER, ALLAN G. B., (1939) "Production, Primary, Secondary and Tertiary", *Economic Record*, June.

GATT, (1985) *Trade Policies for a Better Future: Proposals for Action*, March, GATT, Geneva, Switzerland.

HALL, MARGARET, (1968) "Are Goods and Services Different?", *Westminster Bank Review*, August.

HILL, T. P., (1977) "On Goods and Services", *Review of Income and Wealth*, December.

HINDLEY, BRIAN and ALASDAIR SMITH, (1984) "Comparative Advantage and Trade in Services", *The World Economy*, December.

KIERZKOWSKI, HENRYK, (1984) "Services in the Development Process and Theory of Trade", Discussion Papers in International Economics No. 8405, The Graduate Institute of International Studies, October.

KRAVIS, IRVING, (1983) "Services in the Domestic Economy and in World Transactions", Working Paper No. 1124 (Cambridge, MA: National Bureau of Economic Research).

KRAVIS, IRVING, ALAN HESTON and ROBERT SUMMERS, (1978) *International Comparisons of Real Product and Purchasing Power*, Johns Hopkins Press, for the World Bank: Baltimore.

MEADE, JAMES E., (1951) *The Balance of Payments*, Oxford University Press: London.

PANAGARIYA, ARAVIND, (1985) "Economies of Scale as an Explanation of International Differences in Service Prices and Some Associated Phenomena", University of Maryland, *mimeo*.

SAMPSON, GARY and RICHARD SNAPE, (1985) "Identifying the Issues in Trade in Services", *The World Economy*, 8(2), June, pp. 171–182.

SAMUELSON, P. A., (1964) "Theoretical Notes on Trade Problems", *The Review of Economics and Statistics*, Vol. 46, May, pp. 145–54.

SAPIR, ANDRE and ERNST LUTZ, 1981, *Trade in Services: Economics Determinants and Development-Related Issues*, IBRD Staff Working Paper No. 480, August, Washington D.C., USA.

UNCTAD, (1984) *Services and the Development Process*, TD/B/1008, August 2, UNCTAD, Geneva, Switzerland.

WEISS, FRANK D., (1984) "Scope for Trade in Services", Trade Policy Research Center, *mimeo.*, May.

2

International Trade in Services: Comments

BRIAN HINDLEY, HENRYK KIERZKOWSKI, VICTOR D. NORMAN and SIRI
P. STRANDENES, ANDRÉ SAPIR and JEAN WAELBROECK

BRIAN HINDLEY*

Jagdish Bhagwati's fine paper stimulates comment on many points. I
shall confine myself to just one of these; or at least, to one cluster of related
points.

Whatever the outcome of the US initiative on services in the GATT, the
debate to which it has given rise should have persuaded policy-makers that
the role in the development process of international transactions in the
service sector has been unduly neglected. That is all to the good. I believe
that service sector liberalization holds the potential for substantial
economic gains for developing countries.

But a conviction that liberalization of service transactions will lead to
economic gains for the liberalizing country does not lead inevitably to a
case for rules on services in the GATT. Confusion of these two issues
raises a risk that arguments against acceptance of GATT rules on services
will be treated in developing countries as if they also make a case against
unilateral liberalization.

"Concessions" and the GATT

A trivial difference between unilateral and multilateral liberalization,
true by definition, is that the gains from unilateral liberalization are
available at any time that a government decides to take them. No
international agreement is necessary to realize them. A less trivial
proposition follows from that, however. It is that the case for a government
to enter a multilateral liberalization process must depend upon some gain
from doing so that is over and above the gain available from unilateral
liberalization.

---

*Consultant, the World Bank.

That is part of the role of the "concessions" — reductions in the restriction placed upon one's exports in foreign markets — upon which a GATT negotiations centres. This increased access to foreign markets is conditional upon being a part of the multilateral process (at least for developed countries). Hence, there is reason for a government to prefer multilateral to unilateral liberalization.

The role of concessions in the GATT process, however, runs much deeper than a governmental preference for one mode of liberalization over another. The structure of protection in a particular country at a particular time must be taken to represent the outcome of some process of *political* equilibration. To change the protective structure, therefore, it is necessary to change the factors that support the underlying political equilibrium.

A multilateral exchange of concessions offers one means of doing this. By changing the opportunities available to actors in the domestic political process, the multilateral component changes their economic interests — exporters, for example, have a more direct interest in reduction of their own country's protection against imports when this will reduce foreign protection against their own products. Hence, not only is there reason for a government to prefer multilateral to unilateral liberalization: in practical terms, the choice confronting a government is likely to be between multilateral liberalization and no liberalization at all.

Economists often scoff at the language of GATT negotiations (in which "concessions" are obtained at the "cost" of an increase in the openness to imports of one's own markets). Ricardo's demonstration of the principle of comparative advantage, they say, destroyed once and for all the possibility of regarding increased openness to imports as a cost. From the standpoint of analysis of the economic consequences of trade liberalization, that rejection of the GATT terminology is quite correct. Economic analysis, however, offers no solution to the *political* problem that is addressed by "concessions" in the GATT process.

These aspects of the GATT process are quite general: they apply to goods as well as to services (and, indeed, so far have only applied to goods). The specific problem in the context of developing countries and services in the GATT occurs because, as Professor Bhagwati points out so well, it is not clear what potential for concessions of potential value to developing countries is yielded by the proposed services negotiation.

Services and Concessions

The US Government has proposed that the negotiation should be limited to trade in non-factor services — services that can be supplied from a supplier in country A to a buyer in country B without relocation of either seller or buyer. That position was developed as an attempt to lull developing country fears that a negotiation on services will in fact, through claims of a right of establishment, be about foreign investment. However, it also avoids the symmetrical but even more contentious issues that would be raised in developed countries by a developing country counter-claim of a right to temporarily locate labour in a market for the purpose of supplying a service.

The idea of focusing the negotiation on traded services has been under heavy pressure from US service suppliers, many of whom *do* regard the lack of a right of establishment as the major difficulty facing their international operations. From the point of view of developing countries, however, an equally important property of that focus is that it restricts the negotiation to services (banking and insurance, for example) in which comparative advantage lies predominantly with the developed countries.

Such a definition of "services" therefore excludes any substantial *export* interest on the part of developing countries. Hence, the proposed negotiation holds no concessions of potential interest to them. Nor, currently, do the developed countries display any willingness to contemplate concessions in goods trade to compensate for the lack of them in the services area.

In that case, however, the services negotiation cannot run along traditional GATT lines, which would entail an *exchange* of concessions. The proponents of a services negotiations in GATT seem to face a choice between four alternatives. They are:

(a) to change the terms of the proposed negotiation to include a broadly-defined right of establishment that would embrace a right to temporarily locate labour in a foreign market for the purpose of supplying a service; or

(b) to persuade developing countries that the Ricardian economic benefits from cheap imports of services are sufficient to warrant an opening of their market to imports of services *without* GATT concessions; or

(c) to attempt to force developing countries into accepting liberalization of services — in particular, by threatening to further shut developed country markets to exports from developing countries unless the latter liberalize services; or

(d) to abandon the notion of persuading substantial numbers of developing countries into a GATT agreement on services.

Assessing the Alternatives

My own preference is the same as Professor Bhagwati's and is for an extension of the terms of the negotiation — option (a). After all, the arguments that many of us have developed for the belief that liberalization of service transactions will benefit developing countries also imply that liberalization will benefit developed countries. Moreover, if it is difficult for a bank or insurance company to effectively sell its services, without local establishment, it is impossible for a construction company in a developing country to build a road or a dam at home and export it. But if trade is a good thing, and if it is cheaper to trade by shifting factors than by shifting the goods that they produce, why not allow the factors to move? Or at the very least, why not explore that possibility?

Option (b), of course, raises the paradox of economic gain and political loss that affects the conventional economist's view of GATT. There are potential economic gains for developing countries from liberalization — why then do their governments need "concessions" to persuade them to act? But the question also illustrates the multilateral-unilateral issue. The governments of developing countries have not exercised their option to act unilaterally. The offers of gains that they could obtain through unilateral liberalization seems unlikely to persuade them into multilateral liberalization.

Nevertheless, a successful argument that developing countries should join a GATT negotiation to obtain economic benefits that they could obtain unilaterally would be extensively re-usable. Such an argument could, for example, be applied to the extraordinarily expensive and disruptive protection of agriculture by the EEC and Japan, or to protection of the clothing and textile industries of the US and the EEC. Indeed, the economic benefits that would flow to the citizens of the US, the EEC, and Japan from renunciation of these policies are so well demonstrated that if this tactic is to be employed, it might be better to *start* with agriculture or the MFA rather than with imports of services into developing countries.

The choice to be feared, however, is a negotiation under the threat of further closure of developed country markets. For one thing, it represents a very substantial risk. There are among the supporters of this approach many who *hope* that grounds will be provided to carry out the threat. Their primary interest is not to obtain more freedom for trade; it is to find excuses to block imports into their own markets.

Even for one who believes that liberalization of service transactions would benefit developing countries, however, there are good reasons to reject any attempt to compel liberalization. Even in the most favourable circumstances, a substantial and enforceable multilateral agreement on services is not easy to achieve (as the difficulties of the EEC in liberalizing its *internal* market for services demonstrate).

One large part of the problem lies in the means by which service industries are protected against foreign competition. This is not simply a matter of barriers to establishment, though that is an important issue. The essential point is that services, because of their "invisible" properties, cannot usually be protected by tariffs or quotas — the protective instruments that the GATT process has been successful in removing or reducing. They are instead protected by a range of measures analogous to non-tariff barriers (NTBs) in trade in goods — and the GATT process has not been very successful in removing NTBs. Simple issues might be resolved by negotiation under threat. This is not a simple issue.

Moreover, the services issue *is* important. It is desirable that there should be a multilateral agreement on interventions in service transactions, and that it should achieve a substantial degree of liberalization. A negotiation which must keep unwilling parties on board by threat cannot have this character.

Politics in developed countries may preclude concessions to developing countries that engage their interest in a substantial agreement. In that case, it is better that the negotiation should proceed without the developing countries rather than that they be forced to join at the cost of reducing its value and scope.

The case that developing countries would gain from unilateral liberalization in the service sector is very strong, and countries that have reached that conclusion will be more interested in multilateral agreements. That there should be a substantial agreement for developing countries to join when they are ready is more important than obtaining their accession to an empty agreement now.

HENRYK KIERZKOWSKI*

Professor Bhagwati has done a great service to the profession by producing a stimulating and comprehensive paper on a subject which is likely to dominate international trade negotiations in the years to come. International commerce in services has long been and even continues to be an unhappy orphan of international trade theory. Two of the few authors in the field called one chapter in a book reviewing the state of the art "Economic Theory — History of Neglect." And this appears to be only a slight exaggeration. The Bhagwati paper goes a long way in trying to remedy this situation. Particularly relevant is his focus on the production and trade in services for developing countries and potential gains they might achieve from liberalization of trade and factor movements in this area.

Jagdish Bhagwati concentrates on issues surrounding productivity in

*Professor of Economics, Graudate Institute of International Studies, Geneva.

services. It must be said from the outset that measurement difficulties are much more serious in the case of services than in the industrial or agricultural sectors, and, as a result, productivity trends are more evasive in the former case than in the latter. This stems partly from the ambiguity of definition regarding a service's output. How to measure output for public administration is a case in point. The invisibility of financial insurance or communication services creates similar measurement obstacles.

Even though the estimates for service productivity must be read with a large dose of scepticism, comparisons of the tertiary, industrial and agriculture sectors are inevitably made. For a long time clear consensus existed that productivity in the service sector fell considerably below manufacturing but surpassed that for agriculture.

It was Colin Clark who first provided crucial evidence to this conjecture. But, this view is being challenged today especially as distinctions are drawn between different services. Modern services activities such as telecommunications and banking have demonstrated spectacular productivity gains.

Do theoretical reasons exist why labour productivity should grow more slowly in tertiary than secondary production? So far no hypotheses explaining this phenomenon have been advanced, but market structure may lend at least a partial interpretation. That is, when a particular sector produces services or goods under restricted competition, there may be limited incentives for encouraging technical progress. And, natural monopolies and those created and protected by government policy are not infrequent in the tertiary sector. Why should producers who are in a monopolistic position bother about technical progress? The standard theory of monopoly supplies the answer. However, once the degree of competition is increased through deregulation or liberalization of international trade and investment, the structure of the market is bound to change.

Postal services exemplify very low productivity change or even deterioration. Professor Bhagwati points out that there were 12 mail deliveries per day in 19th century London, and we all know how this contrasts postal services today. Yet, it has to be recognized that a government-created monopoly might lie behind this (as well as excessive trade union power). One cannot help thinking (and hoping) that if private competition were allowed in the provision of postal services, the picture would dramatically alter. Indeed when postal strikes break out, a substitute service is sometimes created, and mail gets delivered more quickly and efficiently.

The example of postal services also reveals another relevant aspect. That is, a broader definition of productivity is needed which could capture changes in the way a service is provided. There were 12 mail deliveries per day in London before World War I, but then telex came along. At present more efficient ways of transmitting "letters" have evolved, involving a combination of computers, satellites and photocopying machines. Today's potential frequency of "mail deliveries" surpasses many hundred times over what it used to be. And that must surely be called technical progress.

To make my point in a more general way, what counts from the social point of view is not only productivity improvements within a particular mode of providing a service, but also changes in the mode itself. Professor Bhagwati has introduced the concept of a "splintering process" to capture the idea that goods may spring from services and services may spring from goods. I wish to broaden his concept by adding that services may also spring from services.

Let me turn now to the issue addressing relative price of services. Why is it that services are relatively more expensive in the developed than developing countries? Professor Bhagwati presents three different theoretical models capable of explaining such behaviour. I find particularly appealing the notion that large endowment differences between the rich and the poor countries result in a relatively cheaper labour for the latter. If services are labour intensive, then they should be less expensive in the developing countries. This explation, however, depends crucially on the factor-intensity assumption. One may wish to question the validity of this assumption with respect to air transportation, shipping as well as other services, but I should think on the whole it holds quite well.

In making international comparisons, one assumes that goods and services are similar across national borders. Quality differences are hardly ever corrected for. However, if quality discrepancies are allowed, yet another explanation of the puzzle emerges.

The model I wish to present draws on my joint work with Rodney Falvey. Suppose that goods are completely standardized and that no quality dissimilarities exist. Services, however, may acquire different quality standards. One unit of the lowest quality, q_1, requires a_{L1} units of labour and a_{K1} units of capital. Assume that the labour requirement remains unchanged for all possible qualities but the capital requirement increases as higher qualities are produced. For the quality level q_2, the capital input coefficient is a_{K2} such that $a_{K2} > a_{K1}$. With no substitution between capital and labour allowed, unit input isoquants are of the Leontief type shown in Fig. 1.

Which quality will individual consumers buy? That depends on their individual income. It is not unreasonable to assume that the higher the income, the higher the quality an individual will select. Given per capita income differences between developed and developing countries, it must be true that demand will tend to concentrate on higher quality services

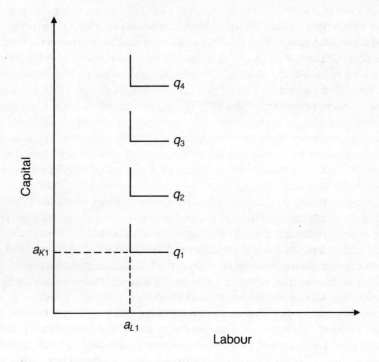

FIG. 1

(such as q_3 and q_4) in the rich countries and on lower quality services (such as q_1 and q_2) in the poor countries.

Now it is quite obvious that prices for high quality services must be greater than those for inferior services. Without an appropriate adjustment for such discrepancies, one is bound to find services relatively expensive in the developed countries.

So, alternative explanations for the price differential are available. I should add, however, that our modelling suffers from one major weakness — we model services as if they were goods. Of course some services do resemble goods, but in such cases the trade theorist meets no challenge. The most interesting services are those that differ from goods.

With regard to trade negotiations for services and potential gains to developing countries, here I go all the way with Jagdish Bhagwati. It is simply wrong to claim that all benefits from trade liberalization and international investment in services will accrue to the North, all to the loss to the South. It is also misleading to argue that because services are so important to the development process they have to be produced domestically.

In 1980 the group of 25 largest services exporters included five developing countries — Mexico, Singapore, South Korea, Saudi Arabia and Egypt. The ratios of services exports to merchandise exports in those five countries were 46%, 33%, 26%, 4% and 60%, respectively. Furthermore, Mexico, Singapore, South Korea and Egypt were net exporters of services.

One can expect that certain developing countries will expand their exports of services for three reasons. First, the fact that the relative price of services is lower in poor countries than in rich countries implies that the former must have a comparative advantage in some services. Second, liberalization of temporary labour movements, discussed by Bhagwati, will again place developing countries in a very competitive position. Third, the importance of physical proximity in the service provision suggests that regional markets are likely to emerge. Certain developing countries could then enjoy a geographical advantage over more efficient producers who happen to be located far away from a particular regional market.

As far as the role services play in development, the analysis is not altogether clear. In many cases development of tertiary production is not a result of growth, or event its concomitant element — it may be one of its preconditions. An efficient and well-run banking system, transportation sector, insurance industry, telecommunications network, and, last but not least, public administration are indispensable conditions for growth and development. Having said that, it does not follow that these services need to be provided by each developing country individually. The relevant question becomes: Given the need to develop a modern, efficient and dynamic service sector, what is the best way of achieving this goal? In some cases it may well be that the optimal solution lies in local production, but in other cases imports or foreign investment may be more efficient.

It has to be recognized, of course, that no country will freely liberalize and deregulate its service industries. There are legitimate reasons which call for government intervention, or at least supervision, and this is true in the developing as well as the developed countries. While it is not possible or even desirable to eliminate all domestic and international barriers, those intended to secure pure profits and monopoly rents harm the development process and ought, therefore, to be discarded.

References

Falvey, R. and Kierzkowski, H. (1984) "Product Quality, Intra-Industry Trade and (Im)perfect Competition;" Discussion paper, Graduate Institute of International Studies, Geneva.

VICTOR D. NORMAN* AND SIRI P. STRANDENES†

Jagdish Bhagwati's highly stimulating paper is one in a series of recent papers on trade in services — several of which have been written by Bhagwati. We have learnt a lot about services and their characteristics from these papers, and the authors have undoubtedly made it easier for policy makers to see the issues involved in liberalizing service trade. In that sense, there can be no doubt that the papers represent a very valuable contribution to the literature on international trade.

What is perhaps less clear, is what we as *trade theorists* have learnt. Are services such as to warrant special attention in terms of theory or analytic tools? Does increased trade in services have general-equilibrium effects that should be looked into? Is trade in services linked to international factor movements in such a way as to blur the distinction between trade in factors and trade in goods? These are the type of questions we shall discuss below. Towards the end, we shall use the answers as the basis for some more specific comments on Bhagwati's paper.

Characteristics of Services

As we see it, there are two things we have learnt from the recent literature on trade in services. The first (which has probably come as comfortable confirmation to most of us) is that there is nothing theoretically special about services — trade theory is as applicable to trade in services as to trade in goods. The second (which may have been more of a surprise) is that there is nothing special about services in terms of empirical characteristics, either.

The applicability of traditional trade theory to service trade is demonstrated in recent surveys by Hindley and Smith (1984) and Sandmo (1984). As they point out, comparative advantage is a sufficiently abstract concept to be applicable to questions of trade gains and division of labour of any sort. The same is true for the more recent theories of trade under imperfect competition. The interesting question, therefore, is not whether trade theory *is* applicable to service trade, but whether services have particular empirical characteristics that warrants attention in applying established theory.

According to conventional wisdom, services are income-elastic, labour-intensive, and have a high value-added share. Not one of these observations is true as a universal characteristic of services, as Tables 1 and 2 — based on Norwegian data — show. For 9 main categories of private

*The Norwegian School of Economics and Business Administration, Bergen.
†The Centre for Applied Research, Bergen.

TABLE 1. *Income elasticities, Norwegian households, 1975–77*

Service	Income elasticity
Medical care	0.872
Maintenance, transp. equipm.	1.356
Public transport services	1.029
Communication services	0.936
Recreation	1.258
Public entertainment	0.793
Books, newspapers	0.701
Personal care	0.830
Restaurant and hotel services	1.215
Simple average	0.999
Variance	0.050

Source: Bioern and Jansen (1982)

TABLE 2. *Production characteristics, Norwegian service sectors*

Service production sector	Index of capital intensity	Index of value-added share
Electricity distribution	394	130
Wholesale and retail trade	13	120
International seaborne transport	376	58
Domestic transportation	93	99
Banking and insurance	67	n.a.
Housing services	18928	115
Maintenance, consumer durables	4	116
Other private services	61	104
Public administration	64	117
Defence	n.a.	83
Education and research	125	125
Public health services	40	122
Other public services	1238	94
Average, excl. housing and defence	100	
Average, exlcuding banking		108

Capital intensities and value-added shares are expressed in per cent of the averages for all Norwegian production sectors.
Source: Data from the Norwegian MSG-model

services, the income elasticity varies from 0.701* to 1.356, with an average of 0.999. The capital intensity of service-producing sectors (excluding housing), varies from 4% of the average for all goods and services to 1238% — and the average for service sectors is exactly the same as the

---

*The inclusion of books and newspapers among services is open to doubt — but that simply illustrates how arbitrary the distinction between goods and services is, and how misleading it can be to think of services and goods as homogeneous aggregates.

average for goods-producing sectors. The value-added share is, on the average, somewhat higher for services than for goods — but some service industries (notably international transportation) have very low value-added shares.

Conventional wisdom also has it that technical progress is slower for services than for goods. Again, empirical analyses suggests important exceptions — seaborne transportation, for example, has had one of the most impressive records as regards new technology; for seaborne oil transportation a rough estimate is 4% annual improvement in technology since the late 1960s.

All of this is probably well known by now. The reason we repeat it, is that it suggests that we may attack the issues involved in service trade from the wrong angle if we continue to search for broad, empirical regularities characterizing services. For *goods*, we have never really attempted to look for common characteristics. Instead, and more fruitfully, we have concentrated on *heterogeneity* and exploited this as a basis for analysis. The fact that aluminium smelting is capital-intensive while shipbuilding is labour-intensive has inspired factor-endowments theories of trade; the fact that the US may have had a technological lead in the production of computers but not in pin-making has been used to illustrate Ricardo-type trade theory; the fact that novels in Dutch are less tradeable than motor cars has enabled trade theorists to study Dutch disease.

A similar approach to trade in services is likely to be the most fruitful one. Norwegian exports of seaborne transport services; British exports of financial services; US exports of computer software; South Korean exports of building services are all examples of phenomena which are difficult to understand if the basic premise is homogeneity of services with respect to technology, factor proportions and income elasticity — but they are easily understood once it is accepted that services are just as heterogeneous as goods.

It should be emphasized that the lack of empirical regularities in service production does not mean that there may not be a higher *incidence* of particular characteristics among services than among goods. As Hindley and Smith point out, we are more likely to find extensive public regulation of service industries than of goods-producing industries — perhaps because important services are characterized by imperfect information on the part of buyers, because there are natural monopolies for some services, or because of important external effects in the production of key services.

This may have important implications for the kind of tools we are likely to need to analyse particular service industries. If the incidence of regulation, imperfect competition, external effects, etc. is lower for goods than for services, we are more likely to find the elementary theory of comparative advantage and gains from trade useful for goods than for services — and to find the more recent theory of trade under imperfect competition, the theory of information, and second-best welfare economics correspondingly more useful for services.

Note, however, that this is a prediction, not a prescription. The heterogeneity of both goods and services implies that the choice of tools to analyse them must depend on the particular characteristic of the good or service one is interested in.

Tradeability

The arguments above are not intended as objections to Bhagwati's search for generality as regards trends in the *tradeability* of services. That search may be fruitful, and it focuses on what is probably the most interesting question in relation to trade in services. It is interesting for two reasons.

One reason has to do with the question of why people concerned with international trade should be interested in services in the first place. It may, of course, have to do with an interest in services as such — for obvious reasons, bankers are interested in banking services, computer specialists are interested in software, marketing people are interested in distribution. For trade theorists, however, that is hardly a reason to be concerned with services. To us, the more interesting question concerns the implications of services for the way in which the economy functions. In that respect, trade theorists have been interested in services because of their traditional role as nontradeables.

Specifically, the lack of trade in services (with the important exceptions that Bhagwati mentions — like international transportation and banking) has created a very large nontradeables sector in most economies; empirically, the nontradeability of services is the main reason why "open economies" like those in Scandinavia have tradeables sectors which only contribute around 1/3 of their national products.

The implications are many, as the substantial literature on two-sector models with tradeables and nontradeables illustrates. One implication, of particular relevance to trade and of specific interest in relation to Bhagwati's discussion of international price difference for services, is that international factor-price equalization is made less likely. This is discussed in detail in a paper by Haaland (1985) and is briefly touched upon in Helpman and Krugman's (1985) recent book. The point is simple: If factor endowments in a country are skewed (as compared to the international average) but factor proportions for nontradeables are not, then the existence of nontradeables will make factor supplies to tradeables production even more skewed. As a result, factor-price equalization becomes less likely.

48   *B. Hindley* et al.

If we are right in asserting that it was the nontradeability of services which made services theoretically interesting in the past, then increased tradeability of services is of interest more because of its implications for the economy as a whole than because of service trade in itself. Stated differently, perhaps the most interesting aspect of increased trade in services is the increased economic openness that will follow.

There is another, and more direct, reason for regarding tradeability of goods and services in general as more interesting than trade in services by itself — viz. the complementarity of goods and service trade. Bhagwati has pointed out that goods and services are often composite goods. We find even better examples of this if we start from the goods side. Can we think of exports of Coca Cola without exports of Coca-Cola marketing? Is trade in Volvos possible without trade in dealerships and maintenance systems for Volvos? In general, if we look at differentiated products, is it possible to separate the production and trade of physical products from distribution and marketing, or from servicing in the case of durable goods? Probably not. If so, tradeability of goods is a prerequisite for many types of service trade; and tradeability of related services is a prerequisite for goods trade.

Conclusions

Our three observations — that there is nothing special or homogeneous about services; that the interesting general issue is tradeability and implications of increased tradeability; and that goods and service trade are often complementary — lead us to conclusions that differ somewhat from those of Bhagwati.

Our first conclusion concerns research. Enough has probably by now been written on general aspects of trade in services. We need more detailed case-studies of trade in particular services. We need more detailed case-studies of trade in particular services. More importantly, however, there is a need for work on the general-equilibrium effects of greater openness. It may no longer be fashionable to see trade theory as the showpiece of general equilibrium — if so, it may be time to turn the trend.

Our second conclusion concerns trade policy. We feel somewhat uncomfortable with Bhagwati's recommendations, because they seem to be based on the premise that there *is* something special about services — or at least that we should accept the political need for distinguishing between goods and services. It is unclear why it should be desirable or necessary to maintain such a distinction. It is true that many services cannot be exported unless the exporter has a physical presence in the importing country. The same is true for many types of goods trade, however — and it is certainly true for the composite goods/services trade typical of differentiated products. We may in the future need a trade policy framework in which this need for exporter presence in the importing country is recognized, and where free trade (in goods and services) is coupled with the right to establish subsidiaries in importing countries and the right to man these — at least temporarily — by individuals from the exporting country. There is no reason for limiting such links to trade in services, however.

Nor do we understand Bhagwati's concern that exports of services from developed countries must be matched by exports of services from developing countries. There may be a political point here, of course. As economists in the tradition of political economy, however, our concern should be to make people understand that inter-industry specialization and trade still provide substantial gains — in that spirit, we should point out that any attempt to reduce the scope for such specialization by linking particular exports to particular imports makes the gain smaller.

The initiative for freer trade in services came from the US; and the skeptical reactions in developing countries and elsewhere is probably better understood as scepticism to US initiatives than as scepticism to free trade in services as such. Our primary function as economists in this respect is to explain that free trade in services (and goods) is advantageous, irrespective of who first proposed it.

References

Bioern, E. and Janssen, E. S. (1982) *Econometrics of incomplete cross section/time series data: Consumer demand in Norwegian household 1975–77*, Central Bureau of Statistics, Oslo.
Haaland, Jan I. (1985) "A note on factor price equalization, specialization and non-traded goods", *discussion paper*, Institute of Economics, Norwegian School of Economics and Business Administration, Bergen.
Helpman, E. and Krugman, P. (1985) *Market structure and foreign trade*, M.I.T. Press.
Hindley, B. and Smith, A. (1984) "Comparative advantage and trade in services", *The World Economy*, Vol. 7, No. 4, pp. 369–390.
Sandmo, A. (1984) *Handel i tjenester*, MU-rapport nr. 1, Centre for Applied Research, Bergen.

ANDRÉ SAPIR*

Services have come to be an intense and exciting area of investigation for trade economists in the last few years. The subject raises important questions ranging from positive trade theory to more practical, policy-oriented issues. The paper by Professor Bhagwati provides an excellent exposition of the entire range of issues. In my commentry, I will discuss further perspectives on this topic.

*Professor, Free University of Brussels.

50   *B. Hindley* et al.

It has become customary in the services literature to distinguish between producer or intermediate services and consumer or final-demand services. My remarks pertain almost entirely to producer services which serve as inputs into other economic activities.

I begin by examining services in their domestic context, where I distinguish between the industrialized and the developing countries. Much has been written about the alleged "deindustrialization" of the industrialized countries. Yet, as Professor Bhagwati has indicated, goods and services are in fact both undergoing a "splintering process" by which goods spring from services and vice versa. I would like to take this argument one step further and suggest that industrialized countries have entered a new industrial era characterized by a greater interdependence between manufacturing and service activities†. In other words, the line between goods and services has often become blurred.

The situation in the developing countries is not quite comparable. Yet, services assume a special importance for these countries. Producer services provide an essential link among economic agents that enable the interdependent functioning of markets. Services like banking, communications, transportation, and so on provide infrastructure services to the entire economy. Clearly, this issue is crucial for developing countries in assessing the role they wish to impart to service transactions in the international division of labour.

Moving to the international scene, the glaring feature of services that comes to the mind of a trade economist is obviously the fact that they tend to be *nontraded*. I think it is important to distinguish between two separate causes for the traditional nontradeability of services:

One is their *nonstorable nature* which implies that many services have to be produced and consumed in the same location and in the same point in time.

The other cause of nontradeability is the *intangible nature* of services by which I mean that uncertainty regarding the quality of services often requires a close and continuous interaction between buyers and sellers. In terms of economic theory, the market for services can be said to be characterized by asymmetric information and a great deal of product differentiation. Moreover, services will tend to exhibit dynamic scale economies of the "learning curve" type*. Obviously, this intangibility will be more or less important depending upon the type of service. Some services are product-like and hence almost tangible.

---

†This conclusion is corroborated in Lawrence (1983).
*This is similar to the model presented in Krugman (1984).

The recognition of these two separate factors is crucial, it seems to me, for assessing the increased tradeability of services made possible by the Information Revolution:

One the *one hand*, the new information technology is enabling to produce services in one place at one point in time and to consume them elsewhere at another point in time — thus increasing trade.

On the *other hand*, the intangible nature of services has remained almost untouched. Hence I suspect that much of the new trade will be in the form of *intra-firm* rather than *arm's-length* transactions. Moreover, the learning-by-doing economies of scale mentioned above imply that higher output now in the domestic market gives firms a base for successful exporting in the future.

I come now to the position of developing countries in the international division of labour and the question of their comparative advantage in services. One of the great developments of the seventies in the trade field has been the emergence of a number of developing countries as major exporters of manufactured products. At the same time, a handful of these newly industrializing countries have made successful inroads in the world market of certain services. The success of these countries in both manufactured products and services derives mostly from their accumulation of human and physical capital and technological capability. Developing countries at the upper end of the spectrum in terms of capital and technology have become net exporters of services to other developing countries while remaining at the same time net importers from industrialized countries and net *overall* importers.*

These issues can be substantiated with the help of two specific case studies. From an extensive study of developing country exports of *engineering services*, I drew the following conclusions:†

1. The revealed comparative advantage of developing countries lies in civil construction projects, with the engineering component embodied into a larger package including construction and equipment components.
2. Developing countries remain very weak in disembodied engineering services which involve more sophisticated technologies.
3. The number of developing countries involved in exporting engineering services remains extremely limited. At the most, half-a-dozen

---

*See Sapir (1985).
†See Sapir (1986).

have made significant inroads on world markets, namely Brazil, India, Korea, Pakistan, the Philippines and Taiwan.

4. The success of these countries is related to the factors I have identified earlier, namely human capital, physical capital and technological capability. In addition, however, I found that the intangible nature of engineering services is such that the successful launching of an export venture requires having established a solid reputation in the domestic market. This is the "learning curve" factor referred to earlier.

5. Nearly 100% of developing country exports of engineering services go to the South. Among the various factors which explain this trade pattern, protectionism plays an important role. Thus, in the area of construction projects, exports have tended to go to the more open markets, i.e. oil-exporting countries with lack of human resources compared to the scale of their civil construction projects. So I cannot but agree with Professor Bhagwati when he states that there is some scope for greater exports by developing countries in the area of construction services.

The second case study is related to *information services*. I briefly summarize the conclusions of an on-going study:

1. The information technology has created information services with substantial scope for international transactions. In turn, transborder data flows have greatly enhanced the possibilities for international trade in traditional services due to their "high information-technology content in both product and process"*

2. As far as information services are concerned, industrialized countries enjoy a clear comparative advantage.

3. Nonetheless, a few developing countries have been gaining a comparative advantage in certain types of services, especially software but at the relatively low end of the spectrum.

4. Comparative advantage in information services hinges primarily on human capital, technological status and a well-developed semiconductor-based hardware sector.

5. The pace of the changes imposed by the technological leaders in the field makes it very difficult for newcomers like developing countries to bridge the technological gap, unless they maintain close contacts with the leaders. This reality is illustrated by India which has recently relaxed her policy of technological self-reliance by liberalizing imports as well as foreign direct investment inflows in electronics. In

---

*See Porter and Millar (1985), p. 154.

particular, the government of India has recently authorized the construction of foreign-owned earth stations aimed at producing software for export via direct satellite relay.

6. As far as the impact of transborder data flows on international transactions is concerned, the fact that information flows relate mostly to firm-specific intangible assets implies that these flows will mostly enhance intra-firm transactions. Hence, transborder data flows are likely to increase *simultaneously* trade and foreign direct investment flows. Indeed, final buyers will tend to purchase services from local branches which belong to a worldwide network and exchange services with their headquarters by means of computer-to-computer communications technology.

I draw three conclusions from the above remarks. The first one is that the infrastructure aspect of services makes the issue of trade liberalization a very touchy one. But at the same time, it means that developing countries need very much to acquire these services. The difficult task for any developing country is to balance properly the various forms of acquisition (namely, imports or local production with or without the participation of foreign firms) in such a way as to fulfil its own development objectives.

My second conclusion is that the issues of trade in services are greatly complicated by the need to tackle simultaneously the problem of movements of labour (like in construction services) or of capital (as in over-the-wire services).

The final conclusion addresses the issue of future GATT negotiations. I share wholeheartedly Professor Bhagwati's concern about the need to enlarge services negotiations as broadly as possible in order to give developing countries a chance to increase their exports of services. Yet, I wonder whether there are indeed sufficient opportunities for there countries to warrant a services-only negotiation. Indeed, despite some impressive forays into world markets, developing countries remain by far net importers of services. My own feeling remains that the harsh reality of trade negotiations is such that developing countries must not only demand to broaden the scope of services but *also* insist on freer access for those manufactured exports where they stand to gain most at the moment. Hence my preference remains for a global approach to North-South trade problems encompassing both goods *and* services.

References

Krugman, P. R. (1984) "Import competition as export promotion: International competition in the presence of oligopoly and economies scale", in H. Kierzkowski (ed.), *Monopolistic competition and international trade*, Clarendon Press: Oxford.

54   B. Hindley et al.

Lawrence, R. Z. (1983) "Is trade deindustrializing America? A medium-term perspective", *Brookings Papers on Economic Activity*.
Porter, M. E. and V. E. Millar (1985) "How information gives you competitive advantage", *Harvard Business Review*.
Sapir, A. (1985) "North-South issues in trade in services", *The World Economy*.
Sapir, A. (1986) "Trade in investment-related technological services", *World Development*.

JEAN WAELBROECK*

I shall seek to relate to the coming GATT negotiations in that area.

A sarcastic observer might be tempted to summarize the state of play as follows. Mr Brock, when he was United States Trade Representative, got a bee in his bonnet that a liberalization of trade in services was in his country's interest. His staff diligently produced a massive volume of papers that, by lumping together in a dubious way data on interest payments and services trade proper, seemed to justify this claim. With the skilful aid of the Big Banks lobby, and of other lobbies in areas where the US is strong, such as communications and miscellaneous services, he did manage to get today's bandwagon rolling, and in particular to have the President commit US prestige to the holding of such negotiations.

The European Community watched this evolution with a mixture of astonishment and concern. Its attempts to liberalize Community trade in services had proved to it how difficult is the taks that the US government wanted it to tackle. The Commission, that has a greater faith in being fast on its feet around the green table than in amassing cubic metres of data, did a bit to fill up the empty files EC trade in services with non member countries, but basically played for time. Hopefully, the US fad would go the way of the hula hoop and of the break dance.

The round on services was however saved by the rise of the dollar and of the US trade deficit, and the pressures for protection that these events triggered. The Commission came to realize that getting a trade round under way might be the only way to hold in check the US Congress' infatuation with protectionist bills. Developing countries, meanwhile, found themselves victims of a very old negotiating ploy. With very real grievances on trade in textiles and clothing and in other areas, but vulnerable to accusations of having quite unenlightened policies on services trade, they felt a little like a wife whose husband sleeps out and is not giving her enough to pay the bills, and yet discovers that, somehow, he has managed to switch the argument to a discussion of why she burnt a cake yesterday. Their concern about a US slide into protectionism was

*Professor at the Free University of Brussels (Centre for Economic Mathematics and Economics).

great enough to convince them that they too had to live with a negotiation agenda that emphasizes services.

So the stage is set. The story is ironic. Somehow, governments have been manoeuvred into tackling an issue that was long neglected and is important. Everywhere — even in the EEC — experts are busy stuffing research papers into files. What contribution does this one make?

The problem about negotiations on services is detail. Not only are these transactions "invisible", to use the apt adjective that economists use to describe them. But they are so diverse that it is extremely difficult to get a firm grasp of the stakes that negotiators have to reckon on. Shipping, tourism, computer programs, traveller checks, satellite communications, fees to consultants and entertainers and many other types of transactions will all have to be discussed, although in each case, the relevant trade barriers reflect institutions that are very specific to each type of trade. The negotiations on tariff cuts of the early trade rounds involved a single policy instrument, and the officials involved could feel that they had a good grasp of what their countries stood to gain as a result of any particular give and take. It was far more difficult already to get such an overall view in the Tokyo Round discussions about codes for non tariff barriers. For services, where issues will be extremely heterogeneous, it may be feared that negotiators will not have the grasp of the implications of proposals for their countries that they need to work out balanced deals. The arguments will be on the trees, not on the forest.

What the paper by Bhagwati achieves is to provide the signposts that are needed to distinguish the forest from the trees. He discusses the secular patterns that characterize service activities and their possible theoretical explanations, casts a refreshing doubt on the very possibility of distinguishing changes in the share of services in trade that are real from reclassifications that result from service activities splintering out of or back into household or industrial production activities, and on the sensitive debates about high tech services and the developing countries belief that they are condemned to take a backseat in the struggle for significant market shares in that area.

Where I wish to focus my attention is however on his opening discussion, where following the excellent paper by Hindley and Smith (1984), he builds up a classification of services according to the nature of the contacts between the parties.

The division is two-fold. First is a distinction between services where physical proximity of the partners is essential, and those that do not require such proximity. The first group may in turn be subdivided according to whether it is the provider who has to move, or the user, or where both parties are potentially mobile.

Such a perspective may be the only way to prevent the negotiations from drifting into a sea of technicalities. The topic is extremely important, yet a successful outcome is not very probable. There is a real danger that the negotiations on trade barriers in services will degenerate into a medley of bitterly fought engagements between the bureaucrats who are responsible for the regulation of narrowly defined areas of services in the various countries. Even those who administer life insurance understand little about the issues involved in industrial insurance, let alone specialists of telephone communications understanding, say, the social security issues raised by migrant remittances. Each is master only of the very intricate legislation that regulates his sector, and as EC experience shows, many will be prone to attribute paramount importance to tiny aspects of these regulations that are unique to his country. These debates will tend to be so intricate that it will be very hard for the leaders of the various negotiating teams to carry out their mission of arbitrating between the issues at hand. Rescuing a foundering Round by, say, a Summit meeting, would be even more difficult to achieve: even more than usual the result would be platitudinous assertions of a common will, that are not precise enough to break any real deadlock. International public opinion, finally, would be too confused to exert a useful pressure for freer trade in services.

I believe that the key to a successful negotiation is to focus it on general rights and principles. The history of the GATT bears witness to the need to organize discussions within a framework of general principles, whether those are the overriding ones that are embodied in the most favoured nations clause, or the rights for a country to establish trade restrictions for balance of payments reasons. Agreement has to be deep. A good illustration of why is the emptiness of the gains which developing countries have secured after decades of effort that earned them only a lip service assent to special and differential treatment.

The experience of the European Community is another illustration of this point. The best example of this is the Cassis de Dijon decision of the European Court of Justice, which decided that for food products, member countries have to accept for consumption goods that have been cleared by the health authorities of the country of production. How that decision has made possible the elimination of a host of often bizarre obstacles to trade is a story that will hopefully be told in detail some day; extending the Cassis de Dijon principle to non food products has been suggested as the only way to make real headway in clearing up the trade obstacles that result from the existence of national norms and standards.

For trade in services, the classification used by Bhagwati suggests the kinds of principles that have to be agreed on before detailed negotiations have a chance of succeeding. Where the nature of the services requires that it is the provider who moves, a consensus is needed about such basic matters as the right of establishment, and about what in the EC is covered by the so-called "plumber directive" that authorize individuals and firms that obtain contracts in another country to bring with them the tools of their trade. Bringing in addition skilled or unskilled staff, as Bhagwati suggests, is an obvious extension of this principle. The consensus needs to be a general one, valid for many types of services, it should not be called into question every time that a new item comes up.

Where it is the user who moves, protection has been less prevalent, because the difficulty of controlling people makes it difficult to enforce (insurance is however an area where the principle is far from being applied). Formal agreement on principles may thus be more easy to obtain, though still worth securing.

The domain where something of a revolution has been taking place is that of communications — one of the cases where, in Bhagwati's list, direct contact between the partners is not necessary to performance of the service. Here the enforceability of the old restrictive regulations is getting more questionable, because satellites that beam their signals over wide areas have given users a freedom of choice that did not exist when messages were carried by more easily controlled wires. The task here is to make laws that are by now out of date provide users with the legal right to choose the cheapest seller that technology is providing them *de facto*.

Are not such principles too far reaching, so that agreement on them could not be secured? The strategy outlined would take time to work out. We can remember how slowly the most favoured nations clause came into general acceptance, but also that there was no real progress in trade liberalization before this acceptance became sufficiently widespread. Let the negotiators have a go at solving problems piecemeal; past experience (of the European Community in particular) does not warrant optimism on the chances of success of this. But let also the debate on rights and principles move centre stage.

3

A Sub-sectoral Approach to Services' Trade Theory

1. Introduction

At a time when the possibility of negotiating a multilateral agreement covering international trade in services is of increasing interest, it is perhaps wise to ask why such an agreement might be desirable. The academic economist's simple answer to this is that the world economy benefits from international trade, a theoretical result supported by the experience of the liberalization of trade in goods brought about in the post-war period through the GATT system.† An agreement on services would therefore be designed to liberalize trade.

Within the trade policy community in Geneva, the seat of the GATT, this simple answer is not generally accepted in the case of international trade in services. Many negotiators instinctively assume that services' trade is a zero-sum game, that if liberalization of this trade led to economic benefits for some, usually assumed to be developed countries, corresponding losses would be suffered by other trading partners.

In addition, the specificities which make services different from goods are often referred to, casting doubt on the applicability to services' trade of economic theories developed with reference to trade in goods, and in particular questioning whether the same notion of trade can be applied to both.

---

*The author works as a trade policy official for the Commission of the European Communities. The views expressed are, of course, his own and not necessarily those of this institution, The impetus for this article has come from the many discussions on the subject of trade in services which have taken place over the last 3 years in international fora. The author's thanks are due to very many participants in these discussions. The errors and misconceptions which remain are the author's alone.

†As the discussion of trade theory will illustrate, no single theory can accommodate the realities even of trade in goods. That the central theory of comparative advantage should have maintained its intellectual dominance is a tribute to the belief that the phenomena which do not fit into it are sufficiently marginal for its main results to hold true sufficiently for policy to be based upon them.

59

Finally, the heterogeneous nature of services, the clear differences which exist between, say, banking services, transport services, and engineering services, have led many to question whether the same trade theory can apply equally to all service sectors.

Until recently, these questions had not received much attention in trade theory, too often services have been relegated to footnotes in a text referring to phenomena drawn from experience of trade in goods, or simply ignored. And yet it is clear that, although policy makers may not often make explicit reference to theory, an academic consensus can have an important impact on the intellectual climate in which they take their decisions. If such a consensus were to emerge on the existence of benefits from liberalization of trade in services, it could not fail to influence international negotiations on the subject.

This paper attempts to indicate some broad lines for work towards such a consensus by examining some of the salient strands of trade theory, looking at the extent to which and the manner in which different services are tradeable, and suggesting how the specifities of different sectors can be accommodated in this theoretical framework.

2. The Tradeability of Services

Recent discussion of the applicability of existing economic theory to international trade in services has been complicated by uncertainty over what exactly is meant by "trade" and by doubts about the coverage of the term "services". A simple definition of trade such as that used in the March 1985 Declaration on trade in services from the US/Israel Free Trade Agreement — "trade in services takes place when a service is exported from the supplier nation and is imported into the other nation[1]" — turns out to be inadequate to the realities of the international services economy and, as Kravis has remarked[2], the services that are the focus of international attention are not identical with those often spoken of in discussions of the domestic "service economy".

In particular, it is clear that government services, most of the domestic distribution sector, and many personal services which require the physical presence of the provider and the consumer in the same place are not prominent in the minds of those who believe the world economy would benefit from the liberalization of trade in services. Hill's definition of services[3] as marketable activities in which production must take place in the presence of the demander is not altogether helpful in this regard, nevertheless it does identify the essential complicating factor which distinguishes many services from goods; their sale often requires a degree of personal contact between producer and consumer.

A good starting point for an analysis of the implications of this phenomenon for tradeability is provided by an UNCTAD Secretariat remark[4] that a criterion for trade can be, "whether or not the majority of the value added is exchanged between residents and non-residents". More simply, this is usually equivalent to saying that if a service cannot be, in this sense, *essentially* produced in one country and sold in another, it is not internationally tradeable*.

It is also helpful to see the essence of international tradeability as lying in the possibility of a domestic supplier of services being exposed to competition from a foreign supplier.

This is most obviously the case for those services which can be sold directly at a distance,† without requiring the presence of the producer in the consumer's country. These may include international banking and commercial insurance activities, trading in commodities, shares, shipping charters, etc. information services, consultancy, engineering, and many business-related services. All require a vehicle for the transfer of information, be it the printed word, the telephone system, or international data transmission using the telecommunications network. And it is the growing quality and efficiency of the latter which is now making an increasing number of services internationally tradeable in this way, a phenomenon for which Bhagwati[5] uses the term "disembodiment" of services.††

The two other major categories of services which can be produced by residents of one country and bought by residents of another are international transport and travel/tourism. Both these sectors are fully internationally tradeable in the sense that suppliers from any country could compete in these markets in a fully liberalized institutional environment. But it should be noted that in each case, the producer and the consumer (or his goods) have to be in the same place at the same time for the service to be furnished.

The necessity for at least some personal contact between buyer and seller is indeed one aspect which has been identified by many authors as a distinguishing characteristic of most services and it is interesting to ask why this is so.

One explanation begins by noting that there is a problem with developing a theory of value for services, as Nusbaumer has explained[7].

---

*Expenditure incurred while abroad for reasons of business travel or personal tourism do not, however, fit in with this simple definition, which is why the UNCTAD formulation is to be preferred.
†Distinguished by Nusbaumer[7] from services traded through incorporation in a material support and services which cannot be furnished other than by contact between producer and consumer, distinctions which the present author believes to be over-simplified.
††Rada[6] has done a sectoral analysis of the impact of TBDF on tradeability.

Very few services are homogeneous products sold on the basis of competition in terms of price per unit. A cursory reflection on the way in which consumers make their choice of plumbers, legal advisers, professional consultants, holidays, etc, is enough to underline the extent to which services are bought and sold on the basis of perceived quality, as well as price. This fact has at least two interesting implications, as has been pointed out by Edvinsson[8].

First, because consumers have extremely imperfect knowledge of the quality of service provided by different suppliers, their judgement may be dominated by their knowledge of those they know and if they are satisfied with their current supplier they may regard experimentation with another as a costly, high-risk alternative. In services transactions there may thus be a bias towards long-term producer/consumer relationships. As Edvinsson puts it, from the point of view of the producer,

"export of invisibles is very much dependent on skill in building business relationships and on social processes between supplier and buyer over time".

This remark leads directly to the second point, to the idea that the very value of the service may depend on the direct interaction between the supplier and the consumer: the value of the service to the consumer may indeed increase with the duration of the business relationship.

These points will be taken up again below when discussing comparative advantage. Suffice it here to note that they underline why, for so many services, it is desirable for the producer's personnel to have at least a temporary presence in the consumer's country of residence in order to be able to render his services.

Although the construction sector is obviously the best example of this phenomenon, it is also particularly relevant for consultancy, engineering, computer software, and indeed for all services where a non-standard product has to be designed and provided to meet the consumer's specifications. A further limiting case is that of certain banking and insurance activities, for which the establishment of a foreign branch, and thus a permanent commercial presence abroad, are often said to be necessary for business to be done.

The conclusion is that for many services a certain commercial presence (whether temporary or permanent) may be necessary in order to facilitate what is *essentially* trade (in the sense of the UNCTAD definition quoted above). But it should be noted that this construction only remains valid if the majority of the value added is still produced in the exporting country.

Deardorff[9] and Kravis[2] offer a plausible explanation for this possibility, in identifying management as the crucial source of comparative advantage in many service sectors. More generally, perhaps, it is particular techniques for manipulating information which may give a company's service product its edge in quality, and this know-how can be "input from a distance," to use Deardorff's term.

Some economists, such as Bhagwati[10], would take this line of argument further and argue that the permanent presence of nationals of one country in the "importing" country, wholly producing their services on the spot and sending remittances to their home country, should also be considered as representing trade in services. Whatever the political arguments for this point of view, this type of activity clearly does not fit into the definition of trade used here and it will not be examined further.

Yet another way of exposing domestic producers of services to foreign competition is to import foreign know-how either in association with inward direct investment or through payments for the use of intellectual property (royalties or franchizing expenditure). In this case as well, because the *essential* factor input moves to the "importing" country, the phenomenon does not fall under the definition of trade used.

Table 1 offers a preliminary breakdown on a sectoral basis according to whether a service can be traded wholly from a distance, tradeable with the help of facilitation by means of a commercial presence in the importing country, or capable of exposure to foreign competition only through movement of essential factor inputs, whether labour, capital, or know-how. Entries in more than one column indicate that more than one possibility exists.

This is not the place, in a general article, to explain each entry in the table. But one or two examples may illustrate one important conclusion. Not only do the results of the analysis vary from sector to sector but also within sectors, depending on the type of activity concerned.

Thus, in the insurance field the coverage of major, commercial risks and reinsurance are services which can be provided through the international telecommunications and postal network without personal contact between assurer and client. The coverage of mass risks such as fire insurance or life insurance and the activities of brokers, on the other hand, are usually distinguished by a considerable degree of personal contact between buyer and seller. Facit: it makes no sense to talk of "the insurance sector" as the subject of this type of analysis.

In the field of telecommunications, basic domestic telecommunications services are produced in most countries by a public monopoly and international services on a co-operative basis between two monopolies. In this case, as Reid[11] has pointed out, there is no question of trade according to our definition taking place. On the other hand, trade is possible for enhanced telecommunications services or VANS (Value Added Networks), if these are provided on a competitive basis using the basic network. Again, what may be true for one sub-sector is not true for another.

TABLE 1. *Tradeability of Services*

Tradeability Sector	Tradeable	Tradeable through facilitation	Non-Tradeable foreign competition through labour movement	Non-Tradeable foreign competiton through investment/ know-how transfer
Travel expenditure	X			
Hotels				X
Restaurants			X	
Travel operators	X	X		X
International maritime and air transport	X	X		
Domestic transport				X
Basic telecommunications				
VANS	X			X
International finance	X	X		
Commercial banking services	X	X		X
Credit card services	X	X		X
Retail banking		X		X
Commercial risks	X	X		X
Reinsurance	X			
Mass risks (personal insurance)		X		X
Insurance broking		X	X	X
Information services	X			
Audio-visual services	X			
Cultural services	X		X	
Construction		X	X	X
Engineering	X	X	X	X
Real estate		X	X	X
Management services		X	X	X
Consultancy	X	X	X	X
Computer services	X	X		X
Software	X	X		
Accountant/audit	X	X	X	X
Legal services	X	X	X	
Advertising	X	X	X	X
Industrial cleaning			X	X
Security			X	X

TABLE 1. *Tradeability of Services* — Continued

Tradeability Sector	Tradeable	Tradeable through facilitation	Non-Tradeable foreign competition through labour movement	Non-Tradeable foreign competiton through investment/ know-how transfer
Medical services	X		X	X
Hospital services				X
Hospital management			X	X
Basic Education				
Specialized education	X	X	X	X
Government				
Personal services			X	
Government services				
International trading	X	X		
Wholesale/retail				X

This conclusion will emerge again in the following section on the application of trade theory.

A further conclusion is that if all those sectors and sub-sectors which on the definition used are not internationally tradeable are aggregated, it can be seen that a very large proportion of any domestic economy is excluded as a potential object of liberalization. This also goes a long way to explaining why the proportion of domestic production of services currently traded internationally is so low compared with that of goods, a fact which is widely remarked.

3. Trade Theories Applied to Services

Traditional economic theory is based upon the premise that economic behaviour can be explained by assuming that individuals and companies behave as a "homo economicus". As consumers, given choice of sources for a given product, they will choose the lowest price on offer, given a single price they will choose the most attractive product; as producers they will attempt to maximize profit by producing at the lowest cost possible, choosing the optimal mix of production factors in order to do so. Although these basic ideas are usually illustrated in textbooks with examples of goods, to claim that they do not apply when the products concerned are services is to assume that homo economicus is schizophrenic.

Traditionally this theory is built upon by adding a series of further assumptions about the characteristics of the markets in which products are bought and sold, about their production functions and demand characteristics. In particular, market transparency and perfect competition are usually assumed. Where there is reason to believe that particular assumptions are too flagrantly in contradiction with the reality of a particular market, special theories have been developed to cope with this.

In this way, separate bodies of economic theory have been developed for, e.g. agricultural markets (in which the vagaries of the weather and the characteristics of reproductive systems make the supply of products subject to particular rules) or land transport (because of the low marginal costs associated with the use of fixed infrastructure).

Land transport is, of course, a service, and yet the economic theory developed for it is based on nothing more than general economic principles and a knowledge of the peculiarities of the market and the product concerned. There seems no reason to believe that this approach cannot be followed for other service sectors.

It is the approach followed by Deardorff[9] in his pathfinding analysis of comparative advantage in the field of services,

> "Select, one at a time, various characteristics that distinguish services from goods, characteristics that intuition suggests may have a bearing on trade and comparative advantage. Build a model that can capture these characteristics and examine its implications."

The analysis which follows summarizes the main theories of international trade and looks at their relevance in view of some of the characteristics of services. It may perhaps serve as a suggestion list for model-builders.

The best-known and most influential theory of trade is undoubtedly the body of theories which build on the original work of Ricardo and were developed formally by Heckscher, Ohlin and Samuelson.

The Heckscher-Ohlin-Samuelson model, which explains comparative cost advantage in terms of relative abundance of factor inputs, is sufficiently well known not to need discussion here. Although Herman and van Holst[12] cast doubt on its validity with respect to trade in services,* the

---

*Their critique is based on what they believe to be the poor explanatory powers of the H-O-S theory in actual cases of services trade. The examples they choose suggest, however, that it may be the difficulty of correctly specifying the inputs to services' production functions, rather than the invalidity of the theory itself, which causes the problem. The specification problem is discussed below.

majority of authors who have examined its applicability (e.g. Sapir and Lutz[13], Krommenacker[14], or Hindley and Smith[15] agree that there is nothing in the theory which intrinsically makes it less applicable to services than to goods, and Bhagwati[10] has not even found it necessary to reaffirm this.

But it is Deardorff[9] whose work has begun the rigorous analysis necessary to show that *specific characteristics* of services leave the theory intact. He examines three cases: the case when trade is in services complementary to goods; the case when a certain commercial presence of the exporting company in the importing country is needed; the case in which the service must be produced in the importing country, even though the input of some factors takes place from a distance.* His analysis, although leaving the theory of comparative advantage substantially intact, does cast doubts on its usefulness "as a guide to empirical reality".

The conundrum which particularly worries Deardorff concerns the case in which the service is "produced" in the importing country, the factor "management" remaining, however, in the exporting country. This situation can lead to trade even though the cost of management is higher in the exporting country, because of the exporting firm's superior technology, a result which is apparently contrary to comparative advantage, unless the know-how embodied in the technology is treated explicitly as a factor input.

This is not the place in which to attempt a courageous rescue of the general validity of comparative advantage. Suffice it to say that Deardorff has identified characteristics of services, recognizable to anyone with a knowledge of the real world, in the light of which the Heckscher-Ohlin-Samuelson model of comparative advantage, viewed as an explanatory theory, may require adaptation and/or extension.† Other such characteristics are examined below.

Before pressing on, it is certainly important to note Deardorff's conclusion with regard to the normative implications of his work,

> "even in the case in which trade might be said to run counter to comparative advantage, there is still a very clear gain from trade for both the countries involved".

This is not, of course, the first time that doubts have been cast on the usefulness of the H-O-S theory, and indeed a whole series of trade models have been developed to provide explanations of certain patterns in goods'

---

*It will be noted that the latter two cases represent particular specifications of the general phenomenon discussed in the previous section on "tradeability". Hindley and Smith[15] also emphasize the practical importance of the phenomenon.
†A result which supports the view of Herman and van Holst[12].

trade. In particular, it became clear many years ago that the massive expansion of intra-industry trade which has occurred in the post-war period required a different approach.

The theory of intra-industry trade usually begins either from the postulate that economies of scale internal to a firm are so large that they are not exhausted in a single national market and thus require trade in order to be fully exploited or by postulating product differentiation associated with Chamberlinian monopolistic competition. As Krugman[16] has pointed out, the two postulates fit well together into a single, more general theory. He points out that this theory explains trade best when scale economies are important and factor endowments are similar, hence its power is explaining trade in manufactures between economically advanced countries.

Is such a theory likely to be more or less relevant to trade in services? It seems doubtful whether economies of scale are likely to be *systematically* more important in the production of services than in the production of goods, although the sectoral analysis below suggests some sectors for which they may be important. But, remembering the previous discussion on the possible importance of quality rather than price in selling many services, it could well be postulated that product differentiation may be a key phenomenon in the services field. As Bhagwati[10] amusingly, but perceptively, points out,

> "It is not uncommon to find travellers who prefer to fly Singapore or Japan Airlines because they have more effusive onboard treatment than on Pan Am or TWA."

And for many non-English speaking consumers, the very fact of a service being rendered in another language is a differentiation of the product contributing significantly to its utility.

Edvinsson's[8] idea of the importance of the producer/client relationship in services has been developed considerably by Bresand and Distler[17], who see the concept of the "made-to-measure" product as being a characteristic of the service economy.

The relevance of product differentiation varies considerably from one service sector to another (see below) but a preliminary conclusion is certainly that theories based upon it may often be of more relevance in the services field than those based on comparative advantage, which assume a single, homogeneous product.

Before leaving the field of comparative static trade theory, mention should be made of two particular cases for which normative theory does not come down on the side of liberalization.

One of the implicit assumptions of the H-O-S model is that the markets concerned are competitive. Hindley and Smith[15] cite the well-known result that an importing country may optimize its welfare by restricting imports even it its own producers are less efficient than the foreign exporter, if the latter is exploiting a monopoly position. They suggest that this scenario is fairly implausible in the area of services, but the attention given to this point by the UNCTAD Secretariat[4] is only one manifestation of widespread suspicion in the trade policy community that this is an incorrect assessment. The increasing use of transborder data flows (TBDF) as a vehicle for trade in services is frequently put forward as a reason, because of the major international economies of scale which may be associated with the international telecommunications system. Thus the UNCTAD Secretariat[4] sees this as an incentive to the growth of a small number of very large transnational service companies, with the attendant risk of collusive behaviour and thus the abuse of a dominant position. And Malmgren[18] suggests, with considerable persuasive power, that such a process is clearly underway in the financial services sector.

On the other hand, Deardorff[9] suggests that the non-competitive situation of multinationals is of no greater relevance for services than it is for goods and Aronson and Cowhey[19] point out that international firms who consume services tend to maintain several sources of supply. This latter phenomenon dovetails well with the argument presented above that long-term producer/client relationships may be typical for services, since a single such relationship may carry a high risk, in terms of opportunities foregone, for the consumer.

The second case in which liberalized markets may not be optimal applies to certain service sectors in which it can be argued that there exist both internal and external economies of scale (the former being the "natural monopoly" argument and the latter the "public service" argument). Not for nothing has transport economics developed as a speciality of its own, rail transport has traditionally been regarded as a sector to which these arguments apply, and the usual policy conclusion has been that a single, usually state-owned, producer should supply the services concerned. Reid[11] has argued convincingly, as noted above, that international trade, under conditions of competition, is not possible under such circumstances.

The arguments for and against the establishment of national monopolies in the case of telecommunications have been well summarized by the OECD Secretariat[20]. What is noticeable is that the arguments in favour of monopoly are based on comparative statics, whereas those in favour of competition are dynamic in nature.*

---

*The present author has argued elsewhere [21] that the importance of relaunching national economies in an era of heavy unemployment, and the consequent importance of encouraging innovation, is beginning to tip the balance between monopoly and competition in telecommunications policy in favour of the latter.

There is in fact a whole series of critiques of the models discussed up to now which are based on the premise that they abstract from dynamic phenomena which are of major importance in the real world. Since some of them may be of particular relevance to services, they need to be addressed here.*

The first critique is embodied in the infant industry argument for protection or subsidization of a national product. Corden's[22] frequently quoted analysis shows that conditions under which the argument holds water: it is necessary, inter alia, that the national supplier(s) experience cost economies over time greater than those of the foreign supplier and that benefits external to the firm accrue to the domestic economy. Krommenacker[23] is sceptical whether the argument is of any more relevance for services that it is for goods, but he does identify "high-technology" industries,

> "where vast and speculative expenditure on research and development are often required",

as those in which it is usually put forward.

Although R+D has often been identified as a crucial component of comparative advantage in services†, it is not clear that this is more important than for goods. Walsh[24] sees this much more as a difference between large and small countries,

> "the smaller or poorer the country, the lower will be the number of fields or industries in which it can undertake R+D and the higher the number of those in which the minimum entry cost will be a barrier".

It has been noted that the infant industry argument requires the development of comparative advantage by the protected producer over time. The likelihood of this is diminished wherever there are reasons to believe that the initial comparative advantage of the foreign producer may be particularly durable.

This argument is associated with the idea that comparative advantage may depend crucially on the possession of a better technology than

---

*Before leaving the field of comparative statics, it is perhaps worth noting which factors have been identified by various authors as likely to be more important in contributing to comparative advantage in the field of services than in that of goods. Sapir and Lutz (13) emphasize physical and human capital, Bhagwati [10] skills in general, Kravis[2] human capital and managerial methods, Krommenacker[14], Krugman[16], and Nusbaumer[7] all mention R + D expenditure, the latter adding O and M (organization and methods) expertise. It is perhaps the combination of personal skills and corporate know-how, which looks remarkably like the "thoughtware" concept developed by Edvinsson[8] which is the common thread. But it is the *a priori* identification of the relative importance of different factors in production functions which poses the difficulty if comparative advantage is to be used as a predictive tool.

† See note, p. 70.

competitors, and that this technological edge can be acquired by R+D expenditure. The result is what Cline[25] has called "arbitrary comparative advantage".* As he puts it,

> "the perception is that in certain manufactured products some countries are artificially achieving a comparative advantage that otherwise would lie with other countries".

The dynamic scenario that most worries certain policy-makers combines this idea with the assumption that the increasing rate of technical change is shortening the lifetime of products. Instead of comparative advantage shifting over the lifetime of a product to reflect (non R+D) factor costs as the knowledge of its technology diffuses, it remains with the original innovator for long enough for him to have used his profits to finance the R+D necessary to introduce a new, replacement product, thereby renewing his competitive edge. Under such conditions the product cycle theory no longer leads to the same results.

The plausibility of this scenario may in fact be even greater in the case of services than in that of goods. A high degree of product differentiation and an associated supernormal level of profits, together with the tendency to long-term producer/client relationships, both increase its intuitive appeal. Clearly, its relevance to particular service sectors will depend crucially, however, on the rate of technological change. This suggests, e.g. that all those services traded through the vehicle of TBDF could potentially be subject to such a phenomenon and thus doubtful candidates for successful infant industry policies.

While on the subject of dynamic phenomena, it should not be forgotten that the principal argument used by policy-makers in favour of increasing competition is that this acts as an incentive to the improvement of quality, the increase of productivity and the acceleration of innovation. This general argument for "deregulation" is increasingly used with reference to service sectors, many of which have traditionally been heavily regulated. And if it is valid for competition in general, it is also true for international competition in particular. This provides an important argument for liberalizing international trade, because of the efficiency gains achieved, quite distinct from the allocative gains associated with comparative static theory.

Before concluding this section on trade theory three further points should be noted.

First, although it is accepted that all goods are tradeable, transport costs represent an inbuilt barrier to trade of a magnitude inversely related to a product's value per unit weight (or volume). This clearly applies equally to

---

*Krugman[16] makes a similar point in describing a "theory of technological competiton."

services, and Bhagwati[9] has noted that where they require personal contact
between buyer and seller, the cost of mobility limits tradeability. This is, of
course, one of the main reasons why TBDF are increasing the tradeability
of services, as costs of international data transmission tumble as a result of
technical change. Perhaps it should be added, however, that to the extent
to which a successful producer/client relationship in the services field may
depend on its being compatible with the local culture (e.g. the language) of
the client, a local producer may have an inbuilt advantage over foreign
producers equivalent to that provided by transport costs in the case of
goods.

Second, several authors, in particular Gray[26], have emphasized the role
of foreign direct investment in providing, in certain circumstances and
under certain conditions, an alternative to trade, and leading to analogous
welfare benefits. Despite the clear relevance of this to services, it is not
pursued here, since it falls outside the definition of trade which has been
adopted.

Third, and of most importance for the section which follows, the
question arises as to the circumstances under which the gains from trade
are greatest, a question of great interest to policymakers. It should be
emphasized at once that analysis of it addresses itself to gains in terms of the
increased economic welfare of consumers participating in the world
economy. The idea of benefits accruing as a result of a net increase of
exports is excluded by this and by the implicit assumption of trade theory,
that exports and imports are always brought into equilibrium by exchange
rate movements.

The magnitude of the benefits from trade, according to comparative
static theories, is related to the magnitude of the differences which would
exist between the products of different countries in the absence of trade
(differences in costs and prices in the case of comparative advantage, and
differences in characteristics and thus "quality" in the case of intra-industry
theories). According to dynamic theories, the magnitude of benefits is
once again dependent on differences between products, these being related
either to the rate of technical change, or to historical circumstances such as
the previous degree of regulation.

4. Sub-Sectoral Characteristics

In policy-making circles it is often asked in which sectors benefits from
liberalizing trade in services can be expected. The economist's answer to
this must always be that the overall benefits arise from the total of trade in
all sectors and that this cannot be attributed to particular sectors. But an
answer to a related question can be attempted: this asks about the sectors
in which trade flows are likely to change most in response to liberalization

thus leading to the multilateral trade pattern which benefits consumers.

The reason why policy-makers ask this question is intimated by Gray[26], when he suggests that negotiations on liberalizing trade in services,

"should be confined in the beginning to those service industries with potential payoffs".

It can indeed be argued that the rationale behind seven successive rounds of tariff-cutting in the GATT was to gradually reduce protective constraints, in particular those which ran most clearly counter to the market. The mechanism to do this consisted essentially of countries trying to obtain "concessions" from their trading partners in precisely those sectors in which they expected the greatest increase in their exports. It therefore makes sense to ask the same question in the case of services, if one assumes that the liberalization of trade in services will inevitably be a step-by-step process, with unequally rapid progress being made in different sectors.

In this section this question is put on a sub-sector by sub-sector basis.* In addition, the probable relevance of particular characteristics of services which have been discussed in previous sections is examined. In the interests of brevity only the most important of those sectors are treated which were identified as being internationally tradeable. But why the sub-sectoral approach? Is this really necessary?

The discussion above has centred on some of the specific characteristics which may distinguish trade in some or all services from trade in goods, and what they suggest about the type of trade theory which may be applicable to services. It is the author's view that considerable empirical work is now necessary on the micro-economic level of the sub-sector, in order for a consensus to emerge on services-specific characteristics. This will then lead to the appropriate development of trade theory. Such an approach to the development of theory, by examining the plausibility of its hypotheses, has been out of favour in recent decades. But the emphasis on empirical varification of the predictions of theory, which has replaced it, is not only impracticable in the field of trade in services—the scarce data which currently exist are simply too unreliable—it also has its own pitfalls, trenchantly summarized by Leamer[27]. And armchair economics based on more or less casual empirical observation has an honorable place in the history of economic theory.

---

*To be more precise, what is examined here is the probable difference between the situations with and without fully liberalized trade. In practice the situation is complicated by the large differences in the degree of protection currently applying to different service sectors. The biggest potential payoffs, in Gray's[26] sense, will presumably be found in sectors with a high trade potential, a high level of initial protection, and a low level of political constraints on negotiability.

4.1. Travel and Tourism

Any application of trade theory to the travel/tourism sector has to take account of certain important specificities. The most obvious is the need for the consumer to be present in the producing country.

In this sector there exist at least three clearly distinguishable markets. The first is business travel, whose magnitude and location is closely linked to the pattern of international economic activities in general, and to trade in other services in particular, to the extent that these require producer/client contact. Gains from trade in this sector will be reflected in the efficiency of the production functions associated with the related activities.

The second market is the mass holiday market, a clear candidate for contributions to overall gains from trade based on comparative advantage, since it is typical of that category of "footloose" services described by Gray[26], which can be produced and consumed in most countries. Comparative advantage is likely to be dominated by two types of input, certain natural resources such as sunny beaches or snow-clad mountains and labour costs. That a certain degree of product differentiation exists is demonstrated by the Club Méditerranée but this seems unlikely to be a major phenomenon. Transport costs are, of course, an important limiting factor.

The third market is that based on location-specific natural resources. The locations of the world's civilizations and of its natural wonders will presumably maintain an absolute advantage with reference to the differentiated products concerned. The opportunities for the exploitation of economic rent by the owners of the resources represent an interesting specificity.

4.2 Air Transport

International air transport is another example of a footloose service, to which the theory of comparative advantage and the efficiency gains attributed to competition could be expected to apply. Comparative advantage is presumably dominated by capital costs (although it may be important that much of the capital is mobile), labour costs, and perhaps operating expertise.*

The possibility of product differentiation has already been noted. But it seems doubtful whether the element of quality differentiation involved in personal contact will be a major characteristic. Indeed this is one of the few services in which price competition for a well-defined product might be the essential norm, were it not often excluded by the existing regulatory framework.

---

*The important cost factor of aviation fuel can be assumed to be the same for all producers.

It may perhaps be doubted whether this is a sector in which a major innovative effect could be achieved by increased competition, since the rate of technical change does not appear to be high. But many economists believe that the traditional heavy regulation of this sector has allowed major static inefficiencies to persist or to arise. As noted above, this would, if correct, provide a good a priori argument for international liberalization. Current US experience with the deregulation of a market of continental dimensions provides an interesting test case.

It should be noted that domestic air transport would seem to be a market with quite different characteristics. In particular, on the definition used, it is not internationally tradeable, since the service cannot be essentially produced by foreign residents, unless it is an extension of an international service.

In passing, it should also be noted that air freight is a special case similar to the business travel market. It is a joint product with trade in some goods as well as with passenger travel.

4.3. Maritime Transport

To the economist the maritime transport market must surely seem to parallel very closely the air transport market in its innate characteristics. But it differs greatly in its regulatory history. Apart from a certain element of cargo reservation, often justified on grounds of national security, the traditional regime was extremely liberal. Although this is now changing to some extent as a result of the cargo-sharing provisions of the UNCTAD Liner Code, this change only affects certain liner conferences and thus scheduled voyages. The bulk market remains substantially free of intervention.

Although international maritime transport is a clear example of one of Gray's[26] "footloose" services,* it has a characteristic which makes it a bad subject for a simple analysis based on comparative advantage but an interesting one for Deardorff's[9] development of it, viz. the ability for labour inputs (still a major element of costs) to be hired in any country. On the other hand, there is no problem with personal contact since the service is concerned with changing the state of goods† rather than of people.

The very existence of liner conferences and the continuing, fierce debate on how they should be regulated are convincing evidence of the

---

*Although Gray himself prefers to place both maritime and air transport in a separate category of "location-joining" services.
†This cursory analysis ignores the passenger transport market, which is relatively unimportant.

importance of economies of scale and of the possibility of the development of non-competitive situations in this sector. It is therefore not surprising that both the infant industry argument and the idea of protection as a defence against monopoly (or oligopoly) supply are often used with reference to it, even if it is not clear that all the conditions needed to justify them are fulfilled.

This sector is not commonly thought of as being subject to major technical change. Yet the still increasing containerization of scheduled services is in fact an important element and the development of multi-modal transport services and the introduction of computerized fleet management techniques may radically transform the industry. If this is potentially the case, the dynamic argument for a liberal regime, based on the stimulus given to innovation by competition may in fact be very strong.

Where coastal shipping services are concerned, remarks similar to those on domestic air transport apply.

4.4. Banking

Banking is not a homogeneous sector but an interlinked network of many different banking services. Nor can there be a single global market for banking services; rather, there exist a series of markets in individual currencies, interconnected through exchange transactions. Perhaps the major sub-sectoral distinction is between an international banking sector, offering complex packages of financial services to firms or individuals engaging in economic activities internationally, and domestic retail banking. Since the latter will almost always require the service to be produced essentially in the country in which it is consumed, it does not seem to be internationally tradeable in the sense used here.

As far as international banking is concerned, the accumulated expertise of certain financial centres is a major factor in determining comparative advantage. But to the extent that this expertise is embodied in individuals, who are potentially mobile, this comparative advantage may not be as stable as it seems.

Currently it is the economies of scale involved in the exploitation of world-wide financial information networks which are causing most structural change within the sector.

One of the most interesting questions is whether the increase in electronic banking which is taking place will in fact significantly reduce the element of personal contact in the producer/client relationship. It is this necessity for personal contact which at present makes the existence of branches or representative offices so necessary for the sale of banking services abroad, making banking internationally tradeable primarily through "facilitation". If the day comes when all or most banking services are carried out via terminals attached to the international communications network, this situation will change.

Given the importance of international economies of scale in electronic banking, the development of non-competitive markets is certainly not to be excluded* although there is currently little evidence of it.

It has been suggested above that many services are bought primarily on the basis of perceived quality. At first sight it seems doubtful whether this applies to banking, in which interest rates on borrowing and lending, which is after all the central activity of banks, are highly transparent. But to the extent that major clients increasingly expect to receive a complex package of different financial services from their banks, a bank's reputation may well be an important factor in its success. In this case, the impact on certain elements of theory affected by a tendency to long-term producer/client relationships may be of importance.

For the world as a whole, so much technological innovation is taking place in the banking sector that increased international competition does seem likely to lead to large efficiency gains from trade.

4.5. Insurance

The main purpose of insurance is the spreading of risk and in so far as national markets may be too small to do this effectively, an international-ization is necessary in the case of large risks. Although this characteristic of insurance is specific to the sector, its economic effects are similar to those of international economies of scale in production in explaining gains from trade.

This argument only applies, however, to large, usually commercial risks. It does not apply to mass risks. Where these are concerned, the case for trade rests on the exploitation of comparative advantage but also on the beneficial dynamic effects of international competition. The quality or price of the product sold by an insurance company depends not only on the performance of its actuaries, but also on its investment expertise, its internal management systems, its skill in risk reduction, and its ability to tailor a policy to the needs of the client. In so far as large differences in this regard may exist between companies in different countries (a question for empirical research), increased international trade may be beneficial for both comparative static and dynamic reasons.

Insurance is often quoted as a service in which personal contact between producer and client is important and a commercial presence necessary in order to sell abroad. On the other hand, the existence of the honourable profession of insurance broker suggests that this is less true than of

---

*As has already been noted above, Malmgren[18] argues in this sense.

banking. It may well be more true for some types of insurance than for others.

Being concerned in essence with the handling of data, insurance is, of course, a sector affected by the revolution in information technology. The impact of TBDF on its international tradeability has already been noted. The other major impact is on the insurance of mass risks, for which the potential for the replacement of labour costs by computer costs, may be leading to considerable changes in the comparative advantage of different countries.

4.6. Construction

Not everyone would classify construction as a service since it produces a tangible good. It is, however, included here because the good is not transportable and hence not tradeable, so it is easiest to regard the international activity in this sector as trade in services.* In order to do so, on the definition we have been using, it is necessary to assume, in particular, that the labour factor services involved on site are only temporarily present, thus making trade possible through facilitation.

One of the preculiarities of construction in practice is that often all production factors do not come from the same country, Unskilled labour from one country may be combined with management and engineering skills from another.

Construction is a basic human activity and has an important share of total world production. But it seems clear that much construction activity, concerned with small projects, is destined to be covered by local supply, because of the cost of international labour mobility and the knowledge of local physical and regulatory conditions which may be required.

But where larger projects are concerned it seems clear that many different building techniques and a multitude of differentiated products exist, with new products being introduced at an impressive rate. This looks at first sight very like the case of manufacturing industry in the industrial world, and yet intra-industry trade between developed countries is very much the exception where construction is concerned. If there are indeed major potential benefits from such trade which remain unexploited because of the overriding impact of obstacles to it, successful liberalization could be extremely beneficial. Whether this is so is clearly another subject for empirical research.

---

*It can be argued, of course, that overseas construction is always, in economic terms, equivalent to the activity of a foreign subsidiary and thus to foreign direct investment, although the absence of any fixed capital in the production process makes this somewhat strange. Clearly construction is *sui generis*, and its inclusion in any broader category of economic activity can only be the result of an agreed convention.

4.7. Information Services

The world is commonly said to be on its way towards an "information society",* in which a whole new range of products based on the processing and transmission of data and other information will play a major part. The growth of economic information services, data banks, etc. is evidence of this phenomenon.

One essential characteristic of information services is that once the telecommunication infrastructure is available and the processed information stored, the marginal costs of a sale to a new customer become very low. In principle, the economies of scale involved are limited only by the scale of the world market, and competition between different producers will only ultimately take place through product differentiation. This characteristic signals both the enormous benefits to be derived for the world economy by exploiting these economies of scale through international trade in information services, and the possibility of the emergence of world-wide monopoly suppliers of particular products.

Another characteristic of the sector is that, because of its symbiotic relationship with the telecommunications network, all its factor inputs need not be located in one and the same place. Hindley and Smith[15] suggest that the crucial labour intensive input function of keyboard manipulation to enter data, will increasingly be drawn from low-wage countries.

Reflection on the sources of comparative advantage in this sector suggests that three peculiarities may be important. First, the existence of an efficient domestic telecommunications network (soon in the form of an ISDN = Integrated Services Digital Network) will be a precondition. Second, because of the importance of economies of scale, the first entrants into the market for a new product are likely to be able to maintain their competitive edge, making the infant industry argument untenable. Third, the rate of introduction of new products may well be very rapid and the ability to develop them a function of the capacity to expend large sums on R+D, again casting doubt on the viability of infant industry policies.

4.8. Other Business Services

Other services sold to business, such as accountancy, consultancy, computer services, advertising, legal services, etc. have a number of characteristics in common. Personal contact between producer and client, perceived quality, and long-term buyer/seller relationships are all important. In most of these services local knowledge (reflecting national

---

*Bressand and Distler[17] provide an unusual and thought-provoking description of this "next world".

regulatory or market peculiarities) may well provide a considerable built-in advantage to local suppliers.

It is difficult to judge how fast these sectors are being affected by technical change, but in view of the fact that they are all highly knowledge-intensive the effect may be considerable. This argues in favour of potential dynamic benefits arising from international competition.

4.9. Cultural Services

The services provided live by members of the performing arts are undoubtedly internationally traded, but their economic importance is clearly less than their cultural.

Of much more economic importance are audio-visual products,* whose provision in the form of a film screening or a television transmission is usually viewed as a service.† It is clear that the economies of scale involved are potentially world-wide and also clear that non-competitive tendencies are present in the market, as the UNCTAD Secretariat[4] points out.

Audio-visual products also have characteristics which distinguish them from all other services. Their consumption is often thought to be associated with the transfer of certain cultural values, a view which makes some governments reluctant to allow the consumer to fully exercise his own preferences. In such a situation, traditional economic theory has little to say, since it is usually based on the assumption that consumer preferences are given. Product differentiation is also the rule, indeed most products can be said to be unique.

5. Conclusions

The above analysis suggests that no single trade theory is likely to be able to encompass all the characteristics which make trade in services such a complex—and such an exciting—domain. But since the same thing already applies to trade in goods, this is hardly surprising. Some of the characteristics of trade in particular goods which have led to the development of partial theories are clearly of relevance for some services, other services may exhibit characteristics of their own for which new partial theories may be needed. It is therefore likely to be some time before the theoretical foundation for predicting service trade flows is fully laid.††

---

*This is a typical example of Bhagwati's[5] "disembodied" services, but to be distinguished from his other use of the word, which refers to the long-distance provision of a service through TBDF.

†Although films are already covered by the GATT, whose Article IV provides for screen quotas.

††It may well be that the improvement in statistics which is also required could take even longer.

On balance the general arguments suggesting that liberal trade brings both static allocative and dynamic efficiency gains seem likely to remain valid, for most sectors or sub-sectors, leaving the normative implications of trade theory essentially intact.

It may well be that major potential benefits to the world economy from liberalizing services trade lie in all those sectors in which TBDF is increasing tradeability and the introduction of new information technologies is revolutionizing production and spawning new products. It is undoubtedly in this large group of sectors that the dynamic benefits of international competition are likely to be most marked, but static gains could also be expected in many sectors at present sheltered from international competition.

In empirical research on the peculiarities of services it will be necessary to descend below the level of a sector in order to identify a homogeneous group of products with common characteristics.

References

1. US/Israel Free Trade Agreement, House of Representatives' document 99–61, 29 April 1985.
2. Kravis, Irving B., "Services in the Domestic Economy and in World Transactions", National Bureau of Economic Research, Working Paper No 1124, May 1983.
3. Hill, T., "On Goods and Services". *Review of Income and Wealth 23*, December 1977.
4. UNCTAD Secretariat, "Services and the Development Process", TD/B/1008/Rev.1, 1985.
5. Bhagwati, Jagdish N., "Splintering and Disembodiment of Services and Developing Nations", *The World Economy*, June 1984.
6. Rada, J. "The International Division of Labour and Technology", Geneva, International Management Institute.
7. Nusbaumer, Jacques, "Les services: nouvelle donne de l'économie", *Economica*, Paris, 1984.
8. Edvinsson, Leif, "Trade in Thoughtware and Internationalisation of Services", unpublished paper.
9. Deardorff, Alan V., "Comparative Advantage and International Trade and Investment in Services", University of Michigan, November 1984.
10. Bhagwati, Jagdish N., "Trade in Services and Developing Countries", Xth Annual Geneva lecture, London School of Economics, 28 November 1985.
11. Reid, Anne Hutcheson, "The Role of Telecommunications and Services in International Trade", OECD, 1985, ICCP(85)12.
12. Herman, B. and van Holst, B., "Towards a Theory of International Trade in Services", Netherlands Economic Institute series on Foundations of Empirical Economic Research, 1981.
13. Sapir, André and Lutz, Ernst, "Trade in Services, Economic Determinants and Development-related issues", World Bank Staff Working Paper No. 480, August 1981.
14. Krommenacker, Raymond, "World-Traded Services: the Challenge for the Eighties", Artech House, Dedham, MA, 1984.
15. Hindley, Brian and Smith, Alasdair, "Comparative Advantage and Trade in Services", *The World Economy*, Vol. 7, No 4, 1984.
16. Krugman, Paul, "New Theories of Trade Among Industrial Countries", *American Economic Review*, May 1983.

17. Bressand, Albert and Distler, Catherine, "Le prochain monde", Coll. Odyssée, Seuil, Paris, November 1985.
18. Malmgren, Harald, B., "Negotiating International Rules for Services", TPRC meeting on "Restrictions on Transactions in the International Market for Services", Ditchley Park, 13–15 April, 1983.
19. Aronson, Jonathan D. and Cowhey, Peter F., "Trade in Services: a Case for Open Markets", American Enterprise Institute, 1984.
20. OECD, DSTI/ICCP/(82)32, "Monopoly and Competition in the Provision of Telecommunications Services: a Survey of the Issues", September 1982.
21. Richardson, John B., "International Trade Aspects of Telecommunications Services", *Common Market Law Review*, 1987.
22. Corden, Max, "Trade Policy and Economic Welfare", Oxford, Clarendon Press, 1974.
23. Krommenacker, Raymond, "Services and Space Technology: the Emergence of Space Generated, Highly Integrated Goods and Services".
24. Walsh, V. M., "Technology, Competitiveness and the Special Problems of Small Countries", OECD, DSTI/SPR/(86)11, 1986.
25. Cline, William R., "Reciprocity and Arbitrary comparative Advantage", Institute for International Economics, Washington, September 1982.
26. Gray, H. Peter, "A Negotiating Strategy for Trade in Services", *Journal of World Trade Law*, September/October 1983.
27. Leamer, Edward E., "Let's Take the Con out of Econometrics", *American Economic Review*, March 1983.

4

The Role of the Service Sector in Economic Development: Similarities and Differences by Development Category

DOROTHY I. RIDDLE*

1. Introduction

The labelling of service industries as "post–industrial" (Bell, 1973) has misled many into believing that service sector development is relevant primarily to the "industrialized" countries. Nothing could be further from the truth. Indeed, the service sector is much more important in developing countries than has often been realized. Service industries facilitate every aspect of social, political, and economic life. Without transportation, communications, utilities, or construction services, little economic activity is possible. An efficient government, a healthy and literate work force, and stable financial markets are as much a prerequisite for economic growth as are the availability of raw materials.

Conceptualizing economic growth as fuelled by the manufacturing sector has overlooked the fact that the initial growth of manufacturing, known as the Industrial Revolution, was itself dependent upon changes in the service sector — sometimes known as the Commercial Revolution. Development of the factories themselves was only possible because of the growth of capital markets. Mass production was dependent on both the changes in transportation that allowed the timely and cost-efficient arrival of raw materials and finished goods, and the availability of large markets developed through international trade.

Our present global economy is one in which economic sectors and national economies are increasingly interdependent. Every nation is involved in international transactions. Some have little in the way of

*Department of International Studies, American Graduate School of Management, Glendale, Arizona, U.S.A.

agriculture or mining activities and import virtually all raw materials. Others have little manufacturing activity and import most manufactured goods. But every nation with an economy that is at all effective must have a functional service sector.

Service industries not only facilitate extractive and manufacturing activities, but value-added occurs primarily in services. Service industries are the primary force for economic growth. They are the major purchasers of equipment and supplies. They initiate demands for new technology. And they create and ensure quality of life.

In order to clarify and underscore the leading role of services in economic development, analyses in this article will distinguish among countries[1] at four levels of development, based on the per capita income categories used by the World Bank in its 1984 *World Development Report:* Low-income countries (LOW); Lower-middle-income countries (LOMD); Upper-middle-income countries (UPMD); and Industrialized countries (IND). From the country groupings in Table 1, it is apparent that there is not a clear dichotomy between developing and industrialized countries regarding size of service sector; for example, a number of the so-called newly industrializing countries (NICs) have larger service sectors than do the industrialized countries. As the data will make clear, there are also important differences among the developing countries, not just between developing and industrialized countries. In addition, high-growth and low-

TABLE 1.   *Countries Grouped by Service Sector as Percentage of GDP: 1981*

%Services	Development Category			
	Low Income	Lower Middle	Upper Middle	Industrial
Under 35%	China			
35–39%	Ghana Bangladesh Somalia	Liberia		
40–44%	Uganda Ethiopa India			
45–49%	Mali Central African Republic Haiti	Indonesia Philippines	South Africa	
50–54%	Upper Volta Kenya Pakistan	Nicaragua Honduras Nigeria Thailand Ecuador Cameroon Tunisia	Yugoslavia South Korea Algeria	

TABLE 1. *Countries Grouped by Service Sector as Percentage of GDP: 1981* — Continued

	Development Category			
%Services	Low Income	Lower Middle	Upper Middle	Industrial
55–59%	Sierra Leone Togo Tanzania Sri Lanka	Peru Yemen Arab Rep Turkey Egypt Sudan Zimbabwe Colombia Congo, P.R. Costa Rica El Salvador Guatemala Papua New G. Zambia Bolivia	Syrian Arab Rep Malaysia	Spain Germany, F.R. Ireland Italy
60–64%		Domin. Rep. Ivory Coast	Portugal Chile Mexico Brazil Uruguay	Finland New Zealand Japan
65–69%		Jamaica Morocco	Venezuela	France Austria UK
70–74%			Israel Jordan	Norway Sweden Denmark Belgium Australia Canada USA Netherlands
75–79%			Singapore Greece Trin/Tobago	
Over 80%			Panama	

Calculated from data in the United Nations, *Yearbook of National Account Statistics: 1981* (New York: UN, 1983).

growth countries in each category[2] exhibit significant differences and will be compared in order to highlight the relationship between services and economic growth.

2. Service Industries in the Domestic Economy

Unfortunately, there is not yet universal agreement on the definition of services and so any discussion of services must begin with a definition of terms. All too frequently, definitions of services reflect inappropriate assumptions about labour intensity, perishability, or simultaneity of production and consumption. In actuality, services may be labour intensive (domestic work) or capital intensive (communications), perishable (cleaning) or durable (education), simultaneous (live concert) or decoupled (computer-aided instruction).

Although some claim that the service sector is too hetereogeneous for proper definition, extractive and manufacturing activities are also quite diverse. It is, after all, the purpose of a definition to delineate common characteristics of apparently diverse activities. Any useful definition of economic sectors must differentiate them on the basis of (a) the nature of the production output; (b) the unique inputs used; and (c) the purpose served by the production process. The analyses in this article are based on the following definitions:

EXTRACTIVE SECTOR: Industries that retrieve raw materials from the physical environment so that they can be used as supplies for other economic activities.

MANUFACTURING SECTOR: Industries that produce tangible goods from raw materials, which then serve as equipment and supplies for other economic activities.

SERVICE SECTOR: Industries that provide time, place, and form utility, while bringing about a change in or for the recipient of the service.

Services are produced by (a) the provider acting for the recipient; (b) the recipient providing part of the labour (self-service); and/or (c) the recipient and the producer creating the service together in interaction (co-production).

Table 2 indicates the classification of industries by economic sector.

By 1981, the service sector was the largest economic sector in virtually every country, contributing a higher percentage of Gross Domestic Product (GDP) than either the extractive or the manufacturing sectors (see Table 3). Those who caracterize Low-income countries as agricultural are usually referring to the percentage of the population employed in agriculture, not to the per cent of GDP stemming from agriculture (see Fig. 1). For all countries, gross fixed capital formation has been occurring primarily in the service sector (see Table 4).

One of the reasons why services are not seen as important in economic growth is the belief that the service sector is not productive. Productivity must always be assessed in the context of national development goals. For example, the fact that the service sector often absorbs excess work force can mean that it is particularly effective in meeting goals of full

TABLE 2. *Classification of Industries by Economic Sector*

	Equivalents in Major Data Systems	
Classification	United Nations ISIC* Category	World Bank Category
Extractive Sector	1 & 2	1 & 2
Manufacturing Sector	3	3
Services Sector	4 – 9	4 –11
Infrastructure	4, 5, 7	4, 5, 6
Trade Services	6	7
Business Services	8	8
Community Services†	9	9 –11
†When data permit, Community Services may be further subdivided		
Public Administration	9 (partial)	9
Social/Personal Services	9 (partial)	10, 11

*International Standard Industry Classification.
†Note: For category definitions see United Nations, *Indexes to the International Standard Industrial Classification of all Economic Activities* (New York: United Nations, 1971); World Bank, *World Tables*, 3rd ed. (Baltimore, MD: Johns Hopkins University Press, 1983).

TABLE 3. *Percentage of GDP and Employment by Economic Sector: 1981*

	Development Category			
Economic Sector	Low Income	Lower Middle	Upper Middle	Industrial
GDP				
Extractive Sector	42	27	15	7
Manufacturing Sector	10	16	21	27
Services Sector	48	57	64	66
Employment				
Extractive Sector	72	53	25	9
Manufacturing Sector	10	14	22	24
Services Sector	18	33	53	67

Calculations based on data from the International Labour Office. *Yearbook of Labour Statistics* (Geneva: ILO, 1983); the United Nations. *Yearbook of National Account Statistics: 1981* (New York: United Nations, 1983).

employment — and hence productive. Given the labour intensive nature of many service industries, static comparisons of employment levels with resulting GDP are often misleading. If instead one compares the average annual increase in workers with the average annual increase in resulting GDP, the ratios for the service sector are considerably higher than those for the extractive or manufacturing sectors (see Table 5) — indicating that the allocation of additional labour to the service sector is more economi-

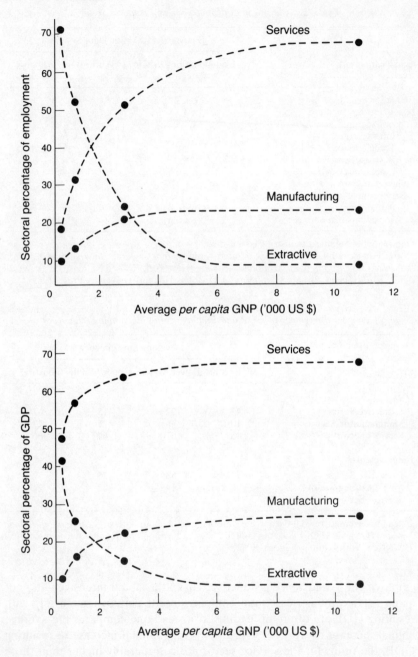

FIG. 1.   Percentage of GDP and Employment by Economic Sector: 1981 (Low, Lower Middle, Upper Middle, Industrial Countries).

TABLE 4. *Percentage of Gross Fixed Capital Formation by Economic Sector: 1981*

Economic Sector	Development Category			
	Low Income	Lower Middle	Upper Middle	Industrial
Extractive Sector	19	26	15	13
Manufacturing Sector	23	22	16	20
Service Sector	58	52	68	66
Infrastructure	31	30	17	20
Trade	4	4	2	6
Business	18	12	21	33
Social/Personal	5	6	28	7

Calculated from data in the United Nations, *Yearbook of National Account Statistics: 1981* (New York: United Nations, 1983).
NOTE: For service subsectors, $\chi^2 = 48.4$. $df= 9$, $p < .001$.

TABLE 5. *Ratio of Average Annual Growth Rates for GDP and Employment By Economic Sector: 1977–81*

Economic Sector	Development Category			
	Lower Income	Lower Middle	Upper Middle	Industrial
Extractive Sector	1.52	1.04	.65	3.41
Manufacturing Sector	.58	.61	1.17	1.54
Service Sector	2.71	7.39	2.31	9.28

Calculated from data in the International Labour Office. *Yearbook of Labour Statistics* (Geneva: ILO, 1983); World Bank, *World Tables*, 3rd ed. (Baltimore, MD: Johns Hopkins University Press, 1983).

cally productive than allocating labour to the extractive or manufacturing sectors.

2.1. Differences by Development Level

In general, any positive relationship between domestic sectoral emphasis and economic growth is apparent only for the service sector, not for the manufacturing sector. For the *Low-income* countries in particular, percentage of GDP from services is positively correlated with average annual growth in per capita GNP ($r = +.80$. $p < .001$). Increased reliance on agriculture is negatively correlated with both economic growth and quality of life indicators (literacy rate, infant mortality rate, life expectancy).

Increased reliance on manufacturing is primarily correlated with shifts in the labour force from sector to sector. Data from the low-income and lower-middle-income countries indicates that workers leaving agriculture move simultaneously into both manufacturing and service sector employment (rather than sequentially into first manufacturing and then services). In other words, both manufacturing and service sector growth are occurring together. From a development perspective, the service sector has the potential for absorbing a large number of workers with relatively little capital investment (other than in education), while the creation of manufacturing sector jobs of necessity requires more capital investment.

For the upper-middle-income countries (often described as the NICS, or newly industrializing countries), increased percentage of GDP from services is correlated with enhanced quality of life (included higher per capita GNP). Although these countries are typically described as manufacturing economies, over 60% of GDP comes from services and the percentage of GDP from manufacturing is unrelated to economic growth indicators. The major distinguishing characteristic of the upper-middle-income countries, constituting a potential development indicator, is the shift in focus of fixed capital formation from physical infrastructure to business services (see Table 4).

In the industrialized countries, sectoral contribution to GDP appears to stabilize at 7% from extraction, 27% from manufacturing, and 66% from services. On the whole, subsectors in the service sector do not vary much in proportion by level of development (see Table 6). Contrary to popular

TABLE 6.   *Service Subsectors as Percentage of GDP: 1981*

Service Subsector	Development Category			
	Low Income	Lower Middle	Upper Middle	Industrial
Utilities	1.5	1.7	2.2	3.3
Construction	4.3	4.7	6.4	6.5
Transport/Communication	6.6	7.3	8.4	7.8
Wholesale/Retail Trade	12.1	16.0	16.7	13.9
Business Services	6.1	10.2	12.6	13.7
Public Administration	12.1	11.2	12.2	14.0
Community/Social	5.5	5.7	5.3	6.4

Calculations based on data from the United Nations, *Yearbook of National Account Statistics: 1981* (New York: United Nations, 1983).

belief, public administration is no larger proportionally than is wholesale/retail trade. The primary growth subsector as per capita income increases is that of business services (often known as producer services) — e.g. banking, insurance, real estate, accounting, advertising, legal services.

2.2. *Differences by Rate of Growth*

If one compares countries that are developing rapidly with those that exhibit negative growth rates, the distinguishing characteristic is the rate of growth in the service sector. In countries like Algeria, Colombia, and the Republic of Korea (South Korea), the service sector grew at an average rate of 7.9% between 1965 and 1981, while per capita GNP more than doubled between 1977 and 1981. In countries like Bolivia, Ghana, and Jamaica, the service sector grew at an average rate of 2.3% between 1965 and 1981, while between 1977 and 1981 per capita income grew very slowly (if at all).

Looking more closely at the composition of the service sector, there is one subsector that differentiates high-growth and low-growth countries — public administration (see Table 7). Efficient public administration is a

TABLE 7. *Public Administration as Percentage of GDP: 1981*

	Development Category			
Growth Rate	Low Income	Lower Middle	Upper Middle	Industrial
High Growth Countries	12	9	11	12
Low Growth Countries	13	13	13	16

Calculations based on data from the United Nations, *Yearbook of National Account Statistics: 1981* (New York: United Nations, 1983).
NOTE: In analysing the rank order of the percentages, U = 0, p = .014.

prerequisite for all economic growth, but excessive public sector control can be counterproductive. While a lack of governmental support services can hamper economic activity, an inefficient bureaucracy can create unnecessary barriers. The consistently larger percentage of GDP from public administration in low-growth countries may be one reason why the public sector is perceived as inherently inefficient.

2.3. Issues in Domestic Service Sector Growth

Typically, the service sector has not been the target of conscious comprehensive development planning. Such lack of planning may result in the initial underdevelopment of key service industries, or poor maintenance of service sector infrastructure once in place. In countries needing external funding for development, development priorities may have been dictated by those funding sources. Until recently, the World Bank and other development agencies have assumed that development occurred through a progression from agriculture to manufacturing, with service sector development being "post-industrial".

For countries that were formerly colonies, that colonial heritage may have created distortions in the service sector. Service sector industries may have been developed in order to facilitate movement of raw materials to colonial power markets and to ensure the prosperity of colonial power firms (e.g. transportation networks), overlooking the needs of the domestic economy. Similarly, some service industries may have been neglected locally because they were supplied from the colonial power (e.g. insurance, professional training).

Public sector ownership of key services industries may be creating inefficiencies. There is a growing trend toward "privatization" of many services, or encouraging competition from the private sector. In areas like transportation, health care, and waste disposal, the growth of private sector firms can enhance the level of services available for all. Sometimes administrations may be able to contract out the provision of needed services so that they are delivered more efficiently and effectively to citizens. While public sector control is often necessary in order to ensure that all citizens receive needed services, private sector alternatives for the more affluent can often relieve demands on public institutions to allow for more effective delivery to less affluent citizens.

Development planning at any level of development must address three separate issues. First, are there needed services that do not yet exist (e.g. business services)? Should there be developed domestically or by attracting foreign firms? Second, are there service industries that exist but could become more efficient through modernization? What incentives are necessary to encourage economies of scale through integration or increased capital intensity? Third, are there service industries whose role has become distorted and hence inefficient in the domestic economy, either through colonial influences or through misguided public policies? For example, service availability in rural areas may need to be enhanced in order to match that of urban areas. Infrastructure maintenance often needs to be asserted as a national priority in industrialized as well as developing countries.

3.   International Trade in Services

The confusion that still exists regarding the role of services in domestic economies is infinitely greater with regard to that of international trade in services. Since discussions of services trade have usually drawn on merchandise trade as the model, the dynamic portions of services trade have been overlooked. Merchandise trade analysis generally assumes that only the product moves across borders, while the consumer and the factors of production remain fixed. In services trade, however, not only the product but also the consumer (e.g. tourism) and the production factors (e.g. affiliates) are movable.

Limitations are placed on services traded only if one assumes that producer and consumer must be in different countries (the "location" definition of trade[3]. If one accepts an "ownership" rather than a "location" definition of traded services, then every conceivable service is capable of being traded. For example, utilities and communications services are sold to foreign companies doing business in a given country.

Acknowledging the mobility of consumers and production factors, four categories of services trade are possible (see Table 8): across-the-border trade; domestic-establishment trade; foreign-earnings trade; and third-country trade. "Across-the-border" trade is the category similar to merchandise trade, in which producer and consumer are each in different countries. In the other three categories, producer and consumer are in the same country but at least one is a nonresident. "Domestic-establishment" trade assumes that the consumer will move to the producer — as is the case in tourism and in foreign study. "Foreign-earnings" trade assumes that the producer must have a presence in the consumer's country in order to effectively deliver the service, while "third-country" trade assumes that both consumer and producer are in a foreign country when the service is delivered (as when a German buys Kentucky Fried Chicken in Japan).

TABLE 8.   *Conceptual Framework for Categorizing Services Trade*

		Factors of Production	
		Don't Move	Move
Consumers	Don't Move	Across-the-border trade	Foreign-earnings trade
	Move	Domestic-establishment trade	Third-country trade

Adapted in part G. P. Sampson and R. H. Snape, "International trade in services: A framework for identifying the issues" (*World Economy*, **8**, 171–181).

3.1. *Differences by Development Level*

Services trade is as important to developing countries as it is to the industrialized countries (see Table 9). The volume of trade in services is lower in developing countries than the volume for industrialized countries, but that is due to the lower volume of exports and imports overall. In 1981, services exports (conservatively defined[4]) averaged 17% of total exports; services imports averaged 18% of all imports.

Services trade is as important economically as is merchandise trade at all levels of development. Balance of trade in services becomes steadily more positive as per capita income rises. Although on the average developing countries are net importers of services, there are a number of countries (e.g. Pakistan, Kenya) that depend upon surpluses in services trade to

TABLE 9.   *Services Trade as a Percentage of Total Trade: 1981*

Services as:	Development Category				Developing Country Average
	Low Income	Lower Middle	Upper Middle	Industrial	
% Exports	14.5	13.7	21.4	18.3	16.5
% Imports	16.2	20.1	19.7	18.1	18.7

Calculated from data in the *U.S. National Study on Trade in Services* (No. 455–773–20145) (Washington, D.C.: US Government, 1984).

offset their merchandise deficits. For the lower-middle-income countries, the volume of services exports is significantly related to the growth of both GDP and per capita income.

3.2. Differences by Growth Rate

If services and merchandise trade are analysed as a percentage of a country's GDP, several interesting facts emerge. Merchandise exports, seen by many as a correlate of economic growth, are more likely to be a correlate of *low* growth (see Fig. 2). For the lower-middle-income countries in 1981, the low-growth countries exported as significantly higher

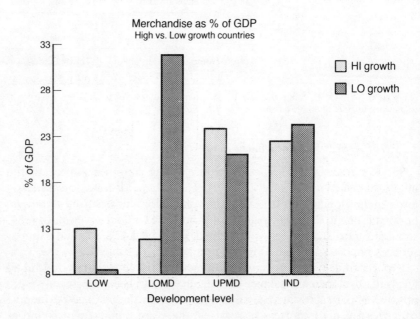

FIG. 2.   Merchandise Exports as Percentage of GDP: 1981

percentage of merchandise than did the high-growth countries ($t = 2.95$, df = 8, $p < .02$). For services exports, the opposite is true (see Fig. 3). A higher percentage of service exports are characteristic of high-growth countries, particularly the upper-middle-income countries ($t = 2.46$, df = 8, $p < .05$).

If services trade is viewed instead as a percentage of total trade, the importance of services in economic growth becomes even more apparent. For the lower-middle-income countries in particular, high-growth countries exported a significantly higher proportion of services (see Fig. 4; $t = 4.45$, df = 8. $p < .01$). Tourism is not the only service exported. There are also significant exports in transportation-related services and professional and business services.

Looking at imports, again services are a crucial factor. Particularly in the developing countries, the low-growth countries imported a significantly higher proportion of services than did the high-growth countries (see Fig. 5; F = 7.25, df = 1/32, p < .05). Many of these services were imported by foreign firms that could not purchase needed services locally. A major growth strategy for developing countries can be the development of business or intermediate services to service the international sector of the economy.

Clearly, services trade plays a crucial role in developing countries. Proportionally higher service exports are characteristic of high-growth

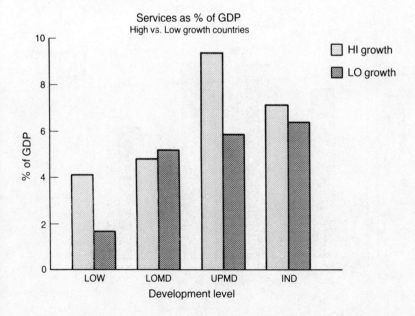

FIG. 3.   Services Exports as Percentage of GDP: 1981

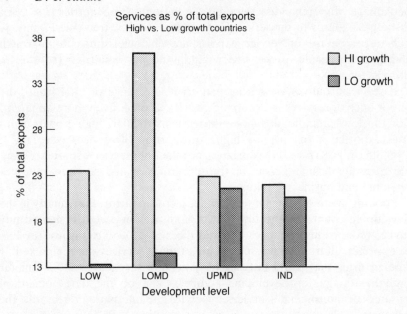

FIG. 4.   Services Exports as Percentage of Total Exports: 1981

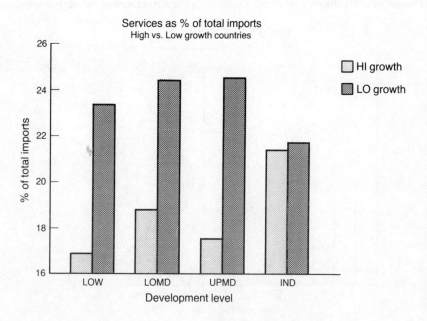

FIG. 5.   Services Imports as Percentage of Total Imports: 1981

countries, while excessive dependency on imported services is characteristic of low-growth countries. Over-emphasis on merchandise exports is
also characteristic of low-growth countries. Effective development planning must include a strengthening of both domestic and international
service sector — to reduce relative dependency on imported services while
providing incentives for services exports.

3.3. Issues in Services Trade

One of the most controversial trade issues at present is that of nontariff
barriers to services trade. The United States and other industrialized
countries have pressed for an extension of a GATT-type discipline to cover
services trade issues, while developing countries have remained apprehen-
sive. Fears on the part of developing countries have included concern that
national treatment of foreign firms would disrupt government control over
development priorities and that a reduction in protectionism would aid the
economic growth of industrialized nations at the expense of developing
nations.

In order to assess the validity of such fears, a framework for analysing
patterns of nontariff barriers is essential, rather than the simple listing of
such barriers as has been characteristic of recent studies. The distinction
between movement of production factors and movement of consumers
made earlier can provide such a framework, resulting in the following
categories (see Table 10 for more detail):

TABLE 10. *Types of Nontariff Barriers to Trade in Services*

	Category of Service Trade			
	"Trade"		"Investment"	
Barrier to:	Across-the-border	Domestic	Foreign-earnings	Third-country
Product Movement	Market access Local purchase Telematics Govt. activity† Technical standards Charges/taxes Intellectual property	Telematics*	Market access Local purchase Telematics Govt. activity Technical standards Charges/taxes Intellectual property	Market access Local purchase Telematics Govt. activity Technical standards
Capital Movement	Currency restrictions	Currency restrictions	Currency restrictions Repatriation of profits	Currency restrictions Repatriation of profits

TABLE 10. *Types of Nontariff Barriers to Trade in Services* — Continued

	Category of Service Trade			
	"Trade"		"Investment"	
Barrier to:	Across-the-border	Domestic	Foreign-earnings	Third-country
Human Movement:				
Labour	Work permits		Work permits	Work permits
Consumers		Visas		Visas
		Departure tax		Departure tax
Producer Establishment			Right of establishment	Right of establishment
			Access to production inputs	Access to production inputs

*In consumer's home country.
†Subsidies, dumping, procurement practices, regulations, monopolies.

Adapted from R. J. Krommenacker, *World-traded Services: The Challenge for the Eighties* (Dedham, MA: Artech House, 1984); R. K. Shelp, *Beyond Industrialization: Ascendency of the Global Service Economy* (New York: Praeger Publishers, 1981).

(a) Barriers to product movement (e.g. market access, local purchase, technical standards, surcharges);

(b) Barriers to capital movement (e.g. currency restrictions, repatriation of profits);

(c) Barriers to human movement (e.g. work permits, departure tax, visas);

(d) Barriers to producer establishment (e.g. right of establishment, access to production inputs).

Barriers to trade in services are particularly difficult to identify because most do not occur "at the border". Many service industries are highly regulated by national governments so that nontariff barriers may be inadvertent as well as specifically designed to exclude foreign competition.

While sufficient data is not available for a global analysis, data from Australia and the ASEAN nations suggests that less developed economies have a greater number of nontariff barriers than do more developed countries (see Table 11). Although a causal relationship cannot be inferred from the data, one can speculate that more open economies have the potential to develop more rapidly. Certainly, such openness mitigates against having to use scarce resources to duplicate services already available at a competitive price on the world market.

TABLE 11. *Analysis of Nontariff Barriers to ASEAN-Australian Services Trade: 1981*

| | Development Category | | | | | |
| | Lower Middle* | | Upper Middle/Industrial† | | Total | |
Barrier to:	Number	Per cent	Number	Per cent	Number	Per cent
Product Movement	25	42	18	44	43	43
Capital Movement	6	10	1	2	7	7
Human Movement	4	7	3	7	7	7
Producer Establishment	25	42	19	46	44	44
Totals	60	101‡	41	99	101	101

*Includes Indonesia, Philippines, Thailand.
†Includes Australia, Malaysia, Singapore.
‡Totals may not add to 100% because of rounding.
Calculated from data in K. Tucker; G. Scow; and M. Sundberg, *Services in ASEAN-Australian Trade* (Kuala Lumpur and Camberra: ASEAN-Australia Joint Research Project, 1983), p. 36. Table 18.
NOTE: The proportion of nontariff barriers in Industrial and upper-middle-income countries is significantly less than the proportion in lower-middle-income countries ($z = 8.16, p < .001$).

4. Developing Comparative Advantage in Services Trade

Conventional wisdom has assumed that industrialized countries have and will continue to have a comparative advantage in services trade. Certainly in terms of volume, industrialized countries continue to dominate world trade in services. But the recent award of a major construction project in the United States to a South Korean firm raises questions as to whether that need be the case.

Industrialized countries have maintained a comparative advantage in services primarily through reputation and competitive costs. Not only have they dominated in terms of sheer volume, but their corporations are also developing organizational forms, such as business format franchising, that reduce producer risk while creating increasing possibilities to achieve economies of scale. While developing country firms are unlikely to match export volume, they are certainly capable of replicating the "franchise miracle".

There are also a variety of other sources of comparative advantage that, once identified, can be developed. The most frequently exploited have been geographical location and natural endowments — exploited in both transportation and tourism services. Other aspects of geographical location that are just beginning to be appreciated are factors such as the ability to communicate worldwide with little atmospheric interference and time zone location. Singapore, for example, is hoping to exploit time zone location as part of a vital link for 24-hour financial transactions.

100   D. I. Riddle

Just as geographic endowments are important, so too is the infrastructure that exists. State-of-the-art telecommunications facilities can constitute a strong incentive for attracting foreign investors. Adequate transportation facilities and efficient customs services also enhance the attractiveness of an economy. To the extent that infrastructure exceeds minimal standards and has excess capacity, countries can potentially have a comparative advantage in facilitating trade and attracting further domestic and foreign investment.

Political milieu includes degree of perceived risk in investing in the country in question, as well the diplomatic alliances that exist; for example, Hong Kong is able to transship from Taiwan and Republic of Korea to the People's Republic of China. India is similarly positioned in relation to the USSR.

Although Bhagwati (1984) has argued that developing countries have lower factor prices and therefore provide cheaper services, this is true only for labour-intensive services. Increasingly, services are human capital (i.e. skilled labour) and/or capital intensive. As the service sector becomes more dependent on information technology, a literate and skilled workforce becomes a definite asset. Language ability can also constitute a potential comparative advantage; for example, both Jamaica and Barbados are promoting their skilled, literate, English-speaking populations. Since telematics technology enables support staff to be located anywhere in the world, telematics training can also constitute a comparative advantage in attracting offshore offices.

Finally, little attention has been paid to cultural differences in service delivery. One might expect that, for example, in service industries where there is a good deal of interaction with customers, cultures that place a heavy emphasis on maintaining good interpersonal relationships (rather than simply task efficiency) could have a comparative advantage. The effectiveness of management training programme in developing countries for persons from other developing countries is another example of potential cultural comparative advantage.

Administrations used to comparative advantage analyses only in relation to manufacturing or extractive activities may be concerned that the allocation of potentially scarce resources to the services sector may not be the most efficient use of those resources. Data from Sweden, however, suggests that service industries *can* provide a better return on capital than the other two sectors (see Table 12).

5. Conclusions

The growth and dynamism of the service sector is a vital key to economic growth. While economies can, if necessary, import agricultural and

TABLE 12.   *Swedish Data on Selected Measures of Capital Input Productivity (Private Sector): 1981*

Industry	Return on Total Capital (%)	Return on Equity (%)	Capital Stock Per Employee (SEK 1000)
Extractive/Manufacturing	7.0	6.7	377
Services Construction	8.0	30.3	58
Commerce	8.2	18.7	107
Transport	6.2	4.9	421
Banking	11.0	28.5	188
Insurance	6.0	10.9	1,607
Professional services	7.0	22.7	114
Other services	15.9	50.4	51

From the *Swedish National Study on Trade in Services* (Stockholm: Swedish Government, 1984).

manufactured goods, all economies need a certain basic services infrastructure in place in order to function at all. Essential services must include efficient delivery — by public or private sector firms — of utilities, transportation, telecommunication, and financial services. Public administrative structures must facilitate economic activity, while ensuring stable and proactive fiscal policies, and effectively delivered health and education services. All too often these basic services have been dismissed as relatively unproductive or unimportant.

The service sector is already the largest sector in virtually all economies; however, it has seldom been the target for careful and comprehensive development planning. Research indicates that economic growth is closely linked to growth in the service sector, both domestically and internationally. High-growth countries are those with vital services infrastructure in place and with services to export.

It makes little sense to continue defining economic growth in terms of "industrialization" — i.e. manufacturing sector growth — when the manufacturing sector plays only a support role (in the sense of providing equipment and supplies for other economic activities). Focusing instead on "servicization" would acknowledge the service sector appropriately as the crucial vehicle for economic growth. Not only is an efficient services infrastructure essential for the growth of other sectors of the economy, but the effective development of business or producer/intermediary services is vital to economic development.

Notes

* Dr. Riddle is Associate Professor in the Department of International Studies, American Graduate School of International Management. Glendale, AZ 85306, USA. The material in

102   D. I. Riddle

this article is taken in large part from her book: *Service-led Growth: The Role of the Service Sector in World Development* (New York: Praeger Publishers, 1986).

1. All research data cited in the paper are based on an analysis of 81 countries (excluding the Eastern European and Middle East oil-exporting countries due to paucity of data) at four levels of development, based on the categories used in the World Bank 1984 *World Development Report*. Constant currency figures were used for Gross Domestic Product (GDP).

2. The five high-growth and five low-growth countries in each development category were selected based on being either above- or below-average regarding both average annual growth in Gross Domestic Product and average annual growth in per capita Gross National Product between 1970 and 1981.

3. "Ownership" definition means that international trade is considered to take place if the firms or consumers involved are of different nationalities regardless of the location; thus, if a French firm in Hong Kong purchased consulting services from a Belgian firm also in Hong Kong, the transaction would be counted as an international trade in services. "Location" definition means that international trade is considered to take place if the firms or consumers are in different nations regardless of nationality; thus, if a French firm in Hong Kong purchased consulting services from a French firm in Bangkok, the transaction would be counted as an international trade in services. Since international trade statistics are generally calculated in order to track currency flows, the "ownership" definition would seem more appropriate.

4. Services trade has been defined conservatively to include only Shipment, Other Transportation, Travel, and Other Services. The controversial categories of investment and government transfers have been excluded.

References

Bauer, P. T. and Yamey, B. S. [1951] "Economic progress and occupational distribution", *Economic Journal*, **61** (December), 741–755.

Baumol, W. J. [1967] "Macroeconomics of unbalanced growth: The anatomy of urban crisis", *American Economic Review*, **57**, 415–426.

Baumol, W. J., Blackman, S. and Wolff, E. [1985] "Unbalanced growth revisited: Asymptotic stagnancy and new evidence", *American Economic Review*, **75**, 806–817.

Bell, D. [1973] *The Coming of the Post-industrial Society: A Venture in Social Forecasting*, Basic Books, New York.

Bhagwati, J. N. [1984] "Splintering and disembodiment of services and developing nations", *World Economy*, **7** (2), 133–143.

Bhagwati, J. N. [1984] "Why are services cheaper in the poor countries?", *The Economic Journal*, **94**, 279–286.

Clark, C. [1940] *The Conditions of Economic Progress*, Macmillan, London.

Cloney, G. J., II. [1981] "The composition and role of trade in services" (Background paper prepared for the International Chamber of Commerce Roundtable on Liberalization of Trade in Services, June, Paris).

Cook, J. [1983] "You mean we've been speaking prose all these years?" *Forbes*, April 11, 142–149.

Devos, S. A. [1984] "Service trade and OECD", *Journal of Japanese Trade and Industry*, No. 4, 16–19.

Fisher, G. [1939] "Production, primary, secondary and tertiary", *Economic Record*, **15** (June), 24–38.

Gershuny, J. I. and Miles, I. [1983] *The New Service Economy: The Transformation of Employment in Industrial Societies*, Praeger Publishers, New York.

Gibbs, M. [1985] "Continuing the international debate on services", *Journal of World Trade Law*, **19** (3), 199–218.

Goh, K. S. [1984] "Public administration and economic development in LDCs", *World Economy*, **7**, 229–243.

Gray, H. P. [1983] "A negotiating strategy for trade in services", *Journal of World Trade Law*, **17** (5), 377–388.

Hartwell, R. M. [1973] "The service revolution: The growth of services in modern economy", in *The Fontana Economic History of Europe: The Industrial Revolution*, C. M. Cipolla (Ed.), Collins, London, 359–396.

Hill, T. P. [1977] "On goods and services", *Review of Income and Wealth*, **23**, 315–338.

Hindley, B. and Smith, A. [1984] "Comparative advantage and trade in services", *World Economy*, December.

Hopkins, M. [1983] "Employment trends in developing countries, 1960–80 and beyond", *International Labour Review*, **122** (4), 461–478.

International Labour Office. [1983] *Yearbook of Labour Statistics*, ILO, Geneva.

International Monetary Fund. [1977] *Balance of Payments Manual*, 4th ed., IMF, Washington, D.C.

Jetro. [1984] *Softnomics: The Service-oriented Economy of Japan*, JETRO, Tokyo.

Khomelyansky, B. N. [1982] "Stabilising the USSR's rural population through development of the social infrastructure", *International Labour Review*, **121**, 89–100.

Kostecka, A. [1985] *Franchising in the Economy: 1983–85*, U.S. Govt., Printing Office, Washington, D.C. (1985–461–105/10192).

Kravis, I. B. [1983] *Services in the Domestic Economy and in World Transactions*, National Bureau of Economic Research, New York.

Kravis, I. B., Heston, A. and Summers, R. [1982] *World Product and Income: International Comparisons of Real Gross Product*, Johns Hopkins University Press, Baltimore.

Oulton, N. [1984] "International Trade in Service Industries: Comparative Advantage of European Community Countries" (Paper presented at an international conference on "Restrictions on Transactions in the International Market for Services", June, Wiston House, England).

Patrick, H. T. [1966] "Financial development and economic growth in underdeveloped countries", *Economic Development and Cultural Change*, **14** (1), 174–189.

Power, K. P. [1983] "Now we can move office work offshore to enhance output", *Wall Street Journal*, June 9, 26.

Riddle, D. I. [1986] *Service-led Growth: The Role of the Service Sector in World Development*, Praeger Publishers, New York.

Riddle, D. I. [1985] "Services: Parasitic or dynamic?" *Policy Studies Review*, **4** (3), 467–474.

Riddle, D. I. and Sours, M. H. [1985] "Service-led growth in the Pacific Basin", in *The Environment of International Business: A Pacific Basin Perspective*, W. C. Kim and P. K. Y. Young (Eds.), UMI Research Press, Ann Arbor (MI).

Riddle, D. I. and Sours, M. H. [1984] "Service industries as growth leaders in the Pacific Rim", *Asia Pacific Journal of Management*, **1** (3), 190–199.

Sampson, G. P. and Snape, R. H. [1985] "International trade in services: A framework for identifying the issues", *World Economy*, **8** (June), 171–181.

Sapir, A. [1982] "Trade in services: Policy issues for the eighties", *Columbia Journal of World Business*, Fall, 77–83.

Sapir, A. and Lutz, E. [1981] *Trade in Services: Economic Determinants and Development-related Issues*, World Bank, Washington, D.C. (No. 480).

Seow, G. F. H. [1981] "The service sector and economic growth", Economic Research Centre, National University of Singapore (mimeo).

Sethuramam, S. V. [1977] "The urban informal sector in Africa", *International Labour Review*, **116** (3), 343–352.

Sieh, L. M. L. [1984] *The Services Sector in Malaysia*, ASEAN-Australia Economic Papers No. 8, Kuala Lumpur.

Swedish Government. [1984] *Swedish National Study on Trade in Services*. Swedish Govt., Stockholm.

Tucker, K. A., Seow, G. and Sundberg, M. [1983] *Services in ASEAN-Australian Trade*, ASEAN-Australia Economic Papers No. 2, Kuala Lumpur.

Umoh, P. N. [1984] "Nigeria's rural banking scheme: A case study in financial development", *The Banker*, September, 75–81.

United Nations. [1985] *National Accounts Statistics: Main Aggregates and Detailed Tables, 1982*, UN, New York.
United Nations. [1983] *Yearbook of National Account Statistics: 1981*, UN, New York.
United Nations. [1971] *Indexes to the International Standard Industry Classification of All Economic Activities*, rev. 2, UN, New York.
United Nations Centre on Transnational Corporations. [1983] *Transnational Corporations in World Development*, UN, New York.
United Nations Conference on Trade and Development. [1985] *Production and Trade in Services: Policies and Their Underlying Factors Bearing Upon International Service Transactions*, UN, Geneva.
United Nations Conference on Trade and Development. [1984] *Services and the Development Process*, UN, Geneva.
US Office of the Trade Representative. [1984] *U.S. National Study on Trade in Services*, US Govt., Printing Office, Washington, DC.
Veil, E. [1982] "The world current account discrepancy", *OECD Occasional Studies*, June, 46–63.
Wells, L. T., Jr. [1983] *Third World Multinationals*, MIT Press, Cambridge (MA).
Willoughby, C. R. [1983] "Infrastructure: Doing more with less", in *Economic Development and the Private Sector*, World Bank, Washington, D.C.
World Bank, [1984] *World Development Report 1984*, World Bank, Washington, D.C.
World Bank, [1983] *World Development Report 1983*, World Bank, Washington, D.C.
World Bank, [1983] *World Tables*, 3rd ed., Johns Hopkins University Press, Baltimore (MD).

5

The Future of Service Employment

JONATHAN I. GERSHUNY*

1. Introduction

Services are taken, almost unquestioningly, as the future of all economic activity. The future locations of production, of employment, and of consumption, are all assumed to be in the tertiary sector. The coming service society is currently, for many politicians and economic comentators a cant Nirvana, in which full employment is magically restored as a result of a growth in the provision and consumption of intangible commodities. But in fact economic thinking is very hazy, not just about *why* this process of tertiarization should be expected to take place, but indeed on the more fundamental question of what exactly services *are*. I have suggested that the three dimensions of service activity — service production, service employment and service consumption — have quite different and distinct patterns of development[1]. And when we come seriously to consider the dynamics of development of the services, there emerges a much less appealing prospect.

I will try to summarize this contrary point of view, by arguing for what in the light of the conventional wisdom may appear to be a rather paradoxical proposition: in industrial societies, though employment may be concentrated in manufacturing, people consume mainly services; in post-industrial societies, by contrast, employment may be concentrated in service industries, but people nevertheless consume mainly goods. And to explain this, I have two social processes, both of which are driven ultimately by technical change. The first is the "*cost-disease*" whereby final services get continuously more expensive relative to other commodities. And the second is partial reversal of the process of the occupational division of labour — the *reaggregation of occupations* within "producer service" and other intermediate service industries.

---

*Professor at the School of Humanities and Social Sciences, University of Bath.

2. When is a Service not a Service?

My paradox — that in post-industrial societies, service industries may be growing but service consumption is nevertheless declining — is like most paradoxes, not really paradoxical at all, but the result of a confusion between the different meanings of the same work, "services".

We can identify three distinct ways in which the word is used:

(a)   It is used to describe particular occupations — thus, people who are not themselves directly involved in the physical manipulation or transformation of materials, are considered to be service workers. The thought behind this term seems to be that services are essentially intangible commodities, so anyone involved in intangible production activities must be producing services; in this sense "service workers" means more or less the same thing as the old-fashioned term "white collar workers" or the new and rather trendy "information workers".

(b)   It is used to cover particular branches of industry — so any employee of an industrial sector which is engaged in producing material goods is a service worker. At the heart of this usage is the same notion, of services as intangibles — but it identifies a quite different group of workers. Service workers in this context are simply a residual category — there are the primary extractive and farming branches, there are the manufacturing industries which we think of as the dominant employers in the high industrial period. . . . and then there are the rest, the residual, the service industries. Of course, when we talk of a residual, we are normally referring to a small proportion of a total. In this case the residual is, in typical developed countries 60–70% of all employment. But it is nevertheless a residual in terms of conceptual development; we have a great body of theory to cover the behaviour of the primary and the secondary sectors, but neither theory — nor even adequately organized data — for the services. Service industries cover an extraordinarily heterogeneous range of activities, and really all that they have in common is that they are "not manufacturing". They dominate the modern economy, but yet are almost completely absent from economic theorizing.

(c)   The third use of the term is to describe a particular sort of final consumption. Yet again, there is the common thread, of intangibility; services are those commodities which we buy, which are consumed more or less at the same time that they are produced. We go to the theatre, we go to hospital, or attend a lecture, or ride on a bus — people produce services which we consume, at the particular instant, on the particular spot. Or if not intangible, service commodities are certainly evanescent, short-lived. People clean our clothes or houses, and they get dirty again; they cook us food and we eat it. Services, in this third sense, are labour intensive production activities, very often having the producers face-to-face with the final consumers.

These three meanings of "services" relate together in an extremely complex manner. Take for example a medical doctor. This is quintessentially a service occupation; the doctor may be employed by hospital — a service industry; and in this case may possibly be producing a final service commodity. But the employer may alternatively be, say, a motor manufacturer and the doctor is working as an occupational safety advisor; here is service occupation, in a manufacturing industry. If the employer makes motor cars, then the "final commodity" that results from the work is a material good, the doctor is a service worker in the first sense, and producing a non-service commodity in the third sense. If, on the other hand, the employer makes buses which are sold to transport undertakings — the work is ultimately consumed in the form of (transport) services.

Or take a skilled metal worker. This is clearly a non-service occupation — but the worker is employed by a contract maintenance company, which is classified as a service industry; if the equipment maintained is in a hospital then final services are produced, whereas, if the equipment is in a factory, the products are final goods. Or consider a copywriter in an advertising agency; is he or she doing anything different from a copywriter in a marketing department in a large manufacturing firm? Or take an electronics expert producing special effects in a theatre — how does his or her employment (and employment prospects) relate to university classmates writing software in an electronics company?

It is all very confusing. Clearly there are different sorts of prospects for different sorts of jobs — but nevertheless the standard classifications of the different parts of the economy seem, sometimes to make meaningless distinctions between activities which are essentially identical, and in other circumstances to group together activities which have widely differing purposes — and widely differing prospects for the future.

Everyone agrees that the "service sector" — using the word in the second sense, of service industries — has been growing, throughout the developed world, that it now dominates all developed economies, and will continue to grow as a proportion of output and employment. But what does this growth mean? Will people consume more final services in the future? Which sorts of service needs will be satisfied? In order to begin to answer the questions, we have to disentangle the various different processes which underlie the development of each of the different meanings of the term "service".

3. The Decline of Service Consumption

What I have described already provides part of the explanation for my

108   *J. I. Gershuny*

first paradox. Service industries do not necessarily produce final service commodities. Growth in service industrial employment, therefore, does not necessarily mean more service consumption.

But nevertheless, we are all accustomed to think of service consumption as inevitably increasing, and therefore providing ever expanding opportunities for growth in labour intensive, and often quite skilled employment. When we actually look at consumption statistics, however, we find on the contrary, that, with a few exceptions, purchases of services by households in most developed countries have actually been *declining* as a proportion of total expenditure over the last two or three decades[2]; and we may be seeing now an overall decline in service consumption. I have suggested that there is a quite clear and systematic reason for this decline.

The explanation is a phenomenon that economists know as the "cost disease"[3] — which is the first of my two sociotechnical processes. Let us start by assuming that service industries, being very labour intensive, and often requiring "face-to-face" production and consumption, show relatively low productivity growth as compared with manufacturing activities. (In fact, as we'll see in a moment, this really only applies to one particular part of the service sector, that of supplying final services to households.) Now consider the processes of wage fixing in the services as compared to the other sectors. Employees in manufacturing industries feel that they deserve a share of the extra value added that comes from this year's labour productivity growth — they engage in *productivity wage bargaining*. Employees in service industries have no equivalent productivity growth out of which they might bargain for an increase of pay; but they do have an argument of equity. Their friends and neighbours and relations with equivalent or identical social and educational backgrounds who happen to have jobs in manufacturing industries, now have more pay. The service workers cannot argue for pay rises on the basis of their productivity — but they can do so on the basis of *relativities with manufacturing industry*. Manufacturing employees have pay rises in line with their productivity growth; service workers have pay rises in line with manufacturing worker's, in spite of low growth in service productivity; obviously, the rise in service wages can only be financed by raising the price of services.

This is the "cost disease". Its results is that the price of final services supplied to households tends continuously to rise over time. (Let me stress immediately that this sociotechnical "cost-disease" process *is* only a tendency, there is no *inevitability* in the rising cost of services. Service industries can adopt tactics to counter the pressure, through resistance to wage rises — easiest in a period of high unemployment — or through technical innovation. But the pressure for wage increases is always present — and the rising relative costs have been a very general feature in most final service industries in most countries.)

The rising cost of services has two different sorts of effect. First, it leads to something we might think of as "self-servicing". The same technology which enables productivity growth in manufacturing industry, also enables innovation at home. Services get more expensive through the cost-disease process — but it also becomes possible, as a result of technical innovations, to avoid purchasing services, by buying equipment that enables households to produce services for themselves. Instead of buying buses, people buy motor cars and produce their own transport services; instead of going to the laundry they buy a washing machine. And so on.

Through such changes in households' consumption and production patterns, a whole sector of the service economy — covering domestic services, short-range transport, certain sorts of entertainment — which once provided maybe one third or one half of all employment in urban areas, has over the last 30 years, almost disappeared.

(I should parenthetically add that this loss was enormously important in generating new jobs in the immediate postwar period. *Direct* employment was lost since fewer people bought these sorts of final services. Instead of buying these final services, people bought durable goods and materials which they used to make the services for themselves — and it was precisely these new markets, for self-servicing equipment like motor cars, washing machines, televisions and so, that were the engines of economic growth during the post war period. But of course the new jobs associated with this production were not in the final service industries.)

This "self-servicing" change is of course getting to be ancient economic history; the second effect of the "cost-disease" is very much more pertinent to present circumstances. The sorts of services that have been subject to the "self-servicing" innovations are relatively simple, straightforward, non-interactive — it is relatively easy to innovate in the process of production of clean clothes so that they are provided by cheap domestic equipment combined with unpaid and unskilled domestic labour. But educational services? Medicine?

Exactly the same "cost-disease" processes apply to these more sophisticated areas of service provision. But in these cases there isn't, or at least until recently there hasn't been, a self-servicing option equivalent to those in the simpler services. There is the same continuous rise in relative costs, in the more sophisticated services, but no real alternative to paying the higher costs. And the situation is complicated by the fact that these same sophisticated services tend to be provided, in much of western Europe, by the State, and without direct charge to the consumer. The rising relative costs are reflected, not in higher prices, but in higher taxes. The "cost-disease" may serve to explain, not just the emergence of self-servicing as an alternative to the private purchase of services, but also, the "crisis of the Welfare State". Consider: we have real and observable productivity growth in manufacturing, at a rate, say, of 3% per year; manufacturing employees accordingly enjoy 3% real pay rises. State employees show no such apparent and observable productivity growth, but they will still, and quite reasonably, expect an equivalent 3% pay rise. What this means is, that even if there is a steady level of state employment, and accordingly a constant level of provision of state services — the state will nevertheless demand *a growing proportion of the national product.* If rates of productivity growth in the public service sector lag behind those elsewhere, then just *maintaining constant levels of welfare state provision demands an ever increasing part of the national wealth.*

This of course creates political problems — that is, people object to paying ever-increasing amounts of tax, to exchange for what they rightly or wrongly see as relatively stable levels of public service provision. By the mid-1970s, almost every developed society experienced some version of the "tax revolt". And the consequence of this is, that the most bouyantly growing employment sector of the 50s and 60s and early 70s, the public service sector, has in most western economies, simply stopped growing during the last 5 or 10 years. So, this "cost-disease" may be an explanation, not just for the decline of large parts of the *private* final services sector, but also for the end of the growth of the *public* service sector.

4. The Rise of the Producer Services

So when we look at final service *consumption*, we can find good reasons to doubt the cosy view that it will continue to grow; the cost-disease means that *ceteris paribus*, we might expect service consumption to decline in the future. (Though of course, ceteris never is paribus — and I'll be returning to the actual choices we have to consider later on.) I have already pointed out that declining service consumption does not necessarily mean declining service employment. This ill-sorted package, "service industries" provides not just "final services" to consumers — but also intermediate services to other producer industries. A large part of the past growth in employment in service industries may be attributable to the increase in the intermediate or producer services sector.

We can explain this growth, oddly enough, by returning for a moment to the first of the meanings of "services" — service occupations. We are all familiar with the process of division of labour, whereby productive tasks are broken down into ever increasingly specialized components. The consequence of the division of labour has been, in the past, to increase the number of people in service occupations employed within manufacturing industry.

But we can now see a rather different process, whereby these increasingly specialized service workers, who might once have been employed within manufacturing industries, now become employed in new and highly specialized "producer service" industries. The work these employees are involved in still contributes to the manufacturing system, to the process of production of material goods, but they are nevertheless classed, in terms of our idiotic national accounting systems, together with all the other "final service" industries. Why should these industries be growing? We can distinguish three interrelated sorts of answers.

The first sort of answer relates to institutional factors. The overhead, non-wage costs of employing labour directly grow continuously. Employer contributions to social security grow as a result of the "cost-disease" processes. Employment protection legislation means that direct employment becomes a fixed, rather than a variable cost. So increasingly employers will rather buy-in component services (just as they will buy-in components) rather than producing them directly. This applies to high skill jobs in design as much as to traditional low-skill bought-in services such as factory cleaning or catering.

But it is not just institutional factors. As tasks become more specialized they require more expertise, and it is not always possible for even the largest of manufacturing concerns to support the new specialities. Particularly where the same specialities are involved in a range of different manufacturing sectors, firms may actually be achieving economies of scale by buying-in intermediate services. This of course applies specifically to high-skill, high-technology services: we find the development of, for example, software services industries which are wholly dependent on the manufacturing sector for their sales. The second explanation for the growth of the producer service sector is simply that the producer services sector is a more efficient way of acquiring component services than producing them in-house.

And the third explanation is simply that the range of component services available to be spun-off into new industries is continuously increasing. Technical change in particular production processes usually means more service-like specialities. And the value of new products consists increasingly of add-on services; thus, for example 60–70% of the value-added in the computer market comes from software or maintenance services rather than manufacturing — these add-ons are provided increasingly by firms in the service sector rather than in manufacturing.

This all adds up to a process that in one sense reverses the traditional process of the division of labour; high levels of occupational division and specialization within manufacturing industry, are followed by a reconcentration of component occupations into specialized producer service industries. We move back, in some cases at least, to the situation where the firm employs just one particular sort of labour; different firms contribute different components of the overall production task. And though I have described manufacturing firms as "buying-in" services, this may give a misleading impression; it may be the producer service, and not the manufacturing industry that is in overall control. Certainly in the UK microcomputer industry, there are a number of examples where service industries responsible for design and marketing functions actually subcontract, "buy-in" the manufacturing function. Here perhaps we have the beginnings of a really radical change in industrial structure; the production of goods dominated by service industries, with only residual and highly automated manufacturing production; service industries, in my second sense, but nevertheless engaged in the production of goods.

I have referred to the final consumer services industries, and to the producer services. There is also a third category that I should briefly mention: the intermediate consumer services, in which I include wholesale and retail distribution, financial, legal and other consumer services. These sorts of services are probably best considered simply as additional component inputs to the system of production (particularly since in most cases payment for these services is hidden in the prices of other goods or services). Clearly, except in a minority of cases (compulsive shoppers, vexatious litigators) no individuals genuinely want to consume these sorts of services as ends in themselves, they are merely *means* to the acquisition of other goods and services. We would certainly have difficulty in envisaging a viable pattern of economic growth based on an increased final demand for these. Again, while these intermediate consumer services have shown substantial growth in past decades, this is for the most part growth in the provision of services ancillary to the system of material production and consumption of goods; expansion of the intermediate consumer services sector is *dependent on growth of final demand for other sorts of commodities*.

So, here is my paradox. In a high industrial society, the dominant image of employment is perhaps the steel mill, rolling rails for the railway, or the machine shop making railway engines. And the housewife, in the high industrial period, what does she buy? She puts on her bonnet, picks up her little basket, and goes to the market to buy . . . a steam engine? Of course the point is that manufacturing employment may have been very important, but nevertheless consumption was very much oriented towards final services. Household expenditure, at least for the richer members of society, would be dominated by the purchase of transport, entertainment, domestic services. And much of the manufacturing industrial production was in fact an intermediate stage in the final output of these services; the employees in the rolling mill producing rails, are playing their part in the final production of transport services.

An in exactly the same way, in our post-industrial society, what does our househusband go to the supermarket to buy? . . . a pound of software services, an industrial design consultant? The labour of these service workers, employees of service industries, is in fact embodied in goods. The producer service industries are busily engaged in making their contribution to our purchases of cars, video recorders, microwave ovens, home computers, and all their ancillary products.

I suggested first of all, reasons for the consumption of final services, whether privately purchased or produced by the state, to decline; and now, reasons for employment in particular parts of the service sector, the producer services, to grow. Thus, post-industrial society has more and more service workers, but less and less service consumption.

Now of course it is possible that a particular nation could specialize in the production of producer services, so that it would not need to worry about its manufacturing industry, but export producer services instead. But this strikes me as a terribly insecure strategy; though the service activities may be "hived-off" by the producer, there is still the closest of relations between the producer industry and the producer services supplier. Often the expertise in the producer service derives directly from its privileged relationship with the manufacturing firm. Often the personnel in the producer service are ex-employees of the manufacturing client; in some countries the manufacturing and producer service will be in the common ownership of a third party, a bank of investment trust. The nation that loses its manufacturing industry stands in peril of losing its producer services industry as well.

And furthermore, the growth of the producer service industry is frequently at the expense of direct employment in manufacturing industry. One more job in the highly efficient producer service industry, may mean two less service workers employed directly by the the the manufacturing firm. Job creation in the service sector may be no job loss for the economy as a whole.

So what does this all add up to? The "cost-disease" process inhibits the growth of both the private and the public parts of the final-service-producing sector. And the past growth in service employment is to be explained, in large part, not by burgeoning demands for final services supplied to consumers, but by the expansion of industries supplying intermediate services, producing inputs to the system of material production.

On this showing the services do not seem to offer a very promising basis for the expansion of employment. There are of course some slightly more optimistic things we might say: particularly about the prospects for encouraging productivity growth in final service production so as to lower prices and stimulate demand. And some people would argue that the experience of the United States has been markedly different to the

114   *J. I. Gershuny*

European pattern that I have been outlining here (though I will argue that this is not so). But I should first present some evidence to support my view of the historical pattern of change in service employment.

5. The Recent History of Service Employment

The attached tables, drawn up from the UK Population Censuses of 1951, 1961 and 1971, together with the 1980 Census of Employment, (using the University of Warwick industry and occupational classifications) illustrate the patterns of development discussed in Sections 2 to 4. I have used the following categories to summarize the data:

Occupational — manual occupations
— intermediate service occupations, including managers, professional workers other than those mentioned below clerical, sales and transport workers
— medical and educational professions
— final service workers; security, catering, cleaning, artists, sports

Industrial — primary and manufacturing industries
— intermediate service industry; including professional business services, legal services, transport and distributive industries
— non-marketed final services; educational, medical and social
— final marketed services; including entertainment, domestic and other miscellaneous services

Of these classifications, the most problematical is the transport industry which supplies both intermediate and final demand. Employment in this industry has declined (by 20%) over the period covered by the tables; the conclusions that follow are not materially altered by placing this employment in the "intermediate" industrial category.

The matrices in Table 1 show the distribution of all employment broken down by the four occupational and the four industrial categories. We see that by 1980, service occupations constitute 60% of all employment, and service industries nearly 70% of the total. But more than half of all service industry employment is in the "goods related" intermediate category (this reduces to just about half when we remember that a part of transport industrial employment should be in the final marketed category). And substantially more than half of the service occupational employment is in the equivalent intermediate service occupations.

TABLE 1. *Small Industry/Occupation Matrix Comparison (% of Employment)*
Occupations

Industries	Manual	Intermediate Service Workers	Med. and Ed.† Workers	Final Service Workers	Total
1951					
Pri and Man*	37.58	6.40	.06	.73	44.76
Producer	15.55	15.22	.18	1.18	32.13
Nonmarket	2.57	3.18	3.90	2.43	23.08
Market	2.22	1.58	.11	7.12	11.03
Total	57.91	26.38	4.24	11.47	100.00
Major Diagonal	63.8166				
1961					
Pri & Man	33.63	8.15	.07	1.13	42.98
Producer	15.42	16.72	.16	1.32	33.62
Nonmarket	2.32	3.19	4.48	3.21	13.21
Market	2.17	2.39	.11	5.52	10.20
Total	53.54	30.45	4.82	11.19	100.00
Major Diagonal	60.3429				
1971					
Pri & Man	28.19	8.77	.13	1.12	38.21
Producer	13.86	18.41	.16	1.52	33.95
Nonmarket	2.16	4.55	5.70	4.83	17.24
Market	2.14	2.53	.25	5.68	10.60
Total	46.34	34.26	6.23	13.16	100.00
Major Diagonal	57.9831				
1980					
Pri & Man	22.64	8.09	.14	1.00	31.87
Producer	13.42	20.38	.19	1.68	35.68
Nonmarket	1.59	5.48	7.16	5.53	19.76
Market	2.11	3.37	.38	6.83	12.70
Total	39.77	37.32	7.87	15.05	100.00
Major Diagonal	57.0175				

*Pri & Man = Primary and Manufacturing Industries
†Med. and Ed. = Medical and Educational

The histogram of occupational employment in Fig. 1 shows some growth in each of the three service occupational categories, with a majority of all growth concentrated in the intermediate service occupations; the industrial category by contrast shows that employment growth is concentrated in the non-marketed service industries.

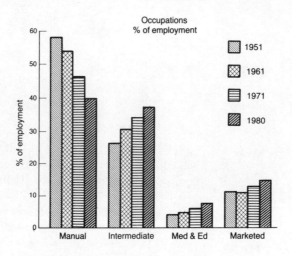

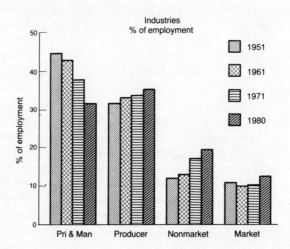

Fig. 1

The explanation for this apparent discrepancy can be seen in Table 2, which summarizes the changes in the occupation/industry distribution of employment over the period 1951–80. The largest single category of increase in the whole economy is the growth of intermediate occupations in the intermediate/producer service industries — an increase of 5% of all employment over the three decades. This is however substantially offset by a 2% reduction of manual employment in the intermediate services industry (largely lost from the railways and the gas industry).

TABLE 2. *Change in % of Employment Occupations*

Industries 1951–1980		Manual	Intermediate Service Workers	Med. and Ed. Workers	Final Service Workers	Total
		1	2	3	4	
Pri & Man	1	−14.93	1.69	.08	.27	−12.98
Producer	2	−2.13	5.16	.01	.50	3.55
Nonmarket	3	−.98	2.30	3.26	3.10	7.67
Market	4	−.10	1.79	.27	−.29	1.67
Total		−18.15	10.94	3.63	3.58	.00

Table 2 suggests that virtually all of the growth of employment over the period can be accounted for by two factors:

(a) Column 2 — the expansion of employment of intermediate service occupations in each industry. This is particularly concentrated in the intermediate services industry.

(b) Row 3 — the expansion of public service provision.

The first of these factors is largely dependent on material production (and largely substitutes for employment in manufacturing), the second on raising the proportion of national income devoted to public service provision: hence my pessimism regarding future prospects for the services as saviours from unemployment.

The data in Table 1 go some-way to support the division of labour/ occupational reaggregation argument in section 4. We can visualize the conventional division of labour as in Fig. 2 as a horizontal spreading out of employment across the occupation/industry matrix, and the reaggregation of occupations as the vertical concentration of intermediate service

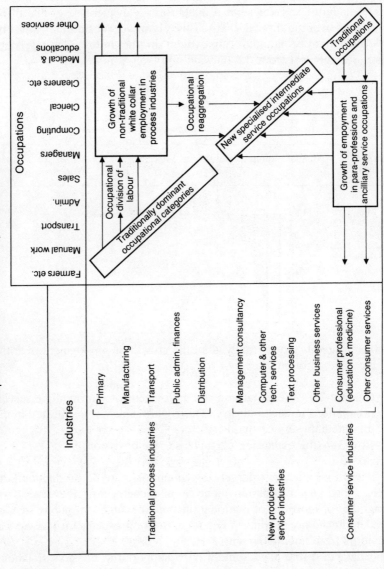

Occupational division of labour and producer services

FIG. 2

workers into the producer service industries. In Table 1, we see that the overall proportion of employment accounted for by the "major diagonal (i.e., top left to bottom right) has been continuously declining over the three decades — this corresponds to the horizontal dispersion, occupational division of labour in Fig. 2. And the slowing of the decline of the "major diagonal" total in the 1970s, reflects the growth of one element, the producer service industry/intermediate service occupation cell — which is the vertical movement, the reaggregation of occupations in Fig. 2.

Fig. 3 compares the changes in occupational and industrial employment

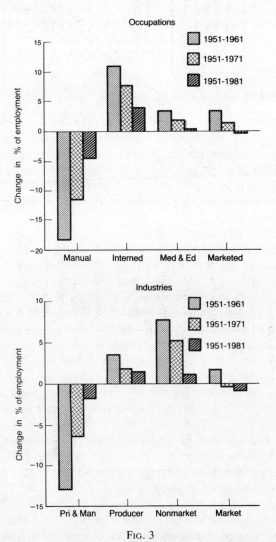

Fig. 3

in the one decade, two decades and three decades from 1951. The regularity of the pattern is striking. It is clear that the 1970s do not represent any radical new departure; if anything, occupation change was faster in the 1960s than in the 1970s. And yet, at the Census of 1971, unemployment stood at about 750,000. We were able to absorb the changes of the 1960s, find new service-occupational jobs to replace the lost manual jobs. There was no argument in the 1960s of a constraint on the supply of labour with latent abilities appropriate for the new service jobs; it would take a very strong (and it seems to me perversely negative) view of the talents of the present cohort of displaced manual workers and unplaced young people, to assume that they could not similarly adapt to service-occupational employment — there is simply no demand for such labour at present.

6. Crowding-out Services (or finding time for them).

Before concluding I would like to insert into the discussion a further consideration, rather unfamiliar, but one that has radical implications for our view of the prospects for the service sector — the proposition that we can generate jobs by working less. Now by this I do not mean a scheme for sharing or splitting jobs. I mean literally that working less during the week, or the year, or the lifetime, may provide more work, and specifically more service employment.

How does this come about?

The argument again starts with the growth of labour productivity in a modern economy. We too easily forget that, if it is not to lead to unemployment, the growth in output per employee, must be matched by an equivalent growth in consumption. Now of course this insight underlies the familiar Keynesian underconsumptionist theories of unemployment. But exactly the same insight also underlies another sort of underconsumptionist argument, that has rather more specific implications for the service sector. It is obviously true, as Keynes (and before him Hobson) argued, that in general we need extra spending power to pay for the society's extra productive potential. More specifically, but for some reason rather less obvious, it is also true that we need extra time in order to consume extra services.

Increases in the efficiency of production must be matched by increases in the scale of consumption; if the free time available for consumption remains constant, then those sorts of consumption that require a lot of free time may get crowded out of peoples lives.

Something rather close to this argument was made some 15 or 20 years ago by the Swedish economist Staffan Linder[4]. He argued that the requirement for increased consumption led to a progressive overcrowding of daily life. In his delightful book *The Harried Leisure Class* he provides us with the following description of the predicament of the averagely industrious consumer:

> ". . . ." after dinner, he may find himself drinking Brazilian coffee, smoking a Dutch cigar, sipping a French Cognac, reading the *New York Times*, listening to a Brandenberg Concerto and entertaining his Swedish wife — all at the same time, with various degrees of success. (Linder *The Harried Leisure Class* p. 79)

Linder describes here the difficulty of simultaneous consumption of mostly consumer durables. The same problems apply even more strongly to the consumption of services. We cannot simultaneously play squash, attend a lecture, visit the doctor. The consumption of goods does not necessarily take any time at all. We can buy things — and then stack them up in the corners of our rooms and not take any notice of them. The consumption of services, however, requires time.

It appears, however, that the way that societies have in the past coped with the requirement for continuously increasing consumption, is not, as Linder suggests, by matching growth in labour productivity per hour with a growth in the density of consumption per hour, but in part at least, by providing more hours for consumption. Throughout the developed world, at least during the postwar years of economic growth, the length of the working day, and of the working life, were in general declining. And this reduction in the amount of work time in the developed world since the mid 1950s, has had some quite specific and positive effects on service consumption and service employment.

Though final service consumption overall has tended to fall over this period, there are nevertheless a few final service-producing industries that have grown over the last quarter-century. The major example of growth in the privately-purchased service category, is leisure and tourist services — restaurants, clubs, hotels. The consumption of the services produced by this branch of the economy require free time; and conversely, particular sorts of free time associate naturally with particular sorts of leisure service. Statutory paid annual holidays virtually demand the consumption of tourist services. The statutory five-day working week may have encouraged the development of particular sorts of weekend sports and recreational participation. Shorter working days may explain the growth in consumption of restaurant and other similar services.

More directly, service consumption can be intentionally *induced* by particular sorts of work-time reduction. For example: reducing time, the length of the working life, by raising the school leaving age (or increasing the proportion of an age cohort that proceeds to higher or further education) provides an immediate increase in the demand for public employment in the educational sector.

These are examples of pieces of social policy adopted quite generally across Europe over the last 40 years, with a wide range of ostensible purposes, which have had the effect — probably unintended of encouraging or constraining people to use time freed from paid workers in the consumption of particular sorts of services. A not insignificant part of current European service employment owes its existence to these policies. And notwithstanding all of the relatively pessimistic things I have written about the "natural trajectory" of the development of services, this use of social policy to stimulate employment in the final service sector does seem still to be an option for the future — if government can develop the political will to promote it.

7. Future Prospects: Coping with "the cost-disease".

Let me, finally, return to the major point of this paper. There are no grounds for assuming that the services sector will necessarily expand so as to produce new growth and new employment. On the contrary, the arguments I have advanced suggest that large parts of the final services sector seem set for a decline in both output and employment. But this decline is in no sense inevitable. The analysis in the foregoing pages suggests a number of alternative possible future lines of development in which new employment might be generated by the expansion of service industries. I shall list four somewhat caricatured possibilities.

The Servant Economy

Much of my argument concerning final services rests on the "cost-disease" process. This process will work in *any* economy under conditions of full employment, since industries and occupations in which pay differentials were not maintained would be unable to recruit staff. With unemployment, however, the cost-disease argument additionally requires reasonable welfare and unemployment benefits, to enable workers to refuse employment that does not provide respectable wage levels. Societies with high unemployment and no such respectable welfare payment systems, therefore may well develop substantial low wage, low price service industries, providing menial services under demeaning conditions of employment. An alternative account of the emergence of self-servicing in postwar economic development, would be simply that full employment meant that the end of the servant class. High unemployment, combined with low welfare payments, might mean its re-emergence. A substantial part of the growth of service employment in the USA over the last decade has been precisely in low paid catering and other personal services. The regeneration of this part of the service sector — forcing the unemployed into service — is certainly possible.

The National Opera Service

In some ways rather parallel to the forced provision of cheap private services, is the forced consumption of expensive public services. In this second case, the allocative consequences of the cost-disease are simply ignored. My example here is the Albanian State Opera Company, whose apparently execrable performances are played to a house filled, not by the bourgeois voluntarist process of subscription, but rather on the socialist principle of conscription (of workers from local factories). They may not like opera, they could not conceivably like *this* opera, but the State provides it nevertheless. Services provided by institutions which are not constrained either by the market or by pluralist political debate, will tend to expand as a result of internal pressures. Our National Health Service, subject to political constraint, cannot expand in the same way that the Albanian National Opera Service can. But, strangely, the USA again provides us with an example; the combined monopoly and monopsony powers of the American Medical Association and the health insurance industry, lead to an unconstrained growth in forced expenditures on medical services which is only slightly less unwelcome than the consumption of opera services in Tirana. Around one quarter of all new jobs created in the USA over the last decade are in medical or health-related jobs.

High Technology Service Production

Both of the preceding examples of service sector growth are of course quite disreputable (though we find them frequently on otherwise respectable political agendas). There is a third way round the cost-disease, which is to reduce costs of production without forcing down wages — by increasing efficiency. And increased efficiency certainly does not mean reduced employment. Just as higher prices reduce demand, so lower prices may increase it. The converse of the "public sector inefficiency" explanation of the tax revolt, is that more efficient public provision of services could mean *more* public expenditure. We might argue as follows: Open University teaching techniques reduce costs per graduate; apply them more generally across the university system, and we could produce more graduates for the same cost; and providing better value in the system might persuade the electorate to raise more tax to pay the university education. Nothing in the preceding pages suggests that *needs* for services are saturated, but only that the cost-disease cuts away at the *means* for service provision — and new technologies may provide new and more efficient means of service production. The new information technologies in particular may in the next 10 or 20 years enable very substantial increases in the efficiency of production of medical and educational services, and the extent of unmet needs in these areas could mean that the more efficient production could lead in turn to more employment.

The Leisure Society

The first three lines of development take price elasticities of demand for services as given, and attempt to stimulate service consumption either by reducing prices, or by suppressing the effects of rising prices. My fourth and final line of argument, is that we can influence service employment by operating on the elasticities themselves. To return to my previous discussion of working time, reduction in working hours is likely to have an effect on the pattern of demand for services independent of the price of services. Some aspects of changes in demand from shorter working hours may possibly have negative effects on service employment — more free time might mean more DIY home maintenance and hence a loss of jobs from the construction industry. But in such areas as leisure, recreation, sports, tourism, education, the effects of shorter working hours — and particularly the effects of shorter working hours without equivalent reductions in take-home pay — are likely to be very positive. Reduction in working time here is a mechanism, providing temporal locations for service consumption. But what underlies this fourth sort of service growth is a conscious attempt to provide people with material circumstances in which they want to consume more service (and also to make the intergenerational and other transfers of access to services involved in a reduction in the length of the working life). Adopting policies which stimulate *wants* for services (and hence new service employment) is very different from forcing consumption of unwanted services.

The rising cost of final services is perhaps the major inhibitor of growth of service consumption and employment. My first two examples of ways round the constraint — forcing service wages downwards to promote unsatisfactory sorts of employment, and enforcing consumption of unwelcome services — are both plausible, if undesirable, future lines of development. But the final two of my alternatives are rather more satisfactory, both in terms of the sorts of services that are envisaged, and in the sorts of employment that are provided. If we want these to represent the future of services — then we must promote the policies which will generate them.

References

1. *After Industrial Society?* J. I. Gershuny, Macmillan, London 1978.
2. *Social Innovation and the Division of Labour*, J. I. Gershuny, Oxford University Press 1983.
3. This term is due to W. J. Baumol; see for example his "The Macroeconomics of Unbalanced Growth", *American Economic Review*, June 1967.
4. *The Harried Leisure Class*, Staffan Linder, Columbia University Press, 1970.

PART 2
Service Sectors Analysis

6

Information Technology and Services

JUAN F. RADA*

1. Introduction

The purpose of this paper is to highlight some of the main impacts of information technology on services and to raise some issues relating to services in general. Interest concerning the role of services on domestic and international economy has increased during the last few years particularly due to the request of the United States to include the liberalization of trade in services as part of the General Agreement on Tariffs and Trade (GATT). Although a number of national studies do exist (about 30 had been presented to GATT at the time of writing) and information has been accumulated on services, the areas of ignorance and uncertainty outweigh those of knowledge. The probelms range from statistics and definitions to a lack of adequate understanding of the interrelationships between the production of goods and services. Apart from the normal *quid pro quo* of international negotiations, there is little understanding of questions as critical to policy as the opening of trade in services and how this could affect other sectors. Also, if services cannot be performed without imported goods, would the liberalization of services eventually lead to the liberalization of goods? On the other hand, as countries develop, they need to consume advanced services in order to produce goods better and more competitively. Lastly, trade in services, contrary to that of goods, often requires the presence of the service provider to consummate the transaction and thus raises issues of right of establishment and foreign investment which normally fall more clearly outside the scope of international bodies such as GATT. In fact, this latter issue will prove the most complex with which to deal and is likely to become the focus of future attention.

---

*Director, International Management Institute (IMI), Geneva. This paper has been prepared for the International Labour Organization (ILO), Geneva, World Employment Programme Research, WEP 2–22/WP 163.

Furthermore, services are greatly conditioned by cultural characteristics, the nature of the nation state and the socio-political system. To further complicate the matter, many services are today part of a total package as they require specific goods to deliver them. This is not only true of banking and other information-intensive sectors but also of fields such as franchising. Contrary to goods, there is a single distribution system for a growing number of services, namely, the telecommunication infrastructure which is publicly owned in most countries.

It is difficult to predict where the current discussions will lead. The obvious short-term outcome is that the increase in knowledge will lead to national policies at least in fields as apparently different as telecommunications and the use of automatic equipment in factories. In the medium term, it will highlight the necessity for a reconception not only of the international instruments currently in place, but also of the very concepts that feed the policy debate in both developed and developing countries.

Current and foreseeable developments in information technology have triggered and focused the debate on services essentially because of their massive impact on the production and distribution of services. Closely linked to this is the growing consensus that employment is unlikely to be generated in agriculture and manufacturing, therefore the service sectors seem essential for employment creation, economic development and general social reasons.

The following is a summary review of issues with no attempt to enter into the debate of the framework of negotiations nor to present the different views in the current international debate. The intention is to gain more perspective on the impact of information technology and some of the ensuing implications. It should be remembered, however, that this is only part of the general impact of the technology which also affects very substantially the production of goods.

Applications of information technology to services are, nevertheless, more difficult to analyse than those on products and production due to the nature of services themselves, which are highly heterogeneous in their production, economies of scale and determinants of competitiveness. There is a lack of knowledge on how developments of what could be called "new" services might affect the international division of labour not only in services but also in goods. What is clear, however, is that services play an increasingly important role in international trade due to their transportability, the increasing service content of manufacturing and the international tradeability of services in general. In this paper emphasis is on trying to understand the relative position of developing countries in the general process of informatization and thus how the changes underway might affect heir position in the international division of labour.

2. The Importance of Services

The conventional view of services, in terms of the evolution of the economic system, has suggested that the growth of this sector is a natural consequence of development. Through time, economies change from "pre-industrial" to "service or post-industrial" economies.[1] A review of the occupational data, either from a strictly "service" viewpoint or in an attempt to reclassify the labour force in terms of the function that it performs regardless of economic sector, would lead one to question, or at least qualify this conventional view.

Reclassification of the labour force, which will be discussed later, was pioneered by Machlup and Porat.[2] Empirical work, done on a wider scale by OECD, groups the labour force into "information and non-information" workers.[3] These approaches document long-term trends that show a change in the content of all economic activities which necessitate taking a new look at the role of services in the economic development process. Analysing occupational data of France, Ireland, Italy and the United Kingdom, Gershuny and Miles reach the conclusion that:

> . . . during the 1960s and 1970s, changes in the occupational distribution of employment have resulted more from changes in occupational structure within economic sectors, than from changes in demand patterns between them. Increased demand for professional, technical, clerical and other specialized service occupations relative to other employees within each sector, accounts for much more of the increase of employment in these sorts of occupations than does the increase of demand for the products of services industries.[4]

The above assessment qualifies the purely "sectorial shift" view which argues that as countries develop, they transfer employment and activities from the agricultural sector to the industrial and service sectors. In fact, it implies that there is also an integration within sectors as the service content of each increases. From the point of view of developing countries and the international division of labour, this is critically important, because it implies a strong organic link between service and non-service activities.

It then appears that services are closely interlinked with the rest of the economy and that they play an active role in the production of goods (e.g. banking). From this point of view, their contribution to the GDP often underestimates their importance. The role of services such as transportation, and utilities in general, are a crucial part of a country's infrastructure. The role of other services such as telecommunications is less well understood. In recent years, a substantial amount of research has shown that their role is critical and increasing in importance due, among other reasons, to the growth of the information content in *all* activities.[5] Other services which can be provided within corporations, have grown, and their importance lies in opening up the possibility of vertical integration as well as geographical expansion.

If services are considered in the context of their linkages with the rest of the economy, and also as a cause and effect of economic development, the impact of information technology has far more importance than might appear at first sight.

Linkages can also be seen from a different angle, that is, the re-grouping of the labour force into "information-handling" activities. The trends derived from these data are in themselves significant *vis-à-vis* information technology, but the use of "information workers" hides, due to its aggregation, the qualitative and quantitative differences in the provision of services. Despite this problem, it is useful to review the findings since they reveal the pervasiveness of information as an essential raw material for many activities. This approach can, nevertheless, be seen as complementary to the one described earlier, namely, that there is a change in occupational structures within sectors rather than among sectors, and that the content of these service occupations has become more "information intensive".

Information occupations and activities are playing an increasingly important role in labour statistics and accounts. It is unlikely that universal agreement will be reached on exactly what the term "information occupations" means, but even if one adopts a fairly restricted definition, the trend towards increases in information occupations is evident.[6]

The first attempts to quantify the information sector or activity date back to the late 1950s when the initial elements of today's debate were identified. A more systematic approach has been taken in the last decade, including pioneering work by Porat for the United States Department of Commerce in 1977. Based on national statistics over a long period, Porat concluded:

> . . . that 46% of the (United States) Gross National Product is bound up with the information activity; . . . and nearly half of the labour force holds some sort of "informational job, earning 53% of labour income.[7]

Porat used the following rather broad definition of information and "information activity", which implies a reclassification of sectors (e.g. office equipment and telecommunications) that are grouped together as "information activity".

> Information is data that has been organized and communicated. The information *activity* includes all the resources consumed in producing, processing and distributing information goods and services.[8]

One of Porat's findings which is of special interest is that the group concerned with planning, decision-making and the control apparatus of the economy, represented up to 21% of GNP in 1967. Furthermore, when the information activity is divided into primary (supplier of information goods and services) and secondary (information produced for internal consumption by governments and non-information firms) and then studied in detail by product category, the findings show that:

— in 1967, around 35 US cents of every consumer dollar paid was for a variety of information services;

— that at the industry level, one US dollar purchase of tobacco contained 11.8 US cents of secondary information, in food the figure was 15.9 US cents and in apparel 18.4 US cents;

— drugs, cleaning and toilet preparations contained 46.9 US cents of information per US dollar. The 46.9 US cents in this case covered R and D, marketing studies and direct advertising;

— the information content of a US $2.00 pharmaceutical product, assuming a 100% trade margin, was as shown in Table 1.

TABLE 1.   *Information Content of a US $2.00 Pharmaceutical Product*

		Secondary Information Component	Non-Information Component (Matter and Energy)
Trade mark-up		US $1.00	0.499	0.501
Producer's price		US $1.00	0.469	0.531
Total consumer price		US $2.00	0.968	1.032

Source: United States Department of Commerce, Office of Telecommunications, *The information economy,* Washington, D.C., 1977, Vol. 2, page 7.

Just less than 97 US cents of every US $2.00 purchase pays for either producer's or retailer's informational requirements. For the producer, the requirements were about 47 US cents, or almost half of the price. This type of exercise, with all its inherent difficulties, simply shows the tremendous importance of the information component.[9]

The difficulties are illustrated by a recent study, again by the United States Department of Commerce, which recalculated and redefined the earlier work of Porat. It argues that the information economy accounted for 30% of GNP in 1958 and 34% in 1980 but qualifies the findings by stating that, depending on the definition, one "can reasonably include up to 46% of the United States economy".[10]

Additional research from a different perspective by Jonscher confirms that the United States' information sector has been growing much more rapidly than the production sector. The information sector value added increased by a factor of approximately 3.7 (in constant US dollar value) between 1947 and 1972 compared to a factor of just over 2 for the production sector. The second outcome of the data, and of special importance for our purpose, is that the output of the information sector is used principally by industry rather than directly by consumers. Final consumption of information items reached US $84,000 million in 1972 compared to US $506,000 million of information services required by the production sector.[11]

The Department of Commerce and Jonscher's data, which were derived by very different methodologies, seem to add weight to the view that the growth of services, especially those with high information content, is more related to a shift in activities within sectors than to the final consumption of services. This further reinforces the view of the growing information content of physical production and material processing.

Finally, Jonscher's data also show that in this input-output structure, the flow that has grown at the most rapid rate between 1947 and 1972 has been input of goods to support the information sector. That input, basically computers, office equipment and facilities, grew by a factor of more than four (constant value) between 1947 and 1972.

In addition to the above there is also a clear link between information intensity, seen as the R and D-intensity of goods, and economic performance. Technology-intensive commodities have out-performed most other goods in international trade. The most important example comes from Japan where the amount of technology embodied in exports more than doubled between 1962 and 1977.[12] Science-based industries can also be seen as knowledge- or information-intensive sectors.[13] This relationship is an important one to consider due to the heavy concentration of R and D activities in only a few countries.

A summary of the above-mentioned trends for the US, Japan and Europe can be seen in Fig. 1 which shows the shifts in the activities of the labour force. The OECD figures are more conservative than those of Porat, essentially, because they use a more restricted definition. These trends can be explained by the growing amount of information required to produce goods and services as well as the development of pure information products. This process, which has been called the "informatization of society", implies a higher technological content in agriculture, industry and services.

The underlying reality is simply a constant growth in the technical division of labour and the spread of specialization which makes production more complex. At the early stage of the industrial revolution, artisans were responsible for the final product or service. As economies have developed, each task has been broken into parts, thus increasing the complexity of co-ordination, and the need to share and exchange information.

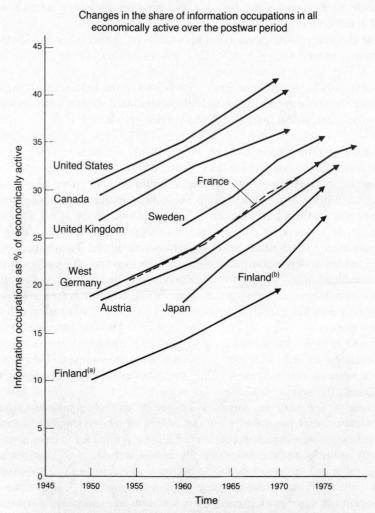

Changes in the share of information occupations in all
economically active over the postwar period

Data for Finland was derived from two separate sources: (a) 1. Pietarisen: (b) The Central
Statistical Office of Finland both sources using a rather more restricted definition of
information occupations than that of Table A1. Absolute values for any given year are
therefore not strictly comparable with other countries although the trend is still of interest.

Source: *OECD, "Microelectronics, productivity and employment",
Paris 1981.*

FIG. 1.   Source: OECD, "Microelectronics, productivity and employment", Paris 1981

All the figures and statistics mentioned, with their inherent imperfections, try to account for information in terms of its economic value. This is difficult to conceptualize, because information does not behave as a traditional commodity.

For the present purpose, the importance of services lies in two basic elements, as follows:

— the growing service content of activities and the linkages with the rest of the economy as illustrated by occupational shifts within sectors;
— the information intensity of the service activities.

The existing data on services are imperfect. At the present time, there is substantial debate concerning the definition of services and even whether a distinction between goods and services should be maintained.[14]

Any definition of services is subject to important qualifications and this is mainly due to their heterogeneity. Kravis, in one of the latest attempts, argues that perhaps the only characteristic of service is the low volume of commodities embodied in them as intermediate inputs. The proportion of value added to gross output is high in services and the proportion of intermediate inputs in the form of services is high when compared to commodity inputs. Even with this observation, Kravis has to allow for an exception in wholesale and retail trade if the distribution of goods are counted as intermediate inputs.[15] One should add that a similar case might be found in some forms of transport, and in forms of advanced financial and banking services. In the latter, the service is indistinguishable from the goods, such as automatic cash telling machines or computerized terminals, that make the service possible.

As technology evolves, more services are subject to a production type of organization and the value of commodities as an intermediate input is likely to increase. In fact in the United States, service firms have invested heavily in the last few years especially in new technologies. Expenditures (after inflation) increased by 145% between 1975 and 1982. This amounts to a 97% increase in investment per service worker.[16] Difficulties of definition are also encountered when attempts are made to characterize services as non-storable goods or simply as intangible goods.[17]

The accumulation of empirical data will condition the outcome of the definitional question and the most likely result will be less aggregated categories and each will be accounted for by specific characteristics. Substantial theoretical work will also be necessary since the distinction between goods and services, and that between "industrial categories" (e.g. banking and retailing or computers and telecommunication sectors) is becoming blurred. In this context, it is legitimate to ask whether the classical distinctions should be maintained or whether a more general organizing concept might be necessary. One avenue to explore, for example, would be to use value added, regardless of whether it is obtained by the production of a good, a service or a combination of both. In turn, this creates difficulties in relation to the theory of value and does not necessarily help in questions related to the regulatory environment. Another suggested possibility is to group activities by functions rather than by characteristics of process. What is clear, however, is that the current debate has exposed flaws in traditional economic and trade theories, and further research will be necessary to approach consensus on questions of definition.

Due to the definitional problem all figures relating to this area should be interpreted with caution. In addition, service activities in the traditional sense may appear understated because many are performed within industrial enterprises. Thus, in national accounts, all services that can be internalized by enterprises such as accounting, design, advertising, R and D, legal services, catering, transport and many others are included as manufacturing output.

But growth in services can also be overstated. This is true when activities that were previously performed within the household, such as child and senior citizen care, are transferred to the money economy. There is not necessarily a substantial "real" growth in output, although it is recorded as such in national statistics.

For the purpose of international comparison, there is little choice but to follow the rather imperfect balance of payments accounts. A broad distinction must be made between "factor" and "non-factor" services. The former relates almost exclusively to investment income. (There is some inconsistency in terms of workers' remittances since it is also a factor which, for balance of payments purposes, is included under "private unrequited transfers" and reported separately from the service accounts.) "Non-factor" services refers to shipping, other transportation, travel, other private services, and other government services.[18]

The General Agreement on Tariffs and Trade (GATT) classifies services by their association with trade in tangible goods qualifying the classification by adding exact characteristics, such as that services are not transferable (e.g. transport service can only be rendered once) and that they have no physical content and, therefore, the unique support of their value is their quality.[19] This approach poses a number of problems, particularly when services, in order to be performed, need a physical carrier which, while essential, is insignificant in terms of value compared to the content (e.g. software tapes) or the definition of quality. In addition to the inherent difficulties in defining services, as mentioned earlier, there are a number of "leakages" in the statistics.

Services are extremely heterogeneous and many of them do not share similar production processes (as steel, textiles, automobiles or wheat), customers, suppliers or markets. This in turn makes difficult international or even national comparison in critical areas such as optimal economies of scale, assessment of market share or relative factor intensity. Maintenance services can be part of an international transaction or purchased locally if they exist in the country. Turn-key plants are an entire package including design, consulting and goods.

In 1981, non-factor services were 16% of total international trade (merchandise, factor services, other transfers and non-factor services) and 22% of international trade in merchandise. If crude oil is excluded from the estimates, the figures are 18% and 27% respectively.[20] Yet only 8% of the total world production of services were traded internationally in 1980. (This figure represents non-factor service debits as a percentage share of domestically produced services.) Comparable figures were 45% for agricultural GDP, and 55% for mining and manufacturing GDP.[21] The low percentage of internationally traded services can be explained by the very nature of the production process of many services which have to be produced and consumed domestically. This is typically the case of governments, education and housing which account for approximately 60% to 65% of service spending in both developed and developing countries.[22]

A further explanation that remains hypothetical at this stage since only circumstantial evidence exists, is that many services have been and are being, replaced by goods which are traded internationally. An extreme example is the substitution of the domestically-produced service of the barber by the internationally traded good of the shaving machine. Similarly, the service of the petrol pump attendant by the internationally traded automatic petrol pump. This type of substitution can help to explain partly the low international "tradeability" of services. It also shows that a "pure" service economy is highly vulnerable to developments in a manufacturing economy. What occurs in this case is that the ultimate "function" is performed by a good rather than a service and therefore transferred to the "goods" statistics.

Services play an important role as a percentage of GDP and employment as shown in Table 2. As one may infer from the data in Table 2, the service sector generates considerable employment in developed and most developing countries. In the former, the labour force in services ranges from 44% in Italy to 66% in the United States and Canada. In developing countries the share of service employment is less than the share of the sector in GDP. The number of people employed in services varies more widely among developing countries than among developing countries than among developed countries: between 5 and 8% in some low-income countries (Nepal and Chad) to 59% or 62% in upper-middle income countries

TABLE 2. *Percentage of Services in Gross Domestic Product and Percentage of Labour Force in Services*

	Services as a percentage of GDP		Percentage of labour force in services	
	1960	1982	1960	1980
Low-income economies	25	31	14	15
Lower-middle income economies	41	42	18	28
Upper-middle income economies	49	48	31	42
High-income, oil-exporting economies	n.a.	25	25	35
Industrial market economies	54	61	44	56
Eastern European non-market economies	n.a.	n.a.	28	39

Source: World Bank, World Development Report, 1984, Tables 3 and 21, Washington, DC, 1984.

(Singapore and Chile). These variants are partly explained by data gathering problems as well as by the existence of structurally different economies.

In terms of GDP, the World Bank excludes electricity, water, gas and construction from its definition of services. If these activities were included under the broad heading of services, the presence of this sector as a percentage of GDP would be much larger in both developed and developing countries. In fact, if construction, utilities and public administration were included, for 1980 the figures would be 67% and 51% for developed and developing countries respectively.[23]

The similarity of the percentage of employment and weight of services in GDP between many developed and developing countries masks profound qualitative differences in types of services and their productivity.[24] Recently, it has been argued that developing countries have a large part of their population working in the service sector and it is precisely this sector that is the most suitable for the massive use of information technology. This attitude confuses services in general with information-intensive services, or people working in services with what have been called information workers.[25] Here, for example, is where the inadequacy of grouping segments of the labour force into "information workers" becomes more apparent because the level of aggregation masks the qualitative differences of information-intensive and other service activities that might have an information component. While it is not possible to go into detail, it should be clear that, by and large, the fact that the service sector is less sophisticated in developing countries is often due to the backwardness of the economic structure, while the nature of services in advanced countries is due to their more mature stages of economic development.[26]

The dominant position of services in the output and employment of developed countries is mainly due to the growth in per capita income, leisure, and changes within sectors such as industry and agriculture, all of which have raised the demand for new services which are complementary to the demand for goods (e.g. maintenance). In developing countries a considerable portion of service activities is of the personal type with very low productivity. In developed countries these activities are often transferred to the structured economy (e.g. cleaning and laundry, and child care). In brief, the nature of services is in general different in developed and developing countries, with the exception of services which are complementary to goods such as transport and insurance and other services which are not, as yet, internationally tradeable on a large scale such as education.

Aside from qualitative differences, the rate of growth in services has been faster in the developed countries. This has given rise to expressions such as the "service economy" or the "post industrial society". In reality those terms refer to a process of change in the technological content and process of production of goods and services which in turn leads to changes in the technical division of labour. In other words, industrial society was not post-agricultural, rather it was agriculture that was industrialized, just as agriculture and industry are now being "informatized". Agriculture and industry will continue to be as essential to individual economies as they have been in the past. For instance, the United States has the largest portion of its labour force in services and, at the same time, is the world's largest agricultural and industrial producer. It is almost impossible to envisage the United States slowly phasing out agriculture and industry. As has been happening in the last few decades, it is more likely that the capital/skill/technology content of those activities will increase, while labour's contribution will continue to decrease in keeping with the historical trend.

While the importance of services to the domestic economies of *all* countries is growing, so is international trade in services. The figures given in Table 3 show the value of service exports in 1980. These figures underestimate, perhaps greatly, the value of international trade in services. There is also an important distortion in the comparison between services and merchandise exports. The underestimation occurs because the figures do not (and cannot, given the statistical base) account for the service content of international trade in goods. Case studies show that the amounts involved might be considerable. According to estimates based on results of Sweden's Office of Statistics' Construction Sector Surveys, about 20% of the export value of construction projects in 1979 consisted of materials and 80% of services. In 1980 and 1981, the material content decreased further. Based on this assessment and comparing it with the construction work

TABLE 3. *Value of Worldwide Service Exports — 1980*

	Value in 1980 (million US dollars)
Service exports	350,000
Merchandise exports	1,650,000
Foreign investment income	225,000
Gross domestic product	9,389,000

Source: The Office of the US Trade Representative, "US National Study on Trade in Services", A submission by the US Government to the General Agreement on Tariffs and Trade, December 1983.

receipts in services, the differences were SKr. 150 million in 1982 between the balance of payment statistics and Statistics' Sweden Survey. The former reported receipts of SKr. 120 million and the latter SKr. 270 million.[27] Numerous studies point out that a considerable volume of service exports is probably reported as exports of goods, particularly in the area of capital goods.[28] In addition, it appears that foreign investment income disguises revenues from foreign services rendered abroad. Buried in the returns on investment there is a substantial volume of trade in services owing to the lack of an appropriate way to list them in the current reporting systems, at least in the US.[29]

The statistics do not (and cannot) account for intra-corporate transactions in services, especially the transportable ones. This is of special importance because, for the moment, most international data links appear to be intra-corporate. Distortions in the comparisons also occurs because of the twelvefold increase in oil prices which has considerably inflated the value of merchandise exports. In fact in 1980, exports of crude oil were 19% of the value of merchandise exports.[30] One can, therefore, safely assume that international trade in services is growing faster than trade in goods or at least that it is substantially more than 20% of world trade.

There is a difference in the growth patterns of developed and developing countries. In industrialized countries in 1982, the largest category of exports in services was "other private services" (approximately US $100,000 million). This category lumps together areas such as banking, insurance, engineering, consulting, data processing and other services. It is precisely in these areas where the most information- and knowledge-intensive services are found, and also where transportability (and thus internationalization) is taking place most rapidly. In fact, historical data for some developed countries (France, Federal Republic of Germany, Italy, England and Wales) show that "producer services" and part of "other services", together with public administration, have grown the fastest in terms of employment creation.[31] For the eight largest service exporting developing countries (defined by IMF as Mexico, Singapore, the Republic of Korea, Greece, Saudi Arabia, Egypt, Israel and Yugoslavia), travel and tourism were the largest exports, together accounting for 36% of export receipts (US $13,200 million), "other private services" followed with 28% (US $10,500 million). Total service exports of these eight countries were US $35,500 million in 1980, or about 10% of the world total.[32]

Services present some distinct characteristics when compared to other activities. Unlike trade in merchandise, the trade balance in services indicates that developed countries are running a substantial (and increasing) surplus in their international exchange of services. The opposite is true for developing countries which are running a substantial (and increasing) deficit in this field. The net deficit for developing countries increased from US $37,000 million in 1970 to US $57,300 million in 1980 — an average annual negative growth rate of 32%.[33]

Due to the link between production of goods and services, a deficit in the latter could be seen as beneficial since it can reinforce the economic production of goods. In this sense, a deficit in itself should not necessarily be viewed as negative. In fact an orthodox policy of import substitution of services could cause more harm than good to development prospects. This is one of the "boomerang" effects that regulations of services can cause. Table 4 provides a view of the evolution of the credit and debit account in merchandise, and factor and non-factor services.

There appears to be a bias in favour of developed countries in international trade in services and this could mean that there is an inherent weakness in the competitive position of developing countries. Due to the mutually reinforcing interaction between the production of goods and of services, if developing countries are not competitive in the production of goods, there will be inevitable implications for the development of a value-added service sector. Furthermore, the development of many services is, in turn, dependent on inputs from the production of goods, particularly of the informational kind (e.g. computers, telecommunication and office equipment), which most developing countries now import.

Weakness in services has wider implications because of the growing relationship between international trade in goods and services. Services are becoming increasingly intertwined with goods, especially in high technology products where the choice of hardware is linked to software and maintenance contracts. This is also true for capital equipment, turn-key projects and, as previously demonstrated, construction.

A survey in the United States conducted by the International Trade Commission on selected service industries, shows some degree of relationship with goods. In some cases, this is strong (construction and management) and, in others, it is weak (education and motion pictures). The survey points out that when it is not possible to quantify merchandise exports, or if they appear negligible, there is nevertheless an indirect

TABLE 4. *Developed and Developing Countries Composition of Current Account, 1975–1980*

(billions of US dollars)

	1975 Merchandise			1975 Factor Services			1975 Non-Factor Services			1980 Merchandise			1980 Factor Services			1980 Non-Factor Services		
	Credit	Debit	Net	Credit	Debit	Net	Credit	Debit	Net	Credit	Debit	Net	Credit	Debit	Net	Credit	Debit	Net
Developed Market Economies	568.7	570.6	-1.9	61.8	52.1	9.7	149.7	147.4	2.2	253.9	1332.7	-78.8	191.2	172.5	18.7	315.8	306.0	9.8
Developing Countries	179.6	157.7	21.9	8.8	19.0	-10.3	27.8	45.7	-17.9	503.2	391.3	111.9	31.1	60.4	-29.2	72.2	129.5	-57.3
Oil Exporting Developing	101.7	53.3	48.4	5.6	7.2	-1.6	5.5	19.8	-14.3	293.3	137.5	155.8	18.0	19.2	-1.1	14.7	65.9	-51.2
Non-Oil Exporting Developing	77.9	104.4	-26.5	3.1	11.8	-8.7	22.3	25.9	-3.6	209.9	253.9	-43.9	13.1	41.2	-28.1	57.5	63.6	-6.1
Least Developed	2.5	5.0	-2.5	0.1	0.2	-0.1	0.7	1.6	-0.8	4.8	11.1	-6.3	0.4	0.3	0.1	1.6	3.5	-1.9

Source: IMF Balance of Payments Type, 1981 as reported in UNCTAD, "Protectionism and Structural Adjustment," March 1983, pp. 48, 59-54. (TD/B/941)

contribution. This is the case for banking and motion pictures, and especially for advertising of US products abroad. Table 5 gives these indications.

TABLE 5. *Relationship of Exports in Selected US Service Industries to US Merchandise Exports (1981)*

	Foreign Revenues from Services (US $million)	Products Exports as a Consequence of Services Activity (US $million)
Communication services	2,700	n.a.
Computer and data processing services	3,000	217.6
Construction and equipment	5,600	22,400
Consulting and management	1,000	5,500
Educational services	1,900	n.a.
Equipment leasing and rental	13,400	57
Financial services	56,400	564
Franchising	2,700	14
Health service	600	56
Hotel/motel services	2,300	18
Insurance services	6,500	n.a.
Motion pictures	1,370	n.a.
Transportation — air	6,400*	57
Transportation — maritime	5,800	n.a.

*US $2,700 million were received from non-US nationals; the figure in the above table is the total international revenue.

Source: US International Trade Commission, "Relationship of Exports in Selected US Service Industries to US Merchandise Exports", Washington, D.C., 1982.

A description of the relationship would not be complete without mentioning services rendered by manufacturers through international transfers within companies. For example, the top ten US computer companies had revenues of software/services of US$5,600 million in 1983, or 9% of their total computer-related revenues. It is not possible to estimate how much of this was obtained overseas. The figures exist only in aggregate form but, of the total revenue, an average of 36% was generated outside the US and services are obviously part of this.[34] Technology, however, permits a degree of substitution and at least part of the services previously rendered *in situ* can now be internationally traded. For example, IBM, Burroughs, Digital and other manufacturers of computers have developed remote support centres to monitor and diagnose problems in computers operated by their customers. Digital has invested considerable sums in remote diagnosis centres in the US and Europe. In the latter, thousands of microcomputers are connected through a network to a centre in Southern France which enables service engineers to determine faults.

This process might require access to data in the customer's computer in order to bring the data to the diagnostic centre.[35] In the computer industry, while goods cannot be sold without services, the opposite is not true.

Another aspect of the same issue is the role of foreign companies which render private non-factor services. For the United States for example, foreign service revenues earned by majority-owned subsidiaries are substantially larger than exports of non-factor private services from the United States. For 1977, the figure amounted to US$280,000 million as compared to US$19,000 million of private non-factor service exports. The service subsidiaries accounted for over 40% of the income of all subsidiaries and 25% of employment. Foreign revenues of the US service sector for 1980 amounted to a total of US$600,000,000 million as compared to exports of US$35,246,000 million for non-factor services during the same year.[36]

Comparative advantage in many of the internationally tradeable services appears to be related to economies of scale, managerial know-how and techniques, as well as to technical knowledge which in many cases is linked to the operation of sophisticated equipment.[37] Studies of such matters are only recently being systematically undertaken, especially for "other private services" and add an important dimension to possible policy revisions since they reveal the micro-economic functioning of services. Past studies in fields such as transportation have also shown the need for economies of scale and considerable know-how. A study of the multinational operations of three service companies in insurance, mass merchandizing and construction engineering, and consulting shows that development of advantage in these fields is "based on the law of large numbers". It further argues that the service technology developed by the companies studied could not have been created in a narrow market base. It concludes:

> This fact alone suggests that many developing countries will need to be part of a high volume market if they are effectively to develop mass consumer and high-technology business service.[38]

The importance of services has been established by illustrating the size of the sector in terms of trade, GDP and employment. It has been demonstrated that multiple links are being formed between services and the rest of the economy, and that there is a growing information content in many services activities. The second part of this paper deals with how information technology is affecting the service sector.

3. The Impact of Information Technology on Services

Developments in office automation and telecommunications have permitted information technology to transform services by increasing their productivity and facilitating their delivery. Information technology makes services transportable due to the extensive digitalization of all types of signals which in turn allows the use of vast networks to transfer, process and retrieve information (e.g. interface of computers-telecommunications (*télématique*)). In addition, dedicated value-added networks have been developed to process information during transmission.

Information technology also increases the use of self-service through remote terminals which allow, for instance, telebanking, teleshopping, bookings and the use of equipment to transfer the manual cost of transactions to users (e.g. automatic petrol pump stations and automatic bank telling machines).

Information technology enhances the replacement of human-to-human services by goods (e.g. film development services by video cameras or electronic photography, the reduction of maintenance requirements due to self-diagnostic systems and modular repairs). It also makes possible the development of new services (e.g. videotext). New services, however, often only consist of transporting existing services rather than inventing new ones. There is, therefore, a process of substitution.

The change in services is dependent on a special infrastructure which is being developed in many countries. The infrastructure is centered around telecommunication systems that include cable television and other forms of broadcasting, coupling of radio with telephone networks and an array of other systems for full exploitation of current products. In many respects, the situation is similar to that of the car at the beginning of the century. Cars were commercially available (admittedly in an immature manner) before there were roads, petrol stations, or garages, let alone skilled mechanics. It was only after World War II that large-scale construction of motorways really got underway and the car began to compete seriously with railroads. The currently emerging social and economic infrastructure will be the "information roads or highways" which will carry services within countries and across borders. The full impact of this infrastructure will only be known when it reaches its future potential.

The essential feature of change is that many services are becoming transportable thus making it possible to create a great number of new services. This is, of course, in addition to the alterations within the production of services themselves through office automation or more self-service. Today, telecommunications make it possible to transport economically the contents of a library to a living room or an office. Similarly, a banking service can be transported to a shopping centre, households and many other places by utilizing automatic cash-telling points which are connected to the bank's computer. As the cost of telecommunications decreases, the number of transportable services increases.

Although there is no detailed assessment of the characteristics of the content of international telecommunications traffic, the volume continues to increase rapidly. The increase is faster than that of national economies or that of international trade. Telex traffic is growing at over 16% per year. 60% of world telecommunications traffic is routed over the North Atlantic and 20% over the Pacific, in line with the main areas of economic activity and trade flows. Europe-Latin America flows grew by 27% during 1974–76 and by 40.7% during 1976–79. In absolute terms the flows increased 9.5 times between 1972 and 1979. For the North America-South America flow, following a period of stagnation from 1973 to 1975, the increase in volume was 35.4% from 1976 to 1979. The traffic, measured in thousands of minutes charged increased 5.2 times between 1972 and 1979.[39] This growth in traffic runs parallel to a sharp decrease in the real price of telecommunications which, for the United States, declined by a factor of 3.5 between 1970 and 1981. Telephone traffic between the United States and the rest of the world increased by a factor of 11.3 between 1970 and 1981.[40]

An analogy from the last century, is the decreased cost of transport brought about by progress in technology which made it possible to move heavy and bulky cargo economically. The consequence was that international and regional comparative advantage in producing goods became evident once distance was no longer a "natural" barrier to trade. Similarly, as telecommunication costs decrease, the relative economic advantage in the production of services, particularly information-intensive ones, becomes evident. Another example from the 19th century is the impact of refrigeration on trade in goods. Before refrigeration, perishable products were only traded locally. Refrigeration made it possible to transport goods over long distances and internationally. The notion of distance is implicit in most activities preceded by the ubiquitous "tele", i.e. tele-vision, tele-banking, tele-shopping, tele-conferencing, tele-text, etc. Before television, theatre performances were only traded locally and supplied *in situ*. Today, they can be transported over distances through live transmission or stocked on tape, film or video disks. At the same time, there is a substitution of goods for services through self-diagnosis and modular repairs as with the use of cartridges in photocopying machines. In that example, a domestically produced service is replaced by an internationally traded good. Similarly photographic and photo development services are being replaced by electronic photography or video cassettes. Sometimes, goods are replaced by services as is the case of certain newspapers and magazines where shipped printed matter has been replaced by transmission through telecommunication channels.

The process of substitution, mentioned earlier in a different context, has fundamental policy implications which have not been properly assessed in the current debate. For example, a liberal policy for trade in goods can make way for substitution of domestically-produced services, whereas a liberal policy in services can generate substantial demand for goods which are normally (but not always) based on electronics. The evidence shows that on the national level, as income increases, the amount of income devoted to human-to-human services tends to remain relatively constant while greater percentages of income are devoted to the purchase of goods to produce the service functions at home or at the working place, thus generating considerable demand for "goods".[41] There is no apparent reason to believe that the same phenomenon does not occur internationally.

The "materialization" of services requires further study since it can affect employment policy in a number of ways and because the organic link and substitution that exists in the interaction between the manufacturing and service sectors ought to be considered. As technology advances (e.g. applications of artificial intelligence), materialization is likely to accelerate and one can speculate that, in the long run, an economy that preserves and enhances its manufacturing base will compete advantageously against a hypothetical "service economy". Furthermore, for the medium term, losing comparative advantage in the production of goods can lead to a double impact: the import of goods *and* the substitution of domestically-produced services by imported goods.

It should be borne in mind that changes in services take place in the context of the growing "service content" of manufacturing and agricultural activities as well as the growth in services in the traditional sense of the "tertiary sector" as previously explained. Furthermore, increasing numbers of capital goods contain a service component in the form of software or links to data bases (e.g. computers, machine tools and Computer-Aided Design (CAD) and Computer-Aided Manufacturing (CAM) systems). This is due to the growing electronic content of products. When products are "electronized", a communication dimension is almost a natural consequence of the evolution of the product. Thus, cash registers change from being sophisticated adding and substracting machines to data entry terminals; word processors can become part of a total office system, or numerically-controlled machine tools can be linked locally or internationally to hierarchy of computers as part of a manufacturing system.

What distinguishes present and future developments from the past is that communications have integrated a growing number of products into larger systems. In industrial processes, the communications between different stages of the process can now be done by machines, domestically or internationally, instead of by people. As most of these services are traded within organizations the real dimension of international circulation of "intangibles" is greatly understated.

The trends described are often combined with self-service and the replacement of human-to-human services by goods.[42] For example, in telebanking or the use of automatic cash machines, the client supplies the input for the transaction (self-service) and the cashier is replaced by the equipment (human-to-human service replaced by goods). New services, such as videotext, exist precisely because it is possible to transport economically vast amounts of information through interacting telecommunication channels. This enables true interaction between provider and user in a fashion similar to human interaction, for instance, over a travel agency counter.

Transporting services and raising their productivity opens new opportunities to combine traditional and advanced technologies, especially in manufacturing and agriculture. Administrative, logistic, marketing and information-gathering activities are important components of manufacturing which can be greatly rationalized internally or put together in the form of a co-operative similar to the common pool of machinery used in some agricultural areas. An example is the experience of the Prato Valley, north of Florence, Italy, where the manufacturing process of woollen clothing remains organized in traditional and small-scale enterprises, while economies of scale have been achieved through the use of networks at the service (e.g. marketing) and logistic levels. Other processes such as cleaning, which are characterized by economies of scale, are owned on a co-operative basis.[43]

In agriculture, the "green finger" experiment in the US and other experiments in France allow farmers to obtain market information and place their products directly without the need of intermediaries. This is a sort of "participatory" commodity exchange. At the same time, farmers obtain technical information and, perhaps more importantly, market transparency in agricultural inputs without being fully dependent on local suppliers. Other experiences include the monitoring of crops and making recommendations to farmers on irrigation and the application of fertilizer or pesticides according to crop conditions. The farmer puts in the data on crop conditions and receives an answer on possible action to take. This has also been done collectively by groups of farmers who share one terminal or take their data to a centralized location.

The transportation of services can also produce a change in distribution systems since in many cases the goods move rather than the consumers (e.g. teleshopping). But more importantly and contrary to the distribution of goods, transported services have a single and unique distribution channel — the telecommunication infrastructure. National and international access to the networks is, therefore, essential. This is one of the important elements in current international discussions and complementary to the question of access to data as such.

It is not possible to give an account here of all concrete applications and chain effects that are occurring in services. The speed of transformation is largely conditioned by the evolution of the telecommunications infrastructure. In this context, the development of the telecommunications infrastructure becomes a central economic issue for the creation of value-added services and employment. This infrastructure could play the role that the building of roads or railroads played in the past, not only because of the labour-intensity of "wiring" countries and cities, but most importantly, because of the service spin-off that it can produce in the long run.

The following list shows the main impacts of information technology on internationally traded services. The list is based on the traditional classification of services. (see p. 149)

The main general consequences of the increasing transportability of services are summarized below. The consequences are not mutually exclusive and, in most cases, are concurrent but they are classified in an order that facilitates comprehension of the implications of the changes underway. They are as follows:

(a) Increase in productivity of service production;
(b) greater "transparency" of markets;
(c) blurring of the borders between sectors;
(d) changes in the barriers to entry; and
(e) further internationalization of services.

3.1. Increase in Productivity of Service Production

The first effect of transportability has to do with the production of the services themselves. In services, there is a reduction of the transaction cost particularly in fields such as banking, insurance and other information-intensive activities. Many services can now be operated unattended for 24 hours-a-day from many different locations including the household. The array of applications of office automation equipment and particularly properly operated on-line systems, increase productivity in all areas that until now had not been formalized and were thus difficult to rationalize. This is the case, for example, of professional and managerial work. The use of on-line systems also increases the mobility of financial resources since they can be easily moved by electronic fund transfer. There is also an increase in the span of control over highly diverse and geographically dispersed activities. While this is not the place to delve into the possible permutations of office automation, it is important to point out that it is increasingly perceived as a source of comparative advantage.

Traditionally, there has been little concern for understanding office work as a specific process in which the technical division of labour, measurements of quality and productivity can differ from those applicable to manufacturing. In the last few years, changes made possible by informa-

Partial list of services activities and some of the effects of technological change

Service	Impact of Technological Change	Comment
Shipping (Freight)	Partial substitution of transport of goods by services.	Substitution of shipped printed matter by sending it through telecommunications.
Other transport (air, rail, road, inland waterways)	As above.	As above. Transport of mail is partly substituted by electronic mail. New logistic systems are emerging where the goods themselves are transferred through telecommunications. This trend will be reinforced through cellular radio.
Travel (passenger transport) applications	Partial substitution especially of business travel.	The use of teleconferencing in specific applications is increasingly substituting for business travel in specific.
Tourism (counselling, advertising, tour operations, hotel/motel services)	Highly transportable.	New systems incorporating videodisc and interactive routines are becoming available. Long distance and international toll-free services will be widely used. Hotel/motel and airline reservations will be far more computerized. The industry will be more internationalized. Some hotels are now offering teleconferencing services between their different locations. Videotext already allows bookings to be made directly for some services.
Insurance and re-insurance	More transportability.	Customers will be able to order directly specific insurance through retailing points or terminals as is now the case in many airports which offer flight insurance.
Banking and other financial services	More transportable.	Automatic cash-teller machines can reach many different places while providing a 24-hour service. Tele-banking is done now at corporate level and in some households. SWIFT will evolve into a worldwide trading network. Banks are also increasingly becoming information suppliers in finance, trade and investment.
Brokerage	More and highly transportable.	This service is heavily based on availability of information. It will become even more international in the future when it will be possible for non-specialists to intervene through terminals, thereby eliminating middle-men in many cases, as already domestically available in the US.

Service	Change	Comment
Accounting	More and highly transportable.	This was one of the first applications of EDP and is used by many transnational companies on an international basis. Many small- and mediumsized enterprises will internalize this service rather than buy it from specialist firms. This is possible because of microcomputer programmes combining accounts, billing and management reporting systems.
Advertising	More and highly transportable.	This will be the case especially with Direct Satellite Broadcasting due to start operations in Europe in 1986–87. Already operational in Canada and parts of the US. International regulations related to the satellite "footprint" when the signal goes across borders, will slow down applications. The main concern is with cultural identity as well as the economic effects when advertising revenues are obtained by a company operating outside the national territory.
Films and TV features	Already highly transportable.	Direct satellite broadcasting will increase transportability while the existence of video tapes will make enforcement of copyright laws practically impossible. "National content" regulations will be difficult to apply except for national broadcasting services.
Wholesaling and retailing	Increased transparency of markets. Goods and services supermarkets.	Easy access to price information and services could increase competition in this sector. Complex delivery systems are likely to be developed. In large supermarket chains, the trend is to offer also a "supermarket of services". Teleshopping is already used for a limited number of goods. This will evolve into a sort of "international mail order" catalogue with direct relationship between the consumer and main wholesaler or retailer.
Construction engineering (management, consulting, design architecture)	More and highly transportable.	The use of CAD systems and remote entry for calculations in centralized systems will increase transportability.
(Professional services)	(More and highly transportable.)	(Remote access to the key in this sector.)
— Legal		Large data bases of a national or international nature (e.g. Lexis). People seeking advice might interrogate bases directly.

Service	Change	Comment
— Economic	More and highly transportable.	Large data bases, both national and international, already exist. This area will expand greatly. There is concern about sovereignty over national data as well as questions pertaining to individual privacy.
— Medical	Transportable.	Remote diagnosis for some types of illness is already in experimental stages. The results of medical exams can now be transmitted in some cases to specialist clinics within or outside the country. This is analogous to processing data abroad.
— Technical	More transportable.	Different technicians operating in distant places can work on the same problem as is now the case with the design of chips. Access to technical data bases has been possible since the late 1960s and developed rapidly during the 1970s. Specific technical data bases are being developed for new manufacturing processes such as machining.
— Education	Highly transportable.	This field is normally under non-marketable services. The use of educational software, teaching machines, interactive programmes and video-cassette is converting a large proportion of this activity into a marketable service, at least as far as "instruction" is concerned. Technology allows the widespread application of the British Open University concept even at the high school level. High quality interactive teaching for remote locations becomes possible.
Repairs and maintenance	Highly transportable.	As equipment includes electronics and self-diagnosis, maintenance and interaction for repair can be over long distance as well as by running recovery routines. Repairs as such have to be done *in situ*, but the instructions come long distance, unless redundancy capacity can be switched on. Modular repairs are increasing the self-service aspect of this activity.

Service	Change	Comment
Data processing	More and highly transportable.	The key in this sector is the ease of data communications. Data can be processed within or outside a country.
— Software	Highly transportable.	Software can be developed and maintained by teams at distant locations. It can be marketed and distributed using telecommunications lines.
— Remote data entry	More and highly transportable.	There is a growing trend to use cheap skilled clerical labour for remote data entry, replacing key punch operators.
Information services — Newspapers	More and highly transportable.	Telecommunications permits the *International Herald Tribune* to be edited in Paris and printed in Zurich, Paris, London and Hong Kong. In turn, videotext will partly do away with hard copies.
— On-line systems	Already highly transportable.	Commodity, stock and financial information. It will develop to provide a more analytical type of information with graphics included.

tion technology have led to a growing interest in the area for several reasons. First, an increasing number of people, especially in the advanced countries, are engaged in clerical work or in activities with some type of clerical/information component. As mentioned previously, the work of OECD has been particularly significant in establishing internationally comparable data in this area. Second, although the usefulness of productivity measurements for clerical work are debatable (due, for instance, to quality considerations), it is assumed that productivity in the office sector lags behind manufacturing and agriculture. (This assumption is not always tenable as it depends largely on the measuring instruments.) Third, the office sector is relatively undercapitalized, with investment per worker at a fraction of that of agriculture or manufacturing.

A higher degree of office automation is possible today through:

(a) Further automation of formalized work (e.g. data and word processing); and
(b) Interaction of equipment through communications which leads to the optimization of organizational systems and increases the effectiveness of people working in environments which are weakly formalized.

The importance of developments in office technology is based on two factors. The first is the capacity to take over four familiar office operations which traditionally required human skills and effort, as follows:

— Information capture: Collecting information or initiating an information-based transaction.

— Information processing: Covering areas as varied as calculation, editing, typing, producing and merging files, etc.

— Information storage: Creating files and storing information in them.

— Information retrieval: Recovering information as and when needed.

The second factor is the capacity to integrate the above functions into a single system, either within a specific location or through a national/international network. Integration can take place within the office functions and/or manufacturing, logistics, R and D, and other functions of the enterprise.

In the long run, the distinction between shop-floor and office work in manufacturing enterprises will be minimal. This is partly due to the trend to operate as single businesses with a closed information loop. One could argue, therefore, that manufacturing automation as well as office automation are transitions to "integrated business systems", a concept made possible by information technology.

The realization of potential depends upon the performance of equipment, utilization of its systems characteristics, quality of the telecommunications services and human/organizational behaviour. It is the latter which, at present, appears to be the most important impediment to applications. Numerous measures have been taken at the country level (e.g. Information Technology Year in the United Kingdom) as well as at the enterprise level, to encourage diffusion.

By using traditional methods of measuring productivity in clerical activities, considerable increases have been recorded. In the case of banking, for example, it is expected that in the United Kingdom the cost of cashing a cheque will be reduced from 29.5p. in 1983 to 14.8p. in 1992. This will be achieved by electronic fund transfers and the use of automatic telling machines (ATM). In the United Kingdom, the volume of transactions is expanding by about 7% a year while the number of bank employees is only increasing by 1 to 2% annually.[44] It is not expected that even that small annual increase in employment will be maintained in the United Kingdom, due to the high market penetration of banks and related services.[45]

There is a growing consensus that, for enterprises, the real benefit of office automation lies in the optimization of the general control and managerial system rather than in specific increases in productivity at the work station or computer terminal level. An integrated system allows companies to reach considerable economies of scale in organization and almost instantaneous control of operations. *It is the communication dimension or the interaction of equipment that makes the real difference in the rationalization of office work.*

The American Express Company is a good example of organizational economies of scale and system optimization. The company has 9 major information-processing centres in the US and abroad, 6 worldwide data and time-sharing network groups, 70 large computer systems and 229 smaller ones. The systems support 17,000 on-line terminals within the company, another 5,700 point-of-sale terminals and over 50 direct links to approximately 30,000 terminals at airlines and department stores. The services and networks rely on every form of communications media: private lines as well as public data networks; cable, microwave and satellite transmission, and, experimentally, optical fibre. The company, of course, uses telex and telephones in addition to on-line data transmission.

However, in the future, private integrated networks will carry both voice and data traffic. The cost of developing, operating and maintaining those information-processing systems and communications networks is over US$300 million per year.

The company uses global communications and the above infrastructure for:

— Processing 350 million American Express card transactions per year.
— Daily authorization of 250,000 of those worldwide transactions within an average response time of 5 seconds.
— Verification and replacement of lost or stolen travellers' cheques sold by more than 100,000 banks and other selling outlets around the world.
— Accessing reservation systems and travel service data bases by American Express travel offices and representatives in 125 countries.
— Rapid execution of approximately US$10,000 million per day in international banking transactions, in the form of money transfers, letters of credit and foreign exchange transactions.
— The completion of 56 million insurance premiums and claim transactions per year.
— Virtually instantaneous response to 500,000 daily messages directing high-speed trading in securities, commodities, bonds, treasury bills and a host of other items.[46]

For multinational enterprises this represents an entirely new process of extending economies of scale in traditional manufacturing, marketing and logistics to the organizational level. In this context, the capacity to control centrally the activities of many dispersed locations increases and the organization itself is altered. For instance, the use of on-line systems for managerial purposes compels rethinking of the centralization-decentralization question since it often becomes devoid of significance when all components of the decision-making process can interact.[47]

3.2. Transparency of Markets

A transparent market is one in which all pertinent information about the goods being transacted in the market is available. This is essential for competition, industrial and individual consumers because a wide variety of choice if offered from which to make a selection. Transparency occurs for goods and services rather than for information products *per se* (e.g. a consultant's report or a market study). Information does not behave like a normal "commodity", because if all the information was available about the information itself, it would become a free good with simple cognition being the only form of consumption. This fact has caused considerable discussion on the nature of information itself and the economic theory needed to treat it as a "commodity".

Access to vast pools of information operates de facto in many areas as an electronic yellow-pages directory. Data bases increase information regarding alternative sources, prices, qualities, etc. and thus widen choices and increase transparency of markets. This in itself has important consequences because it shortens the response time to changing market conditions, and lowers entry barriers to markets, where it is necessary to diffuse quickly and massively information about a given product or service. One example of this is Reuter's commodity and stock market information terminals which operate practically in real time throughout the world. This type of system is very successful when the time factor is essential and most of the information being supplied is perishable. In the future, there will be systems which offer both perishable and more permanent types of information, particularly with the widespread use of cable, local networks and a combination of powerful processing/archiving technology.

Transparency of different markets will grow with the entry into services of more on-line data bases and transaction systems. Table 6 shows growth in revenues for the on-line data base market. The rate of growth varies from 30% in the US to 62% in Western Europe for the period 1980–85. As of 1981, one half of 965 internationally traded on-line data bases contained business and industry information, followed by science and technology as the second most important category. Out of the 158 million records added in the US in 1981, 61% were in the area of trade, in Western Europe the figure was 7 million records of 16% of new records.[48]

TABLE 6.   Estimated revenues for the on-line data-base market, United States and Western European countries, 1980 and 1985 (Millions of dollars)

Country	Year		
	1980	1985 (estimated)	Average annual growth rate, 1980–85 (Percentage)
United States	1,170	4,227	30
Western Europe	123	1,398	62
United Kingdom	54	397	49
France	12	305	91
Italy	10	110	61
Germany, Federal Republic of	7	149	84
Other	41	437	61
Total	1,294	5,625	34

Source: INPUT, International market opportunities for on-line database services (Palo Alto, INPUT, 1980), as quoted in UNCTC, Transborder data flows: access to the international on-line data-base market, New York, 1983.

The effect of more transparent markets on the international economic system is not yet clear. On the one hand, there are substantial positive effects in at least two areas. One is the increased choice for the national, corporate and individual consumer. Secondly, there is an easy and economic mechanism for producers to expose their wares on the market thus decreasing barriers to entry. This can be important for developing countries because it lowers marketing costs and the exchange of commercial data can encourage South-South trade. On the other hand, concern has been expressed (particularly by the Bank of International Settlements) that transparent markets in the absence of a regulatory framework can lead to rapid and sharp fluctuations of currencies and other financial instruments. It could even lead to the destabilization of institutions if inaccurate or incomplete information is instantaneously circulated throughout the world commercial channels.[49] Indeed, the credibility and importance information is essential to a transparent market.

3.3. Blurring of Border Lines Between Sectors

The classical case here is the merging of banking, financial services and retailing. In Europe and the United States many large supermarkets and department stores use interactive point-of-sale systems, have their own "in-house" credit cards or standard credit cards, which leaves the banks with only the monthly cheque or giro payment to settle aggregate purchases. In the United States, Sears Roebuck is one of the most advanced in implementing this type of innovation with "in-store financial centres" which offer a range of products from stocks and bonds to life insurance, saving certificates or car and house loans.

There has always been the possibility of organizations outside the banking system providing what amounts to payment systems without being classified as banks. Shops cash cheques for their customers, and other institutions will occasionally use their own bank accounts on behalf of their customers by drawing cheques to third parties in return for cash. These services were provided rarely and only as a special favour because payment services were a costly business protected by the entry barrier of the branch networks. The significance of electronic fund transfers and networks in general, is that they have made it profitable for outsiders to provide substitutes for normal payment and other services. Outsiders can compete effectively because banking is closely regulated and has substantially fixed assets in buildings and installations that require amortization. That partly explains why there are such pressures to deregulate the financial services industries and why banks are diversifying into additional value-added services.[50]

While the case above refers to the blurring of lines between different service providers, the same occurs between industry and services. A classical case here is the computer industry and the telecommunications industry which were distinctly different in the past, but are now becoming one. Computer companies are offering telecommunication services or local area and international networks while telecommunication service suppliers are entering the computer field. Bank and financial service institutions are also selling equipment which is necessary for the provision of their services.

The blurring of lines between sectors confirms how intertwined goods and services are becoming in many fields. This has policy implications particularly in the field of service regulations. It also increases the complexity of data gathering procedures and of neatly distinguishing between goods and services in international trade. One of the important effects of sectoral convergence is an increase in economies of scale through vertical integration as evidenced by the products offered. The trend in most areas is to offer total packages that can be a combination of an array of goods and services. This is valid for the service area and increasingly for manufacturing. This process will concentrate activities and increase barriers to entry in many fields.

3.4.   Changes in the Barriers to Entry

There are two main types of changes here. One, where the barrier to entry for services suppliers is lowered, and the other, where the barriers to entry increase for mass consumer services or where industry intertwine their offer of goods with services. Entry barriers are lowered when the telecommunication infrastructure is used to market and/or distribute services. Connection to a network can make heavy investment in branch offices or localized services unnecessary. The cost of the network in turn is shared by all the users, suppliers and consumers. This is analogous to the role played by motorways or railroads that gave producers in remote locations easy and economical access to large urban centres. Through telecommunications clients can be reached without the physical presence of the seller. This is particularly true for information-intensive services such as software houses, time-sharing services or data bases which can enter markets through telephone lines. The investment needed by a small bank or other institution to offer its services on a public videotext system is comparatively small. There are greater chances for small banks to broaden their market by using the wired infrastructure than by installing automatic cash teller machines in different areas. These machines can only be maintained and justified on the basis of a large volume of transactions.

While growth in employment and diversification of services might occur due to lower entry barriers, it is also true that certain services enjoy increased economies of scale both nationally and internationally. For insurance, large volumes provide a better spread of risk; for financial and credit card services they reduce the cost of transactions due to the economies of scale in data processing and telecommunications. When goods are intertwined with services, the barrier to entry is considerably increased especially because captive markets can be created when the consumption of goods is tied to the consumption of services.

The lowering of entry barriers has a considerable capital saving effect and also enhances the replacement of existing services by new ones. Postal services with their expensive infrastructure and operational cost are partially replaced by electronic mail,[51] and newspapers and journals are transmitted through telecommunications to be printed in various locations. In the latter, a new form of logistic infrastructure emerges, where not only the services are transported but the product (i.e. a newspaper or journal) remains in an intangible form for as long as possible in order to save on transport costs and to gain time. In the future, the electronic newspaper will remain intangible unless the customer chooses to have a "hard" copy printed.

Although connection to a network might not require a lot of capital, the production of many services does require considerable investment and economies. A study of the international on-line data base situation shows that developing countries are hardly represented in this field, mainly due to high barriers to entry in the production of this service. The reasons are high investment cost in hardware and software, high operational cost, economies of scale, and competition with established producers. This assumes that adequate domestic technical, organizational and human infrastructure exists.[52]

3.5. *Internationalization of Services*

The consequences of the process of transportability of services mentioned above, inevitably bear directly on international aspects. Internationalization of services increases as more services become tradeable through improvements in telecommunications, as more services are embodied in goods, and finally, as services are fully contained in physical carriers (i.e. tapes, video disk, etc.) or substituted by goods. Despite the multifaceted impact of technology on the internationalization of services, research has mostly concentrated on the role of data transmission in old and new services. This is not surprising since transmission of data across borders (transborder data flows) offers the most striking example of change in the means and content of international trade. The acknowledgement of that change has caused countries to review their policies towards data transmissions in order to maximize national benefits and discourage possible adverse effects. The evolution of the policies remains in a state of flux since, in many cases, they imply tariff and non-tariff barriers to trade in services which are just beginning to be discussed at an international level.

There are three main issues in the transmission of data across borders. The first relates to the protection of individual privacy which, to a great extent, has been partly resolved in the developed countries through the adoption of the OECD privacy guidelines and the resolution of the Council of Europe.[53] This issue has not been dealt with in the developing countries.

The second issue, which is far more complex, relates to national sovereignty, cultural identity and vulnerability arising from the fact that crucial data pertaining to a country, a company or a subsidiary, can be kept abroad and could be withheld for political, economic or other reasons. The classical example here is the case of Dressner Industries in France which was obliged by the French Government and according to French Law, to honour its contract with the Soviet Union to supply compressors for the construction of the Siberian pipeline. Dressner-France ground to a halt simply because the US administration ordered the company headquarters in the US to terminate engineering and other services and information flows from Dallas. As a consequence, Dressner-France was confronted with cancellation of contracts, particularly from Australia, since the buyer realized that without access to the central data base, the French subsidiary was virtually paralysed. Dressner works through a complex network of telecommunications and satellite links from its central data base in the US to offices and construction sites in about 100 countries. The data base carries up-to-the minute design information, financial data, personnel files and inventories listing all crucial data for the operations of the subsidiaries.[54] International agreement on access to data has thus become essential in order to avoid inconsistent and contradictory national rulings.

The third issue, and the most important for the purpose of this paper, relates to the economic effects of the internationalization of services. Countries have reacted in two distinct ways.

Most developed countries have followed a policy of encouraging the supply of information-intensive goods and services through special government programmes, financial incentives and R and D. There are only a few specific instances where governments have explicitly regulated telecommunications flows to protect infant industries or employment. However, the international flow of machine-to-machine or machine-to-human communications increases, new legal and administrative measures could be introduced. Measures under discussion range from straightforward prohibitions to differential applications of rates and access to lease lines. However, changes in accounting practices so as to quantify the flow of information (now largely underestimated) could be more important in the long run than technical monitoring systems. The French Madec report advocates carrying out "informatic audits", which essentially implies that technical means of control will be largely unnecessary.[55] The need to assess current practice related to fiscal and accounting principles used for information flows, has been recently suggested by the OECD Secretariat in order to "identify the issues to be treated in this field".[56]

The second main form of reaction has been the explicit regulation of data-flow mechanisms as part of a general informatic policy to encourage the production of information goods and services. That type of policy amounts to a programme of *import substitution of services*, similar to past policies of import-substitution of manufactured goods. The only clear example in this field is Brazil. On average, the traffic volume of the international data transmission links in Brazil increased by about 56% per year up to 1985, with an increase of a little less than 50% foreseen from 1985 onwards.[57] Brazil has been actively pursuing a policy of encouragement and protection of its informatic industry. The policy includes hardware as well as international data links. The reasoning is related to the balance of payments, the development of local industry, the protection of national sovereignty and the avoidance of dependency on foreign-based information-processing systems. The policy, which has been transformed into law and is already operational, prohibits teleprocessing abroad, the import or export of software through telecommunications, the use of foreign software or data if a national equivalent is available and the transmission of data important to national security or individual privacy.[58] Table 7 shows the main characteristics of the Brazilian on-line transborder data flow policy.

A classical example of the process of internationalization that illustrates the changes underway is banking. Technology is accelerating the process of internationalization and transportability of services in this industry. As with credit cards, banking also shows the economic importance of information exchange as such, although it is very difficult to attach a specific monetary value to information transactions.

International telecommunications networks have drastically increased with the internationalization of banking. During the 1960s and the beginning of the 1970s, US banks, followed by the top Western European and Japanese banks, opened branch offices all over the world. The major factor was the growth of international trade. This led to an increase of financial transactions since a large part of global exports was financed with trade credits arranged by major banks. Another key factor was the internationalization of production and the concurrent increase in the overseas investments of the large industrial corporations. This made the system of doing financial business from the home office or through correspondent banks inadequate. "Banks had to provide more information

TABLE 7.   *Brazilian transborder data flow policies**

| | | Category of on-line transborder data flows | |
		Corporate	Commercial
On-line use of transborder data flows	Data communications	Person-to-person communications are not restricted	Brazilian PTT only; co-operation agreements possible
	Data-base access	Copy of data base in Brazil, whenever reasonable	Encouraged, but in co-operation with Brazilian institutions, preferably with copy of data base in Brazil. If no local copy, services are provided by PTT, although co-operation agreements are possible
	Data processing (including use of software)	Not favoured abroad if reasonable local alternative exists	Not allowed abroad, except in exceptional circumstances

*As regards the criteria to approve individual leased voice-channel links; other aspects of the country's transborder-data-flow policy are not presented here.

Source: Special Secretariat of Informatics, as quoted in UNCTC, *Transborder data flows and Brazil*, New York, 1983, page 135.

on the changes of business abroad, and they could only provide such information if they themselves were represented abroad."[59]

The dependency of banking on telecommunications and information exchange is summarized as follows by the Vice-President of Continental Illinois in testimony to a United States Congress Sub-Committee on Transborder Data Flows:

> As an international bank, our business is entirely dependent upon the free flow of instantaneous communications. In the course of our banking business, we need to have minute-by-minute intelligence from the money markets across the world. In addition, we need to be able to provide fund-transfer services to our customers who move large amounts of funds on a day-to-day basis from one country to another. These same customers need immediate information about their account balances in different parts of the world, the state of the world foreign exchange, the interest arbitrage markets in the major parts of the world, and so forth.[60]

In order to provide dependable communication services, banks also developed private communication networks that handle large volumes of transborder financial data flows. It should be noted that this process coincides with a strong degree of concentration in banking. The fact that information technology or large-scale banking applications are so capital-intensive is one of the important contributing factors. The application and development of international telecommunications networks give substantial advantages to large banks. However, the smaller banks could provide services in certain specialized areas utilizing interbank networks such as the Society for Worldwide Interbank Financial Telecommunications (SWIFT).

SWIFT was born in the late 1960s when a group of large Western European banks studied the possibility of improved procedures for international transactions and came to the conclusion that international banking needed an accurate, rapid, safe and standardized funds transfer system. The network became operational in May 1977. In 1984, SWIFT carried over 250,000 messages daily. Since 1977 the connection cost to the network has decreased approximately forty times to about US$5,500. This makes it possible for relatively small and specialized banks and financial services to extend their activities internationally.[61] By 1984, SWIFT connected over 900 banks in 30 countries through operating centres in Belgium, the Netherlands and the US. Processed transactions fall into four main categories: customer transfers, bank transfers, foreign exchange confirmations and loan/deposit confirmations.

In manufacturing, similar developments to those of banking take place through the extensive use of company networks. This is the case of Motorola, one of the largest producers of electronic components in the US. Motorola uses a central manufacturing and ordering system to schedule component production for worldwide shipments and to process customer orders in individual plants around the world. Subsidiaries have terminals linked via telecommunications to the parent company where the information is processed and stored. If, for any reason, the company were unable to use the telecommunication system for data transmission, the manual, traditional alternative would be too costly and slow to allow them to remain competitive on a worldwide basis. Some of the consequences for Motorola would be that inventories "would rise dramatically" since levels of stock could not be optimized; the number of people required to process information would at least quadruple, giving rise to problems of information consistency; the quality of services to customers would deteriorate, while capital expenditure and costs would increase as a consequence of the decentralization of activities. The company would have to reorganize its operations using a different pattern of information flows.[62]

The case of Motorola is by no means unique. Almost all multinational companies have some form of network which uses different types of telecommunications channels. Time-sharing remote CAD systems are already available; new services of this type are constantly appearing on the market. Ordering terminals that link directly to the suppliers' computers are penetrating rapidly, especially in retailing and the automobile industry.

Large car producers, such as General Motors and Ford, have asked all their major suppliers of components, national and international, to connect to their Computer Aided Design system in order to reduce design time and increase quality. Earlier, the example of remote diagnosis of equipment was mentioned which is yet another dimension of the process of internationalization of services. What characterizes these types of service is that they are, for the most part, intracorporate and thus not registered as international trade in services. The economic and employment effects of these trends remain, at this stage, under review and it is not possible to assess the relative position of a country except by proxy, since, for developing countries especially, the number of data links are very limited. It is clear, however, that data links will increase the economic integration of OECD countries and will enhance the effectiveness of large companies. The most unfavourable effects appear in the area of technological autonomy of local units, as was the case with Dressner-France; the most favourable in enhanced competitiveness.

A study of Brazil shows that, by 1982, the impact of data links in terms of economic and employment effects was by and large neutral, as shown in Table 8. The study covers only 26 links and Brazil tends to be exceptional among developing countries in terms of the size of its economy and the fact that it has implemented a policy in the field of international data transmission. The study also bears out the assertions made earlier that most links are of an intracorporate nature.

In the Brazilian study the US emerges as the country where most information resources are located. Similarly, the areas of fastest growth, for which future-oriented value-added services are important, are heavily

TABLE 8. *Transnational non-governmental computer-communication systems: summary of estimated impact on Brazil, various areas, March 1982*

(Number)

Area of impact	Estimated impact		
	Favourable	Neutral	Unfavourable
Balance of payments	2	16	3
Autonomy of unit	1	15	5
Employment	4	14	3
Competitiveness	19	2	-
Technological capacity	4	13	4
TOTAL	30	60	15

Source: Estimates of the technical staff of the Special Secretariat of Informatics, as quoted in UNCTC, *Transborder data flows and Brazil*, New York, 1983, page 171.

concentrated in that country. Of the publicly available on-line data bases, approximately 50% are in the US; they contain 63% of the records or information items, as shown in Table 9. In fact, the US position in international trade in services has been decreasing in the past few years with the exception of "other private services" which are precisely those which are undergoing the greatest transformations.

The development of telecommunications will greatly condition the trends in this field. Growth is expected to accelerate due to the multiplication of satellite links, cable TV, value-added networks and cheaper telecommunication tariffs. Those factors and the concentration of information resources, are producing concern about the economic impact in the long run. The current situation between Europe and the US illustrates the problem, especially in relation to on-line services which is the fastest growing sector. The President of the European Information Providers' Association summarizes the situation as follows:

> More than half of the European on-line market has been won by three US companies. European exports to the US market are swamped by a reverse flow of information sold by US suppliers to their European users.[63]

4. Transportability of Services and the World System

There is a growing gap between developing and advanced countries in terms of the material base and infrastructure to support "information-intensive" services and industries. Worldwide, there is an extremely uneven distribution of the systems and infrastructure necessary to increase the productivity of production and services, as well as the capacities for transportation and development of new services.

In addition to this quantitative difference, there are qualitative ones such as skill levels, support infrastructure, and organizational systems. The gap can only be measured by rough general indicators since no detailed breakdown exists of all the various types of equipment in different markets (see Tables 9 and 10).

Two important points emerge from this purely quantitative check. First, the participation of developing countries in the computers and telecommunications aspect of the process of "informatization" is indeed very small. Second, as time passes, the investment gap in these fields widens. In fact in the 1980s, the "gap" will most likely grow by a factor of two. Figures for telecommunications expenditures are more predictable than those for computers, essentially because of longer planning and investment cycles. Projections in terms of more precise telecommunications investment are shown for selected regions in Table 10.

Differences in the amounts of investment in data transmission and satellites are even greater when considering the total telecommunications

TABLE 9. *Worldwide telecommunications equipment markets**
(US$1000 million)

	1980	%	1985	%	1990	%
Developed countries	36	90	53.5	89	75.4	86
Developing countries	4	10	6.7	11	12.1	14
TOTAL	40	100	60.2	100	87.5	100

Includes: Telephone, telegraph, telex, data communications, satellite communications, mobile radio and radio telephone, radio paging, cable television.

Source: Derived from data from Arthur D. Little Inc.

TABLE 10. *Selected "informatics" indicators*

	Telegraph, telex and data transmission system (US$ millions)		Satellite communications (US$ millions)	
	1980	1990	1980	1990
Africa	48.4	97.3	3.0	10.5
Latin America	106.5	189.0	14.0	34.9
North America	2481.4	6000.5	122.8	463.7
Europe	733.9	1984.1	59.0	189.2

Source: Derived from data from Arthur D. Little, Inc.

markets. The combined Latin American and African market represented 5% of that of North America and Europe in 1980. The market includes telex, telegraphic and data transmission equipment. In 1990 the predicted figure is just over 4%. This expresses the level of development and the structural weakness of developing countries. Furthermore, it might imply that they will have a very small role to play in the internationalization of transportable services.

The number of telephones per capita is unevenly distributed; two-thirds of the world population has no access to the service. Differences in the quality and capability of the services from country to country also have an important impact on economic development.[64] It is not possible to say how much of the increased volume of traffic indicated by the investments in telecommunications relates to imports or exports of services, whether professional, financial or other. It can be assumed that part of the increase reflects the type of phenomenon described earlier. As telecommunications costs decrease and new satellites, earth stations and submarine cables enter into service, the growth will probably accelerate further, allowing at the same time transfers of full information packages (i.e. voice, image, graphics, motion). Developing countries are totally dependent on the international public telecommunication networks through the INTELSAT system. The figures given above are in the context of changes in services and information flows, they should also be borne in mind in relation to office work.

In fact, computer applications in developing countries are mostly data processing and will remain so for an extended period. In advanced economies, the trend is towards information processing, as explained earlier.

Some developing countries, such as India, have been able to export some "information-intensive" products, especially software. This has been possible in the context of a relatively large domestic electronic industry (by developing countries' standards), with production worth US$1,200 million in 1982 backed by a government programme to encourage the industry.[65]

5. Concluding Remarks

There are three elements to highlight concerning services. The first is the growing importance of services, together with a different understanding of their production in the overall economy. For the purpose of assessing relative comparative advantages, it appears that the organic link between production of goods and services is a key element. This link mutually reinforces the relationship. In this context, losing comparative advantage in the production of goods could affect the demand and type of services required by an economy. The reverse process can also occur due to the multiplier effect of services on the production of goods. Further research will be required to establish clearly the precise mechanisms of these links and how they are affected by changes in technology.

The second element is that, at this stage of research, the greatest impact of information technology on international trade in services is the enhanced transportability of many services. This also creates conditions for the emergence of new services essentially because services can be traded internationally through the telecommunication system. This phenomenon is especially important in the light of the role of services and the relatively rapid growth of the latter in international trade.

The third element is that the international situation in services significantly favours developed countries. This appears to be true of world trade and also for the increasing differences in equipment and infrastructure so necessary to increase productivity, and that allow the transportation of services. The internationalization of services either through telecommunications or through their more modern and economic production (e.g. office automation) poses issues for developing countries that are not only new but substantially more complex than the types of problems usually faced during the early phases of "industrialization". This is due to the "informatization" of goods and services.

Explanations for the current position of many developing countries in this field are numerous and more research is needed to clarify the point. To advance a hypothesis: one possible explanation is the lack of explicit policy in the service sector, in contrast to the agricultural and industrial sectors. Some specific fields, such as shipping, are exceptions to this general lack of policy. For more advanced developing countries, the explanation could also lie in the fact that the policies of import substitution of goods were never accompanied by a corresponding policy in services.

As countries enter more complex and difficult stages of development, a policy in services will be necessary to encourage the development of the sector, and to maintain and promote the manufacturing and agricultural base. The exact content of these policies will depend on each country's specific conditions.

The impact of information technology on services well-illustrates the horizontal effects of the technology and the fact that the changes caused by it cannot be narrowed to the field of electronics.

Notes and References

1. Antecedents to this discussion can be found in Fisher, A., "Primary, Secondary and Tertiary Production", *Economic record*, June 1939 and Clark, C., *The Condition of Economic Progress*, London, 1951. More recent contributions include Kuzuets, S., *Economic Growth of Nations*, Harvard University Press, 1971, and Fuchs, V. R., *The Service Economy*, National Bureau of Economic Research, New York, 1968.
2. — Machlup, F., *The Production and Distribution of Knowledge in the United States*, Princeton University Press, 1962. This work has been reviewed and updated by the author in Machlup, F., *Knowledge and Knowledge Production*, Princeton University Press, 1980, Vol. I.
   — US Department of Commerce, Office of Telecommunications, *The Information Economy: Definition and Measurement*, OT Special Publication 77–12(1) by Dr. Marc Uri Porat, Washington, D.C., 1977.
3. OECD, *Microelectronics, Productivity and Employment*, Paris, 1981.
4. Gershuny, J. and Miles, I., *The New Service Economy*, Frances Pinter, London, 1983, page 48.
5. International Telecommunications Union (ITU), "The Missing Link", Report of the Independent Commission for Worldwide Telecommunications Development, Geneva, December 1984.
6. For a brief discussion on this point, see OECD *Microelectronics, Productivity and Employment, op. cit.*
7. US Department of Commerce, Office of Telecommunications, *The Information Economy: Definition and Measurement, op. cit.*, page 1.
8. *Idem*, page 4.
9. *Idem*, Vol. 2 page 7.
10. US Department of Commerce, International Trade Administration Office of Service Industries, "The Interrelationships of the Services, High-Technology and Information Sectors in the Private Sector Economy of the United States," Washington, D.C., 1985.

11. Jonscher, C. "Information Resources and Economic Productivity", in *Information Economics and Policy*, Vol. 1, No. 1, North Holland, 1983.
12. US Department of Labor, Bureau of International Labor Affairs, *Trends in Technology Intensive Trade*, Washington, D.C., 1980, page ii.
13. This is one of the assumptions made by the Information, Communications and Computer Policy Series (ICCP) of OECD.
14. Rada, J., "Development, telecommunications and the emerging service economy", Intergovernmental Bureau of Informatics (IBI), June 1984 (mimeo).
15. Kravis, I., "Services in the domestic economy and in world transactions", National Bureau of Economics Research, Inc., Working Paper Series, Working Paper No. 1124, May 1983.
16. Inoussa, M., US Department of Commerce, International Trade Administration, Office of Service Industries, in *Business America*, July 8, 1985.
17. *Idem*, page 5.
18. World Bank, "Trade in non-factor services: past trends and current issues", World Bank Staff Working Paper, No. 410, Washington, D.C., 1980.
19. See GATT, "International trade in services and the GATT", Geneva, 1981, (mimeo). For a detailed discussion of this and related issues, see Nusbaumer, J., "Les services: nouvelle donnée de l'économie", *Economica*, Paris, 1984.
20. Based on figures from Nusbaumer, J., "Les services: nouvelle donnée de l'économie", *op. cit.*, and United Nations, *1982 Yearbook of International Trade Statistics*, Vol. II, New York, 1984.
21. UNCTAD, "Services and the development process", TD/B/1008–2, August 1984, Geneva, page 5.
22. Kravis, I., "Services in the domestic economy and in world transactions", *op. cit.*, page 6.
23. UNCTAD, *Protectionism and Structural Adjustment — Production and Trade in Services, Policies and Their Underlying Factors bearing upon International Services Transactions*, Geneva, 1983, page 21.
24. Abundant literature exists on this point, especially in relation to what has been called the "informal urban sector".
25. This confusion is typical in popular writings such as Serven-Schreiber, J. J., *Le défi mondial*, Paris, 1981 and Toffler, A., *The Third Wave*, Collins, 1980.
26. On this point see, for instance, World Bank, *World Development Report*, Washington, D.C., 1978, pages 8–9.
27. Joelson, K. and Persson, N. E., "Sweden's invisible foreign trade in the 1970s", Sveriges Riksbank, Occasional Paper 2, Stockholm, March 1984.
28. Economic Consulting Services, Inc. *The International Operations of U.S. Service Industries: Current Data Collection and Analysis*, Washington, D.C., June 1981. Also see, Joelson, K. and Persson, N. E., "Sweden's invisible foreign trade in the 1970s", *op. cit.* page 57.
29. Economic Consulting Services, "The International Operations of US Service Industries: Current Data Collection and Analysis" — prepared by the US Department of State and Commerce and the Office of the US Trade Representative, June 1981.
30. United Nations, *1982 Yearbook of International Trade Statistics*, Vol. II, *op. cit.*
31. Gershuny, J. and Miles, I., *The New Service Economy*, *op. cit.*, pages 52–54.
32. The Office of the US Trade Representative, "U.S. national study on trade in services", a submission by the US Government to the General Agreement on Tariffs and Trade, December 1983.
33. UNCTAD, "Protectionism and structural adjustment", TD/B/941, March 1983.
34. *Datamation*, June 1, 1984.
35. *Transnational Data Report*, Vol. V, No. 2, March 1982.
36. Kravis, I., "Services in the domestic economy and in world transactions", *op. cit.*, pages 4 and 20. Also see on this point, Krommenacker, R., *World Trade Services: the Challenge for the Eighties*, 1984, especially Chapter 2.
37. Shelp, R. K. *et al.*, *Service Industries and Economic Development*, Praeger, 1984.
38. *Idem*, page 15.

170   J. F. Rada

39. Asghar, M., Senoma, Y. and Pinez, R., "Work of the world plan committee for the development of telecommunications, Paris, 1980 and the evolution of telephone traffic", extract from the *ITU Telecommunications Journal*, Geneva, September 1980.
40. Antonelli, C., "Multinational firms, international trade and international telecommunications", in *Information Economics and Policy*, 1 (1984), page 335.
41. Gershuny, J. and Miles, I., *The New Service Economy, op. cit.*
42. *Idem.*
43. Mazzonis, D., Colombo, U. and Lanzavecchia, G., "The Prato system: an example of integration of old and new technologies", Italian National Commission for Nuclear and Alternative energy Sources, Rome, 1983 (mimeo).
44. Economist Intelligence Unit, "Microtechnology in banking", Special Report No. 169, London, 1984, pages 3 and 77.
45. Rajan, A., *New Technology and Employment in Insurance, Banking and Building Societies*, Institute of Manpower Studies, London, 1984.
46. Freeman, H. L., "A user's view of international communications", in Rada, J. F. and Pipe, G. R. (eds.), *Communication Regulation and International Business*, proceedings of a workshop held at the International Management Institute (IMI), Geneva, Switzerland, April 1983, North-Holland, Amsterdam, 1984.
47. Rada, Juan F., "Trends and effects of information technology", in Rada, J. F. and Pipe, G. R. (eds.), *Communication Regulation and International Business*, proceedings of a workshop held at the International Management Institute (IMI), Geneva, Switzerland, April 1983, North-Holland, Amsterdam, 1984.
48. UNCTC, *Transborder Data Flows: Access to the International On-line Data-base Market*, New York, 1983, pages 27–28.
49. The circulation of inaccurate information might have been one of the factors contributing to the collapse of the Continental Illinois Bank in 1984.
50. Revell, J., "The consequences of electronic fund transfers", paper read at the Annual Meeting of the Norwegian Bankers' Association, Oslo, 1982 (mimeo).
51. Indication of rapid diffusion of electronic mail can be seen in the use of local area networks and data bases. See, for instance, the reports of Strategic Inc., Denmark, and Euronet, *Diane news*, Luxembourg, several issues.
52. UNCTC, *Transborder Data Flows: Access to the International On-line Data-base Market, op. cit.*
53. OECD, "Guidelines for the protection of privacy", 1982, reproduced in Rada, J. F. and Pipe, G. R. (eds.), *Communication Regulation and International Business*, proceedings of a workshop held at the International Management Institute (IMI), Geneva, Switzerland, April 1983, North-Holland, Amsterdam, 1984.
54. As reported by the *New York Times*, 13 March 1983, page F.1. For a commentary on some of the implications, see, Bhagwati, J. N., "Splintering and disembodiment of services and developing nations" in *The World Economy*, Vol. 7, No. 2, June 1984, pages 139–140.
55. See Madec, A. J., *Les flux transfrontières de données*, La Documentation Française, 1983.
56. *Transnational Data Report*, Vol. VIII, No. 6, September 1985.
57. *Transnational Data Report*, Vol. IV, No. 5, July 1981.
58. UNCTC, *Transborder Data Flows and Brazil, op. cit.*
59. Junne, G., "Multinational banks, the state and international integration", in Beyme, K. von (ed.), *German Political Systems*, London, 1976, page 120, as quoted by Hamelink, C., *Finance and Information: a Study of Converging Interest*, Instituto Latinoamericano de Estudios Transnacionales, Mexico, 1981, page 63.
60. United States House of Representatives, *Hearings before a Subcommittee of the Committee on Government Operations*, Washington, D.C., 1980, page 112.
61. The Economist Intelligence Unit (EIU), "Microtechnology in Banking", Special Report No. 169, London, 1984, page 43.
62. United States House of Representatives, *Hearings before a Subcommittee of the Committee on Government Operations*, Washington, D.C., 1980, *op. cit.* pages 629–631.
63. *Transnational Data Report*, Vol. V, No. 2, March 1982.

64. International Telecommunications Union (ITU), *The Missing Link*, Geneva, 1984, *op. cit.*
65. Government of India, *Annual Report of the Department of Electronics, 1982–83*, New Delhi, 1983.

7

Services and Space Technology: The Emergence of Space Generated, Highly Integrated Goods and Services (IGS)

RAYMOND KROMMENACKER*

1. Introduction

It is now commonplace to consider services as increasingly linked to new technology, which affects directly their development. In fact, the fusing of new technology into services engenders integrated, technologically complex, goods and services which could be called, for convenience sake, IGS. This note first discusses the patterns of three specific IGS — direct broadcast satellite services, satellite and shuttle launch services, and space station services. The note analyses the arguments invoked by governments to justify their interventions in the field of services and space technology, and points to the existing or potential trade issues perceived in each of the IGS. The note also examines the competiveness and technological capabilities in these three fields of space activities while stressing that government-industry co-operation is the main factor influencing the pace and direction at which the technological change is introduced. After having introduced a prospective analysis, because economic behaviour should be analysed in the context of the rapidly changing conditions of a global and interdependent economy, the note concludes that new mechanisms might be delineated for instilling concrete business considerations in international public policy choice.

---

*Counsellor, Gatt. Lecturer (*Cycle Supérieur de Sciences Economiques*) at the *Institut d'Etudes Politiques* of Paris. The author is grateful for the comments received from R. Blackhurst, A. Lindén, J. Nusbaumer and J. Richardson, but he remains responsible for any views expressed.

2. Direct Broadcast Satellite Services

Direct broadcast satellite services (DBS) are among the activities which will introduce dramatic developments all over the world in the day-to-day life of every human being. These services have not yet been "contaminated" by a vast array of restrictions. However, the cultural and social sensitivities argument will be invoked more and more frequently in connection with the foreseeable growing impact of DBS services. This argument behind government intervention is the only one of the usual arguments that is noticeably more important for services restrictions than for goods restrictions.

Most of the known motivations concerning trade in goods are equally applicable to explaining restrictions on trade in services — for example balance-of-payments control, protection of domestic consumers from risk, infant-industry argument, and employment argument. A second category includes motivations that are relevant to both goods and services trade but that at the same time may be relatively more important in the services area. First, the national-security argument, often mixed with the economic-security argument and the domestic-sovereignty argument, is invoked by governments that intend to have key industries domestically owned, particularly in industries producing high-technology goods and services. Second, the cultural and social sensitivities argument, which calls for the right to preserve one's heritage, will represent one of the most frequently invoked motivations with the growing use of satellites — for example, the direct-broadcast satellite-to-house television networks that have already started and the space platforms.

Direct broadcast is a dramatically new technology. With satellite transmission of broadcast signals over large areas and with the possibility of direct transmission to homes, and even to individuals with devices no larger than pocket pagers, governments will find that they no longer possess the means to control regulations and the authority to regulate reception within their own territory. In addition to its technological novelty, direct broadcast presents a unique interplay of three competing interests: the free flow of information, cultural and social sensitivities, and national sovereignty. How these three interests are accommodated in a regulatory scheme will determine the future role that direct broadcast will play in international society.

2.1. Direct-Broadcast Satellite-to-Home Television Networks

In July 1982 the US Federal Communications Commission (FCC) authorized for the first time the sales of channels on direct-broadcast satellites (DBS), a move that allowed private companies to buy rather than lease slots on the satellites. This decision of the FCC opened the way to the creation of a direct-broadcast satellite-to-home television network in the United States. A transponder on a direct broadcast satellite, located 36,000 km above the equator on a geostationary orbit, acts as a transmitter, beaming television programmes into homes equipped with special dish receivers. As of May 1983 four private US companies have received FCC permission for direct-broadcast satellites. In July 1985, FCC authorized private firms to launch communication satellites for linking the United States, South America, Europe and Africa.[1] Before this technology was a reality, issues engendered controversy, centering in the United Nations Committee on Peaceful Uses of Outer Space (Outer Space Committee) with intermittent attention from the International Telecommunication Union (ITU) and other forums. While the Soviet Union and developing countries emphasized the intrusion of direct broadcast to national sovereignty, Canada and Sweden stressed the technology's threat to cultural integrity. The principle of free flow of information was put forward by the United States. On 10 December 1982, after 10 years of discussion, the United Nations adopted non-binding principles governing national use of artificial earth satellites for direct television broadcasting. As a result of the vote (88 to 15 with 11 abstentions), no nation shall establish a broadcast service except on the basis of agreement with a receiving country, assuring the recipient veto power. In addition, the principles, which attempt to control the content of foreign broadcasts, provide that direct satellite transmissions must pay due respect to the political and cultural integrity of nations and adhere to the principle of nonintervention. Finally, governments are held responsible for broadcasts coming from their territory. A major principle requires exclusions from DBS of:

> Any material which is detrimental to the maintenance of international peace and security, which publicizes ideas of war, militarism, national and racial hatred and enmity between peoples, which is aimed at interfering in the domestic affairs of other States or which undermines the foundations of the local civilization, culture, way of life, traditions and language.

The 15 countries that voted against are the EEC, Israel, the Nordic Countries, and the United States. Eleven countries abstained from voting.

2.2. Avoiding Disputes through Block Allotment Planning

If politically no unanimous views can be brought on this issue of the "Information Order" that was debated in UNESCO and in other fora, at least a possible solution can be foreseen in the ITU through block allotment planning. The block allotment planning proposal represents a compromise between the goals of equitable access and efficient utilization of orbital locations of the frequency spectrum. Where countries cover large areas as in North America, the domestic concern over unauthorized radiation or spillover is not as acute as in cases where many countries are within close proximity. In this regard, it has been suggested that two or more geographically adjacent countries combine their resources to design a multinational system. It is unclear whether such a proposal is politically tenable. In 1985 Space World Administrative Radio Conference discussed this issue further and tried to find a satisfactory solution. One crucial issue was to what extent the ITU was competent to grant permanent property rights in the geostationary orbit, since the granting of such rights would necessitate an extension of sovereignty into outer space. Interest of developed and developing countries were reconciled within the existing régime on a first agreement on a fundamental principle that each country had the right for at least one orbital frequency. This compromise offered by Australia gives developing nations a chance to reserve space in the orbit. Even with this agreement, the conflict will not be resolved soon, as the details of the Australian plan will not be worked out until the next conference in 1988.

A number of questions are still unresolved: will the regional spectrum allocation of ITU permit an easy control of all direct broadcasts? If a nation ignores its ITU obligations, would broadcasting be technically possible or would it introduce major disturbances? How will the United Nations convention be implemented? Are its non-binding provisions sufficiently explicit to handle apparently apposed principles such as national sovereignty, cultural integrity, and free flow of information? Is the United Nations mechanism of "peaceful settlement of disputes" workable? Is there any need for more detailed standards, multilaterally agreed and having a binding effect on the parties to the agreement?

The way in which these questions are solved will influence the attitudes of governments regarding the invocation of the cultural and social sensitivities argument in the near future. Cases may arise in which direct broadcast would be outlawed. The question would then be whether the government concerned possesses the appropriate means to put pressure on the foreign country owning the satellite, in order that the broadcast is amended or stopped.

Satellites are in little danger of colliding, but there is risk of frequency interference, the overlapping and garbling of radio beams. The congestion is worst over North America and Europe. In 1982, India had to bargain with Intelsat for an orbital slot and has since had to make expensive, time-consuming adjustments on its communications satellite, Insat, to avoid an overlap of frequencies. Insat, which cost $130 million, relays telephone calls and links thousands of Indian villages to television. Land-based telephone lines could have performed those chores, but would have cost $1 billion, the government estimated. Moreover, Insat watches the weather, photographing the snow pack on the Himalayas, for instance, to provide early flood warning.

Mexico, Brazil, Indonesia and a group of Arab countries also have satellites. Indonesia's Palapa-A and Palapa-B, for instance, link a vast area that includes Malaysia, the Philippines, Thailand and Singapore. The United States, Japan and Western European countries argue that voluntary co-ordination of satellite launches and traffic has worked well so far and that advances in technology, including the use of higher frequencies and more antennas, would insure fair access to popular places in the orbit.

But developing nations, complaining that such technological improvements are too costly and difficult, have sought confirmed reservations for lower-frequency satellites. Colombia's proposed Condor satellite would provide service to Latin America. Although developing nations support the Australian plan, it seems that it does not meet all their demands. For one thing, the first-come, first-served rule would still apply to positions in the highly used C-bands, a frequency range about 40 times higher than that of an FM radio receiver. But the developing countries would be able to reserve slots in a C-band expansion made possible by better technology, and in the higher frequency K-band, which is used heavily by the Soviet Union. The United States, the biggest user of satellite communications, grudgingly supports the Australian plan. The United States has long been opposed to a priori planning, not because it's fair or unfair, but simply because it's wasteful. The geostationary orbit cannot seriously be cut up without knowing the characteristics of the satellites that are going into that orbit. A less favourable solution was, however, apparently better than none.

A typical example of the kind of disputes which would emerge at an increasing rate in the near future is found in the Pacific region where an issue concerning a direct broadcast satellite opposed South Korea to Japan early in 1984. With the launching of Yuri 2A using foreign technology on 23 January 1984, Japan's National Space Development Agency (NASDA, the Japan's NASA) set the stage for the country's first practical satellite TV broadcast system aimed directly at the homes of individual viewers. The day after, the authorities of South Korea expressed their great concern and pointed to the cultural aggression of Japan which had not consulted with the South-Korean authorities about DBS impact on sovereign nations before the launching of the satellite. The Prime Minister of South Korea gave instructions that counter-measures be studied. In the meantime, two of the three transponders of the satellite failed and it was only able to broadcast a single channel. This is the first example of intergovernmental disputes arising for reasons of direct broadcast satellite services.

In Europe, the 1984 EEC "Green Paper on the establishment of the common market for broadcasting, especially by satellite and cable" endeavours to present ingredients of a solution in the light of the current TV overspill in Europe.

This new phenomenon of the so-called breach of the cultural and social sensitivities might extend to all regions of the world with the effect of causing growing acrimony in trading relations. *Countries affected by the direct broadcast satellite services could retaliate by closing their domestic market to products and services originating in countries owning the satellites.*

3. Satellite and Shuttle Launch Services

Today the main trade issue with respect to satellite and shuttle launch services concerns their pricing by existing holders of this specific technology although derived problems of space insurance could influence holders' attitude *vis-à-vis* the marketability of their services. Underwriters face a major crisis, deppened recently by the failure of the two United States Hugues Leaset spacecrafts and the failure of a European Ariane booster. Let us simply recall that satellite manufacturers have insisted on delivering the satellite to their customers on the ground, leaving the risk of launch and successful operation to satellite owners. The satellite owner has little control over the design and quality of manufacture of the satellite or launch readiness of the mission. This attitude looks like selling an aeroplane to an airline without proving it can fly. The European consortium Arianespace is now setting up its own insurance affiliate in order to counter the prohibitive premium rates.

Concerning the issue of pricing launch services, the United States Administration set up a new pricing policy for space shuttle launch customers, starting in October 1988, that would keep orbiter mission costs low enough to compete with the European Ariane rocket, but high enough not to hurt United States private boosters. The pricing decision follows the settlement of the investigation by the US Trade Representative of a complaint brought by the first privately owned US spacecraft launch services company against 11 European countries and Arianespace. The decision of the US Administration for a new pricing policy would also maintain a strong level of competition between the US shuttle and Ariane expendable launch vehicle, both of which are seeking commercial customer payloads.

In what could have triggered a new trans-Atlantic trade dispute, Transpace Carriers Inc., the US company offering space launch services, had charged that the European consortium Arianespace (36 European aerospace companies, 11 banks and the French Centre National d'Etudes Spatiales) was engaging in predatory pricing practices. Transpace, in a petition filed on 25 May 1984 under Section 301 of the Trade Act of 1974, charged that Arianespace was offering its launch services to potential US customers at subsidized prices 25 to 30% below prices quoted to European customers also seeking to launch satellites. In its complaint, Transpace asked that the US President seek the immediate discontinuance of the alleged two-tiered pricing policy, the elimination of the cost-free or below-cost support in facilities, services and personnel, and the subsidization of mission insurance rates. The Section 301 action could have led to retaliatory action if a formal investigation by the Trade Representative's Office subsequently showed that the charges were justified.

Transpace plans to launch satellite with Delta rockets made by McDonnell-Douglas Corp. which are being phased out by the US National Aeronautics and Space Administration (NASA). According to the Chairman of Arianespace, the consortium's price for a launch on the Ariane rocket, totalling about $25 million a launch, was below what it charged European customers participating in the programme, but the launch price also was roughly equivalent to the per-launch rate quoted by NASA for its space shuttle launch service. The Arianespace Chairman considered that neither Arianespace's quoted price not NASA's reflected the real development costs which stemmed from government subsidies in both cases. The problem according to him was that both agencies were competing for similar contracts. European and American trading partners held several consultations, and in July 1985, the US President decided not to give effect to the petition filed by Transpace Carriers Inc.

Subsequently, the US President decided on a base price of $71 million (in 1982 dollars) running through 30 September 1988, as the cost of a full shuttle cargo payload in an effort to maintain the strongest US shuttle competitive position against Ariane. Starting on 1 October 1988, the base price will be $74 million (in 1982 dollars). The US Administration is of the opinion that the Europeans are expected to price their launch services slightly under the shuttle no matter what fee the US selects. Further, it is considered that the higher the shuttle price, the easier it will be for Arianespace to substantially underprice the US system and gain a stronger competitive advantage. The shuttle price will be a base figure, and individual payloads consuming only part of the cargo bay will pay a price pro-rated on their specific weight and size.

Negotiation for the new price structure were held by the White House Senior Interagency Group for Space (Sig-Space), a committee with senior management membership from all the federal agencies involved with shuttle operations and pricing issues. According to available information, at least three different views were expressed as to how the launch services should be priced.[2]

The Transportation Department was tasked with helping to facilitate the development of a US commercial expendable launch vehicle market. It recommended a shuttle price of about $129 million. This was a realistic estimate of the price required to make the shuttle pay its own way and enabled a more competitive stance by commercial expandable booster operators. The Transportation Department argued that the planned NASA price structure would not lead to full cost recovery, and subsidies for space commercialization should be diverted to basic science and research and development of commercial processes rather than to the transportation component of commercial space costs. The similar, ground-launched rockets could offer more economical access to orbit than the fancy, crew-tended shuttle. It was like comparing a trucking service to a chauffeured limousine. The disadvantage of this option was that it would give Ariane a stronger competitive position and impose higher commercial launch costs. The Commerce Department recommended a price of about $65 million, which represents a turnaround from an earlier position in the interest of maintaining a better US competitive position versus the European rocket. The NASA gave a shuttle pricing recommendation of $72 million per shuttle flight starting in October 1988 which was keyed directly to underpricing Ariane. The Defense Department which initially sided with the agencies seeking higher shuttle prices tempered substantially its opposition toward a lower level. NASA and the Defense Department had their own agreements on how much would be charged for military shuttle missions. In return for a relatively lower price, the Defense Department agreed to fly a minimum number of flights per year on the shuttle.

A Congressional Budget Office study established a set of cost bases for its analysis of shuttle pricing ranging between $42 million and $150 million per flight.[2] Three assumptions were made. First, the shuttle flight rate, especially for full cost prices, is assumed to be 24 flights in 1989. Second, the financial interest rate and depreciation period used to calculate the annual capital charge are set at 4% real interest and a 25-year system life. Third, NASA's operational cost estimates are accepted and divided equally between fixed and variable costs. The study tested each pricing policy against a number of policy objectives and listed the probable consequences as follows:

(1) Short-run marginal cost pricing would lead to maximum use of the shuttle and the likely end of the domestic launch business. Shuttle would compete directly with Ariane and foreign launchers. If NASA's costs are understated, revenues will not cover cost. (2) Long-run marginal cost pricing should maintain shuttle's current market share and generate federal revenues. Domestic launch firms would have little chance of success. (3) Full operational cost pricing should have implications similar to long-run marginal pricing. Cost per flight would rise to $98 million if flight rate falls to 18. (4) Full cost less development will cause shuttle to lose more or less market share depending on price increases by Arianespace and other efficient competitors. Prospects for domestic launch firms would be improved but still uncertain. NASA will have excess shuttle capacity. Price per flight would be $129 million at 18 flights per year. (5) Full cost pricing will cause shuttle to lose all but specialized foreign and commercial payloads. Flight rate will be below efficient level. Net federal revenues will be reduced. Domestic launch vehicles will do well if Arianespace increases its price to or near shuttle price. Investors in new space processing and services may reduce planned spending.

It seems that the final Sig-Space recommendation to the President boiled down to finding a middle ground between the Transportation Department's high price recommendation and the Commerce Department's low recommendation. It was believed that while the higher cost was more in line with full shuttle cost recovery, it went too far toward government support for small commercial expendable rockets, at the expense of the large commercial payload sector and US competitiveness.[3]

Competition in spacecraft launch services is spreading worldwide, beyond the United States, Europe and the Soviet Union as other nations seek to stake a claim in what is viewed as possibly the next economic frontier.[4] China is now ready to join the space haulage business and will compete on the world market for the launch of communications satellites by Long March rockets and the construction of space shuttles, according to the director-general of the Chinese space ministry's foreign affairs bureau, Zhang Jiqing. Mr. Zhang said China could provide almost all commercial services in space, ranging from the manufacture of rockets and ground stations to the recovery of satellites already in space, as well as having the capability to carry out a space exploration programme. China will concentrate its efforts on projects needed for developing the national economy, including launching communications, broadcasting, earth re-source survey, meterological and other scientific experimental satellites. China will attempt to underprice the European Ariane, the US shuttle and expendable boosters to garner a share of the international launch service market, according to Sun Jaidong, president of the Chinese Academy of Space Technology (CAST), an agency that functions as Chinas's NASA. Since 1970 China has launched 16 successful spacecrafts. New rocket engines could provide a Saturn-1 class launcher for the later 1990's. Presently, the CZ-2 rocket, for moderate low altitude payloads, and CZ-3, for small geosynchronous payloads, will make up the primary marketing emphasis. China's Beijing Wan Yuan Industries has signed with the Space Vector Corporation, Northridge, California, to market the CZ-3 launch services along with launch services for the smaller CZ-1 booster. Launch on the small CZ-1 could cost as little as $4.1 million. Near-term modification to upgrade CZ-2 and CZ-3 booster capabilities will enable China to place about 5,000 lb. in low earth orbit and 3,000 lb. in geosynchronous transfer orbit. Early 1986, the Swedish Space Corporation signed a one-year launch reservation agreement with China for the potential use of Long March 2 vehicles to orbit Sweden's proposed Mailstar small electronic mail satellites and is working with the Chinese on designing a small propulsion system to boost Mailstar to proper orbit after its release from the launcher.

In 1987, Japan will boost into orbit its first test satellite with a Nissan Motor engine at its launching pad of Tanegashima, an island south of Kyushu. The satellite is being built by the Mitsubishi Electronic Corpora-tion, using Ford technology. It will carry eighteen transponders developed by Nippon Telegraph and Telephone. The first commercial satellite of

Japanese design, to be launched in 1988, will also be the first ever to use gallium arsenide solar chips which will convert the sun's energy into electricity to drive the satellite 50% more efficiently than silicon cells currently in use. The real test will come with Japan's next generation of satellites, which should compete head-to-head with some specific United States space IGS.

India and Brazil are also developing their own rocket launching capabilities in a desire to become technologically less dependent, to gain the economic benefits that derive from space technology and to be regarded as "space powers". It would then seem that competitive strategies based on price or superior technology alone would not prevent foreign entry into the business of the launch services.

4. Space Station Services

The United States is designing the world's most technically advanced manned space station for launch in 1994. The project to develop a $12 billion international space station presents a bigger challenge than the effort two decades ago to put a man on the moon according to NASA. Japan, Canada and the 11 European countries under the auspices of the European Space Agency have agreed to help in the design phase. A total of seven shuttles would be required to lift components of the space station into orbit. Space construction workers would then be required to bolt or weld the sections together. The European Hermes manned shuttle, which would fly in 1997, would be used for missions such as transfer crew and equipment to the manned space stations, in-orbit repair of satellites and servicing of unmanned space platforms. A related point of contention should be resolved with respect to the NASA's requirement that any vehicles, station element, shuttle or free-flying platform, approaching within 20 km of the space station will be under NASA's control for flight safety considerations. The Europeans see it as a problem, especially when they begin servicing free-flying platforms from the space station.

Space services, such as the availability for private firms of the space processing of semi-conductor materials, pharmaceuticals, protein crystals, biotechnology, advanced metals, alloys, glasses, ceramics, polymer and organic chemistry are currently embryonic but will become significant in the future. In the field of materials processing in space, zero-gravity, micro-gravity and weightlessness often are used interchangeably. In truth, there is no such thing as zero-gravity. The earth's gravity stretches to infinity, although it tapers off with the inverse square law. What a spacecraft in orbit experiences is free fall. The net effect is that nothing appears to have any weight, weight being a function of man and acceleration. Actually, acceleration levels are zero only at the spacecraft's centre of gravity. At any distance from the centre an object is in a slightly different orbit and is either pushed or pulled by the structure on which it is mounted. The environment is called microgravity or low-g and is measured in fractions of one earth gravity. For most activities, this effect is not noticeable. For materials processes, it can be intolerable and is exacerbated by thruster firings and crew motions. Materials processing is likely to take place on the co-orbiting platform because the materials processing community will want to attain the lowest level of gravity for hundreds of hours.

For example, significant advances are expected for the electronics industry. Gallium arsenyde crystals grown in space will be used to make more efficient semi-conductors than today's silicon chips. Experiments under way in the growing of mercury-cadmium-telluride crystals will lead to superior infrared detective and photovoltaic material. Ultra-pure glass could improve laser technology, which in turn would advance the communications industry and further work in fusion reactors. The mechanisms of how additions of strontium and antimony to aluminium-silicon-megnesium alloy can dramatically change a metal's structure and micro-gravity tests will indicate how the added alloys modify the overall structure of the base alloy. Another available service would be provided by a large canister called the industrial space facility, which could be hired out to private companies interested in micro-gravity processing.

Donald H. Bunker gives a banker's perspective of the situation being faced by the participants in the commercialization of space. An analysis of the past experiences and the present attitudes and positions provide the conventional wisdom which must be understood if space ventures are to be successful.[5] (1) Banks will under no circumstances accept any abnormal risk in space ventures. (2) Underwriters will no longer subsidize the commercialization of space activities. (3) Governments, who for nationalistic or other reasons, wish to encourage commercial ventures in space (which are not otherwise financeable), will have to provide their sovereign credit as collateral. (4) Operators pass their costs on to consumers. (5) Consumers and governments are the ultimate underwriters of the high costs of commercial space activities. (6) Higher insurance rates and launch and equipment costs are ultimately passed on to the consumer. (7) Consumers generally have alternatives to space generated goods and services. (8) Self-insurance might eliminate the small operators and could lead to the further weakening of the insurance industry. (9) The limited nature of manufacturers' warranties with respect to space equipment is extraordinary.

If the banks refuse to finance space projects without adequate insurance cover, and if underwriters refuse to provide that coverage without a change in the attitudes of operators and manufacturers, then it would appear that the onus is on the operators and governments sponsoring space activities to initiate a programme whereby there is a conscious effort by the participants to re-evaluate their respective positions and requirements taking into consideration those of the others. Efforts should be made to redistribute the risks of space activities more equitably among the parties and to reduce all the risks in the aggregate wherever possible. Donald H. Bunker suggests, *inter alia*, new terms for insurance or co-insurance policies, the creation of a pool of self-insurance by satellite owners, the possibility that governments write supplementary insurance, the delivery of satellites on orbit by manufacturers and the extention from aviation to space of the activities by surveyors and adjustors' firms.

New space commercialization revenue projections continue to show strong business potential for this area.[6] This situation might also cause trade disputes when companies draw benefits from their value-added business. For example, space processed materials would be sold in greater quantities and at much lower prices than somewhat similar earth processed materials. This means that any country could accuse these space processed materials of injuring domestic firms producing similar products on earth, in order to preserve from space competition its traditional producing industries which will have become obsolete before having had any profit-earning capacity. If the importation of such products would cause market disruption in the import country, the traditional trade rules about safeguard measures would be applicable.

Two recent elements influence the framing of space policies. First, changes in civilian budgetary policies for reduced overall public expenditure have increased the financial constraints and given rise to trade-offs such as the dropping of certain scientific programmes and limitations on the diversification of projects. Second, space activities as a whole still have a rapid rate of growth with favourable demand prospects although for certain segments of the space market, trends are still shrouded by uncertainties. In reaction, governments are seeking to increase the proportion of international co-operation programmes in order to reduce financial burdens. For example, Canada, Japan and the member countries of the European Space Agency have agreed to participate in the development of the manned space station. Governments also encourage private investment in space by using incentives and therefore increase industrial opportunities.[7]

Development and production of space IGS have so far depended to a very large extent on public investments. However, like in aviation, where the aircraft manufacturing at its start was entirely publicly-funded while the aviation transportations service grew with private entrepeneurs, privately-owned and operated satellite systems become more common and the launching of those satellites are more subject to competition. Given the high cost of finished space IGS and their high R and D content, the space market structure mainly reflects the effects of size, the technical experience of firms and their advance in the field. It also reflects the importance of the role played by national civilian and military programmes rather than differences in organization, management or financial risk-taking. Access to R and D, the creation of expertise, and more generally the development of the firms' production capabilities are all influenced by these programmes. This influence is even stronger because trade in IGS is still limited.

, In the three IGS which this note covers — direct broadcast satellite services, satellite and space station services, and space station services — two more arguments are invoked by governments to justify their interventions in the field of services and space technology. Besides the cultural and social sensitivities argument, reference is often made to the infant industry argument and to the national-security argument.

5. Infant Industry Argument

Efforts to promote the high-technology sector often amount to the use by some countries of a rationale for trade restrictions and subsidies that are normally associated with the developing countries, namely the infant-industry argument for protection.[8] Similar trends have recently emerged in the field of telematics, which combines technologies in informatics and telecommunications. In most instances, the term is used broadly to refer to trade in both equipment (computers, word processors, communication equipment, software, etc.) and the information that is processed or transmitted by the equipment or just the processing service.[9]

Such trade often confronts certain problems that, while not being unique to information-processing and -transmitting equipment, are frequently especially important in that sector. A leading example is the repercussions of government efforts in several countries to maintain or achieve a leading position in the production of high-technology products.

The infant-industry argument, which was endorsed by John Stuart Mill, is undoubtedly now one of the most widely accepted arguments for protection in developing countries, just as it has in the past been used to justify protection in the United States, Canada, Australia, and some Western European nations. An increasing recourse to the infant-industry argument is presently made by certain developed countries as a way of promoting high-technology industries. Two distinctions have to be made in order to analyse this argument clearly. The first distinction is between economies of scale and economies of time. The former result in falling costs as a scale of output at any point in time increases, while the latter (called dynamic economies) result in falling costs as the length of time over which output has preceded increases. The second distinction is between

internal and external economies, the question being whether the economies, whether of scale or of time, are internal or external to the decision-
making unit, namely the firms.

The infant-industry argument is advanced when newly established firms
and industries require protection in their early stages so that they may grow
and learn and eventually take their places in the ranks of efficient and
competitive industries. The argument implies that the necessity or
justification for protection is temporary and that the protection should be
removed as soon as the industries have reached a viable level of maturity.
It is necessary for the argument to be able to show (1) that the industry will
achieve self-sufficiency with protection, (2) that it could not achieve self-
sufficiency in the absence of protection, and (3) that costs of production
will be low enough, once it reaches maturity, to compensate society for
paying above-world-market prices during the period of infancy.

The infant-industry argument is an argument for temporary protection.
Hence, time must enter the argument in some essential way; the argument
cannot rest solely on static economies of scale, whether internal or
external. Furthermore, it is an argument for intervention to alter the
pattern of production and thus can be justified only if there is some kind of
distortion, imperfection, or externality in the system somewhere — in
other words, that an absence of government intervention would lead to a
suboptimal pattern of production. These two requirements of a time
element and an imperfection or externality element govern the subsequent
discussion.

An argument for temporary protection can be built in two main ways:
one resting on dynamic internal economies and the other on dynamic
external economies.[10] Max Corden shows that dynamic internal economies
do not provide an argument for protection. There should be no case for
intervention through tariffs or subsidies if three conditions are fulfilled: (1)
finance is freely available to the firm at a rate of interest that correctly
indicates the social discount rate; (2) the firm has correct expectations
about the fruits of the learning process and (3) there are no uncorrected
divergencies of any kind in the economy. If there are dynamic external
economies, a firm finds that, as it increases its output over time, its costs
curves shift down because suppliers can provide materials at lower
cost, transport and utility services are used more intensively, worker
productivity rises, etc.

The germ of truth in the infant-industry argument applies when the costs
involved in establishing the industry cannot all be recouped by those who
have made the initial investments. Some form of externality must be
present. To take an example from the setting of developing countries,
workers gain by the skills learned during industrialization. These skills,
deemed a gain to the community, can be transferred to other industries —

that is, the entrepeneurs in a particular sector may undergo costs of training the labour force and then lose those workers to other industries before they can recoup the training costs. If so, it is maintained that protection should be given so as to allow the firms to charge higher prices during the training period, thus allowing them to "simultaneously recoup" the training costs. In fact, tariffs may not be the best protection instrument. The situation calls for a change in production but not in consumption; thus using a tariff involves a loss that would not result if a production subsidy were used instead. However, many developing countries argue that their fiscal systems preclude their using the "first best" production subsidy alternative. The difficulty with the infant-industry argument lies in identifying those industries that are likely to experience significant dynamic external economies and in ensuring that the infant-industry argument is not simply a rationale for the continued protection of inefficient industries. Also, the shield of protection tends to reduce the incentive for the technological change and cost cutting that are part of growing up. As a result, the list of protected industries that have announced their maturity and renounced their protection is notoriously short; and the actual experience with infant-industry type of protection results in severe problems.[11]

It may seem surprising that the infant-industry argument for protection is currently used to advocate and justify protection of certain industries in some of the most developed countries. The industries concerned are the so-called high-technology industries, principally the computer industries, where vast and speculative expenditures on research and development are often required. This is one of the main ways in which protectionists thinking manifests itself at present.

Research and development (R and D) expenditures are expenditures on investment in learning, with a very long period of installation and gestation and with costs having to be incurred for many years before significant fruits emerge. Second, there is usually great uncertainty about what will come out of R and D. Finally some of the knowledge generated may be useful for other projects, so there may be considerable external effects.

A crucial issue is whether there is a case for government assistance. Where does the possible need for government assistance or protection come in? The very fact that the investment expenditure required are vast may mean that an ordinary private capital market would not be willing to supply the funds. If the capital market is unable to deal with a very large demand for funds and yet these funds are available to the government, the authorities should invest them only if they expect rates of return (discounted for risks) that are comparable with returns on other government funds and with returns on private investment. These funds could always be channelled to the private capital market. Thus, in this case, there may be an argument for government intervention in the form of public investment or subsidization but not for protection at the border. Moreover, given that most capital markets are truly international, it has become increasingly difficult to argue that private capital markets cannot provide adequate amounts of capital to projects judged to be potentially profitable, regardless of their size.

6. National-Security Argument: How to Avoid the Domination of High-technology Services

Most countries see the domestic development of high-technology industries, access to foreign technologies, and trade in goods and services embodying advanced technologies as essential to their national interest, in particular in the context of the most recent developments in the United States Strategic Defense Initiative or the European Eureka programmes. At the same time, they impose restrictions for national security reasons to protect the national development of productions considered as sensitive in such fields as telematics, robotics, biotechnology, aerospace, etc.[12] In recent years, the outflow of technology has been retarded by national controls.[13] It is clear that defence and security arguments have played a major role in deliberations and that general economic, commercial, and technological interests of the exporting country have been left aside.[14]

In the case of the United States, the government has responded to emerging industries primarily through its national defence and aerospace programmes. These programmes have contributed to US leadership in world sales of aircraft, communication satellite technology, computers, semiconductors, laser, fibre optic, robotics, optical instruments, scientific instruments, radio and television communication equipment, and many other products. Government funding exceeds two-thirds of the total of broad-based and theoretical experimentation for basic research. Japan applies the same type of relationship. Although further behind in the development of many of these technologies, the European countries also assist their emerging high-technology industries in becoming internationally competitive.[15] However, some observers are of the opinion that the United States has responded inadvertently to the problem of its emerging industries. The programmes have tended to be disconnected from the commercial strategies of competitive firms within the international economy and have failed to promote economic adjustment. Recent data show that the competitiveness of US high-technology products and services has been declining for a number of years.[16]

As to the future, a recent report[17] points out that present trends make the United States more dependent on foreign industry for military technology and could reduce US control over the transfer of technology to third countries. The study calls for the US government and private industry to foster advanced-technology industries as a top national priority. Development of high-technology is essential to the economic and military security of the United States, but the nation may lose its world leadership in this field because of inadequate national planning. Concurrently, Japan's leadership in a great number of high-technology sectors, particularly in advanced computer memories and possibly in artificial intelligence, is maintained.[18]

Until the early 1970s France pursued an industrial policy of selecting and launching major projects in certain sectors that were given priority status, such as aerospace, large computers, and nuclear technology. At the beginning the projects reflected a concern for technological independence, without much regard to profitability. Since 1976 this approach has been partially replaced by a more selective policy, and emphasis is shifting from major projects to specific areas of activity that are considered to be of strategic importance. At the same time, relations between the government and firms receiving public aid are increasingly governed by multiannual contracts.

In developing countries, especially the newly industrialized ones, restrictive policies in the field of telematics are justified by referring to such notions as "resistance to the threat to national sovereignty" or "domestic effort to ensure that the country is not critically dependent on the West for the computing and data processing needs".[19]

In the light of the existing policies in high-technology, there appears no clear distinction between the national-security argument, the economic-security argument, and the domestic-sovereignty argument. The three types of arguments are often mixed. Most governments have long-standing measures to prevent public disclosures of information related to national security. Some governments argue that their economic security or their broader national security requires restrictions on the international transfer of high technology. Finally some governments have placed restrictions on transfers of certain types of high-technology goods and services in order to protect the sovereignty of the economic activities of their citizens.

7. Conclusions

With regard to the new technological developments in direct broadcast satellite services, satellite and shuttle launch services and space station services, government-industry co-operation is the main factor influencing the pace and the direction at which the technological change is introduced. The emergence and the development of space generated, highly integrated, goods and services is linked with the strategic planning of investments by private firms and governmental administrations. Private and public investments in space technology would benefit from a reduction of the existing uncertainties. Trade policy issues linked to space technology should be dealt with in the existing multilateral frameworks suited for commercial diplomacy if bilateral consultation mechanisms did not settle the disputes. However, if it is felt that these fora are no longer able to minimize the spillover effects into the international trade arena of the potentially conflicting national trade and economic actions, then thought should be given to the possibility of establishing a global set of rules and obligations that could respond to the emerging preoccupations as well as to future challenges of interested trading partners, be it in space technology or in telematics. One major characteristic of this newly created agency or forum should be an appropriate representation of both business and governments participating in the discussions, consultations, arbitrations and negotiations so that greater opportunities be offered to compromise and that the best working procedures drawn from public and private sectors be maximised. Such an explicit strategy and an ongoing exchange process would change a zero-sum international conflict into a positive-sum enterprise for world growth.

Notes

General note. This paper was finalized early January 1986. In the light of the developments following the space shuttle accident at the end of January 1986, nuances might be introduced in assumptions made throughout this paper, in particular those concerning the competition in spacecraft launch services between the United States and the European countries.

In addition, the most audacious dreams, worked out prior to January 1986, did not dare anticipate a quasi-monopoly (on a temporary basis) of the People's Republic of China regarding satellite-launching services following the Titan rocket explosion on 18 April 1986 and Arianespace flawed liftoff on 30 May 1986. Three initial launch reservation agreements — two with United States companies and one with a Swedish company — have been signed in 1986 as well as a letter of intent with Iran. Discussions are being held with Australian communications agency, Aussat, which is due to commission a communications satellite for August 1991 and another for early 1992. On 15 August 1986, President Reagan announced that the United States space agency was taken out of the commercial satellite business, although NASA would provide places on the new shuttle for the most important commercial payloads for which contracts had already been signed. NASA payloads would be devoted primarily to national security and space exploration purposes, and occasional commercial satellites would be accepted "in the interests of foreign policy". In December 1986, in a reversal of policy, the US Defense Department asserted its right to prevent the United States from entering a joint management arrangement with foreign countries, inconsistent with potential US military research activities on board the space stations. Martin Marietta and General Dynamics are two of the big United States companies — not to mention several smaller ones — that have their eye on the satellite launching services now that NASA's monopoly is ending. The Soviet Union, which is forbidden by United States export-control laws to launch American-built satellites, still could blast United States companies out of the international launch services. Glavkosmos, a Soviet civilian aerospace agency created in 1985, began marketing the Proton rocket after the Challenger explosion. Although Japan is prevented by a United States technology-licensing agreement from launching non-Japanese

1. Bert W. Rein, *et al.*, Implementation of a US free entry initiative for transatlantic satellite facilities: problems, pitfalls and possibilities, *The George Washington Journal of International Law and Economics*, vol. 18, no. 3, 1985, pp. 459–536.

2. This data was cited by *Aviation Week and Space Technology*, 18 March 1985. See also, Shawn Tully "Europe blasts into the space business", *Fortune*, 27 May 1985, pp. 78–80; *Financial Times*, 20 May 1985, and *Commercial Space*, Fall 1985.

3. Space shuttle marketing managers were able to beat European Ariane booster marketing initiatives to win shuttle launches for six future Hughes spacecraft by offering a new block-buy discount and adding an additional discount for flexibility in determining when the spacecraft would be launched. The block-buy discount could be a significant new shuttle marketing tool on future launch competitions. The spacecraft were new Hughes HS-393s. The shuttle and Ariane came in with the base launch prices for the satellites that were extremely close. The shuttle base launch price for each Hughes spacecraft was $26.1 million in Fiscal 1982 dollars. Marketing features that won the competition for the shuttle were: (1) *block-buy discount*: since Hughes was willing to buy the launches as a package deal, NASA worked out a sliding scale discount on each launch that progressed as high as 10% off the base price for later launches in the package; (2) *stanby discount*: Hughes also accepted a NASA offer to discount the launch price of two or three of the spacecraft by as much as 10% off the base price if Hughes would agree to standby launch scheduling. Under this plan, NASA agrees to launch the spacecraft within a given year, but the agency is given flexibility in determining exactly when during the year the launch will occur. This is in contrast with contracting for a more specific launch date. *Aviation Week and Space Technology*, 4 November 1985.

4. See *Financial Times*, 13 June 1985.

5. Donald H. Bunker, *Space opportunity, risk and liability: a banker's perspective*, McGill University, Institute of Air and Space Law, Mineograph, 153p., 1985.

6. The Center for Space Policy, a Cambridge Massachusetts-based commercial space study firm directed by David Lippy, has performed an analysis that shows that gross annual revenues for all US commercial space endeavours should total between $44.5 billion and $53 billion by the year 2000. Of such revenue, the Center estimated that gross annual sales for space pharmaceutical production alone could be $20 billion, with another $5 billion for materials processing, $15.20 billion for commercial communications, $2 billion for remote sensing and $800 million to $2.2 billion for servicing satellites in orbit. While these numbers might be questionable, they nevertheless reflect the magnitude of some expectations. These data are quoted by D. H. Bunker.

7. Issues related to government policies and strategies of firms are referred to in "The Space Industry", an OECD report (1985).

8. Brian Hindley, *Economic Analysis and Insurance Policy in the Third World*, Trade Policy Research Centre, London, Thames Essay No. 32, 1982, p. 38: "It is the nature of things that insulating an infant-industry from foreign competition is the surest way of keeing it in diapers forever."

9. L. William Fishman *et al.*, "Introduction to Transborder Data Flows," *Stanford Journal of International Law*, vol. 16, Summer 1980, pp. 1–200. See also L. Harry Freeman, "Impeding the Flow of Information Damages National Interests," *Transnational Data Report*, vol. 6, no. 1, p. 19. A convincing description of the forthcoming, high-technology world or Technopolis is given by Albert Bressand in *Le Prochain Monde*, Ed. Seuil, 1985.

10. Max Corden, *Trade Policy and Economic Welfare*, Oxford: Clarendon Press, 1974, pp. 250–279.

11. Martin Bell, Bruce Ross-Larson, Larry E. Westphal, "Assessing the Performance of Infant Industries", World Bank Staff Working Papers number 666, 1985, 43p.

12. *Trends in Technology Intensive Products*, Washington, D.C.: US Department of Labor, Bureau of International Labor Affairs, 1980.

13. George Tolley, "The Foreign Dependence Question," *Journal of Political Economy*, vol. 85, no. 2, April 1977, pp. 323–347.

14. *Technology and Trade Policy: Issues and Agenda for Action*, Malmgren Inc., Washington, October 1981.

15. B. Robert Reich, "Making Industrial Policy," *Foreign Affairs*, vol. 62, Spring 1982, pp. 852–881.
16. Davis A. Lester, "New Definition of High Technology." *Business America*, 18 October 1982. See also Christine Alexander, "Preserving High Technology Secrets: National Security Controls on University Research and Teaching," *Law and Policy in International Business*, vol. 15, no. 1, 1983, pp. 173–240.
17. *An Assessment of United States Competitiveness in High Technology Industries*, Washington, D.C.: US Department of Commerce, 1983.
18. Imai Ken-Ichai, "Some Proposals Concerning Japan's Telecommunications Policy." *Hitotsubashi Journal of Commerce and Management*, vol. 17, no. 1, October 1982, pp. 2–24. See also Gene Bylinsky, "The Next Battle in Memory Chips," *Fortune*, 16 May 1983, pp. 152–156. Exchange of views that the author had in Tokyo in 1986 with experts of NTT Musashino Research Center and with Dr. Kazuhiro Fuchi, director of the research centre of the Institute for New Generation Computer Technology (ICOT) conforted his analysis of Japan's leadership in a number of high-technology sectors.
19. Raja C. Mohan and Vishnu C. Mohan, "The Information Revolution," *India Quarterly*, New Delhi, vol. 38, no. 1, 1982, pp. 1–19. See also Karl P. Sauvant, *Transborder Data Flows: The Basis of the Emerging International Information Economy*, February 1983, mimeograph.

8

Liberalization of Trade in Services — The World Insurance Industry

ANTONY M. BAKER*

1. The Size and Growth of the Insurance Market

The insurance industry is vast and very important in terms of the services it provides, the funds it makes available for investment, the people it employs and the general impact it has on economies. It is one of the largest industries in the world with insurance premiums for most developed countries accounting for in excess of 5% of gross national product.

Total world premium income for life and non-life business in 1984 was in

TABLE 1. *Distribution of the World's Total Insurance Premiums 1970–1984**

	1970	1984
North America	63.5%	54.1%
EEC	21.2%	19.7%
Rest of World	3.4%	4.2%
Japan	7.0%	14.8%
Other OECD countries	1.9%	1.9%
Total OECD Countries	97.0%	94.7%
Developing Countries	3.0%	5.3%
Total All Markets	100.0%	100.0%
World Premium Income US$ Million	110,000	498,000

*Tony Baker is Manager of International Affairs for the Association of British Insurers. He is the author of a number of papers on liberalization of insurance and services and represents ABI (Association of British Insurers) on several outside committees including the Liberalization of Trade in Services Committee of the British Invisible Exports Council. He writes here in a personal capacity.

**Unless otherwise stated all statistics have been compiled from the Swiss Re publication SIGMA.

the region of US$500,000 million. Of this total North America accounted for 54%, the EEC 20%, Japan 15% and other markets 11%.

Note:

In Table 1, the data has been adjusted to make it in as consistent a form as possible. Insurance premiums comprise the total for both life insurance and non-life (general) insurance. Life insurance includes all life, health, pensions and investment plans and long-term disability insurances of insurance companies. Premiums paid to the state for social security benefits are excluded. Non-life insurance embraces all individual classes such as motor, fire, liability, marine and aviation. Unless otherwise stated the EEC totals exclude figures for Spain and Portugal. A number of interesting points emerge from table 1:

— Although the North American Market dominates the world market its relative share has fallen continuously. In the 1950s the North American market accounted for approaching 75% of world premium income compared with 54% in 1984.

— The EEC share has been remarkably constant over the period. This is perhaps a reflection of the different sizes of markets which comprise the EEC. Certainly growth rates of individual countries have varied considerably over the period.

— Japan's share has increased dramatically, 20 years ago they accounted for only around 2½% of world premium income; by 1970 their share had increased to 7% and by 1984 around 15%.

— The total for OECD countries as a whole is in the region of 95%. There has been a small drop over the last 15 years but the figure remains remarkably high. This is pontentially most important for discussion on liberalization of insurance. The OECD must not be overlooked as a readily available forum for such discussions. Indeed much useful work has been achieved in the last few years.

— Developing countries represent a little over 5% of the world market. There has been a near doubling of their share in the last 15 years. This results primarily from the growth in the GNP's of OPEC countries, certain dynamic financial services economies in the far east and expansion in one or two other major markets such as India.

st life and non-life insurance markets in the world in

's Ten Largest Insurance Countries in Terms of Premiums in 1984

	World Share:		
	Life %	Non Life %	Total %
1. USA	43.5	56.6	50.9
2. Japan	23.9	7.8	14.8
3. West Germany	6.2	6.8	6.5
4. Great Britain	7.2	3.8	5.3
5. France	2.7	4.7	3.8
6. Canada	3.3	3.1	3.2
7. Australia	1.2	2.2	1.8
8. Italy	0.5	2.3	1.5
9. Netherlands	1.3	1.2	1.2
10. Switzerland	1.3	1.0	1.1
Total — 10 Largest Countries	91.1	89.5	90.1

The ten largest insurance markets in the world represented about 90% of the world total for both life and non-life business. There are, however, significant differences between countries in the size of their life and non-life business. Important features are:

— For the USA, France and Italy their share of world non-life premiums is considerably higher than for life business.
— For Japan and Great Britain the reverse is true with both having a considerably higher share of the world life market than for non-life business.
— In the case of Great Britain, in particular, it must be pointed out that the figures relate to the size of the domestic market only and exclude the international business of domestic insurers. Otherwise the Great Britain non-life figure would be approximately double the figure shown.

For the world insurance market as a whole, life insurance as a proportion of total premiums in 1984 was 43.5%. In the 1950s, 60s and 70s the life percentage gradually declined, but over the last few years the trend has reversed slightly. The opposite trend has obviously applied to non-life insurance.

There are many reasons to explain the trends but two are particularly important. Firstly, state social security systems grew throughout the world from World War II to the late 1970s. Since then an ageing population and a rising unemployment has caused some governments to look for ways of encouraging the private insurance sector to take on a greater role. This has been particularly true in the fields of health and pension insurance which have been growing at a faster rate than other classes. Secondly, the recessionary forces of the early 1980s had an important impact on non-life business. Demand for insurance fell which resulted in increased competition for existing business and a general reduction in rates in many countries.

Research indicates that there is a close relationship between the growth of insurance premiums and increases in gross national product. It is possible to calculate "insurance multipliers" which are the percentage increases in insurance premiums for each percentage increase in GNP.

In the medium to long-term it has been estimated that for each 1% increase in GNP, insurance premiums increase by something in excess of 1%. In general the more developed the country the closer the figure is to 1% and the less developed the higher the multiple. In a market such as the USA the "insurance multiplier" is around 1–1¼%. For developing countries it can be as high as 5–6%.

This conclusion has important policy considerations for liberalization of trade in services. As developing countries grow it is likely that their insurance industries will grow at an even faster rate. Therefore, anything that can be done to stimulate growth in the world economy should be beneficial to the insurance industries of all countries but more particularly so for developing countries. There is considerable potential in this respect as can be seen from Table 3 which is an analysis of premiums as a percentage of GNP for a selected list of developed and developing countries in 1984:

TABLE 3.   *Total Premiums as a Percentage of GNP in 1984*

	%
USA	6.9
Great Britain	7.1
Japan	6.2
West Germany	5.9
Australia	5.5
France	4.3
Colombia	1.4
India	1.1
Brazil	0.9
Indonesia	0.8
Pakistan	0.7

The scope for growth can also be seen from an examination of the premiums per head of the population in 1984 for the same countries:

TABLE 4.   *Premiums Per Head of Population in 1984 (US$)*

	Life	Non-Life	Total
USA	397.7	672.9	1070.6
Great Britain	277.1	191.4	468.5
Japan	431.2	181.9	613.1
West Germany	217.9	313.5	531.4
Australia	166.0	395.8	561.8
France	105.2	242.0	347.2
Colombia	3.1	12.2	15.3
India	1.6	1.1	2.7
Brazil	1.0	6.4	7.4
Indonesia	1.0	2.6	3.6
Pakistan	0.8	1.3	2.1

The average premium volume per head of the population can be seen as the "insurance density". It indicates the spread of insurance and the willingness and ability of the population to take out private insurance. The main determinant is the amount of disposable income. Thus countries with very high disposable incomes come out highest in the ranking with the developing countries at the bottom of the table. Again it illustrates the potential growth that exists in the world insurance market which should come from developing countries as they expand their economies and increase disposable income.

In looking at the overall statistics for the growth in world premium income it is meaningless to make comparisons based on nominal growth rates because of the considerable differences in the rates of inflation in individual years. In the 1950s, 60s and 70s nominal growth rates continued to expand but actual growth rates after taking account of inflation were remarkably steady at around 5–6% per annum. In the 1980s the rate of growth has fallen to approximately half of that level as a result of the recession and overcapacity in the industry.

The 1980s should also be noted as providing an exception to the "insurance multiplier" observations made previously. The insurance multiplier theory works over the medium to long term but over a period of 2/4 years it is possible for there to be notable differences. Thus in the United States and Great Britain it seems likely that a negative multiplier was in operation during the early 1980s i.e. for each percentage increase in GNP insurance premiums grew at under 1%. The position has changed considerably in 1985 and 1986 with insurance premiums rising considerably faster than GNP. Some dramatic premium increases have hit the headlines.

Overall there has been a notable increase as companies have been forced to increase rates in view of heavy underwriting losses and a reduction in the significance of investment income.

In the 1960s and 70s a major influence on the non-life insurance industry was a tendency for companies to take on business for "cash-flow" i.e. to quote premiums anticipating an underwriting loss which would be compensated by investment income resulting from investing the premiums before claims were paid. Many companies underestimated the size of their underwriting losses. Overall results for the industry declined to the point that in 1984 and 1985 several major markets incurred operating losses i.e. the investment income was not sufficient to compensate for underwriting losses. It will take some time for the market to move back towards a position of equilibrium. High real interest rates continue, combined with buoyant stock markets which have encouraged a high level of supply of insurance. Demand has also been slow to pick up. Nowhere has competition been more intensive than in international insurance business.

2. The Changing Competitive Environment in International Insurance Markets

Important structural changes have been taking place in international insurance markets over the last 20 years. The most important factor has been over-capacity in both domestic markets and in international insurance. This has had a major influence on the growth of the industry and its results. Insurance has become increasingly international.

In recent years the number of insurers operating internationally, direct and by way of reinsurance, has increased rapidly; 25 years ago British insurers were virtually unchallenged internationally as far as direct business was concerned. The main competition came from a handful of American companies, a few major European insurers and one Japanese insurance company. In addition large reinsurance companies (particularly from Switzerland and Germany) were important but they did not compete directly for business in overseas markets.

The situation is very different today. Many examples could be given of insurance companies from both developed and developing countries which have expanded overseas. In the developed world the growth has mainly been in European, American, Japanese and Australian companies. In the developing world often it has been the largest domestic insurer which has looked to create international links. In some countries, such as India, insurers have established overseas companies in several different countries to the extent that the premiums they write overseas are considerably larger than their imports of insurance.

The reason for this change is not difficult to discover. Competition in domestic markets has made growth difficult. Profit margins have been reduced particularly with the effects of inflation. This has steered many companies into looking for improved opportunities overseas.

This expansion has been encouraged by a "soft" reinsurance market i.e. the ability to buy insurance protection at a low rate. In addition, many of the companies new to international insurance business have entered by way of reinsurance. Such a route avoids the need to set up costly establishments in the country of risk.

A further important reason for the trend has been the increased severity of underwriting cycles. Large insurers have found it uncomfortable at times to be operating only in one country. Such companies have thought that by international expansion they will benefit from a broader base with poor results in one area being offset by good results elsewhere. This used to be true but it is no longer. Results tend to be bad everywhere at the same time. This is a consequence of the very internationalism of the insurance industry.

The capacity of the market has also increased by the formation of captives. This results in a creaming off of good quality risks from the traditional markets with a consequent general worsening of insurance portfolios. Furthermore many captives have entered the open market actively competing with other insurance companies. They have done this in order to legitimize themselves for tax purposes and to increase the volume of business they write. In Bermuda alone it is estimated that in excess of 1,000 such captive companies have been established.

For the last few years, up until the early part of 1985, the most important single factor concerning the world insurance market has been over-capacity. There has never been a time when the capacity of insurance markets has not been increasing. There have always been new entrants to the market. Existing companies have expanded their capital and their ability to transact more business. The difference over the last few years has been that the amount of business available to the world market has not been increasing owing to the low level of economic activity. The result has been intensified competition for what business has remained. The increased capacity has been chasing too little premium income. The consequence has been heavy undwriting losses in virtually every market in the world. Table 5 shows the underwriting results for a number of important markets for total non-life business written.

Although the results have been extremely bad they could perhaps have been worse if Japanese insurers had been more inclined to pursue foreign expansion. To date their expansion has occurred in only two areas. Firstly, where Japanese corporations have set up establishments overseas Japanese insurance companies have ensured that they provide the required

TABLE 5.   *Total non-life business: underwriting results 1979–83 (percentage)*

	1979	1981	1983
USA	− 0.6	− 6.0	− 12.0
UK — domestic business	− 2.8	− 1.1	− 7.0
— foreign business	− 3.4	− 12.1	− 13.2
West Germany	+ 1.0	− 0.4	+ 0.7
Japan	− 0.6	− 0.6	+ 1.0
France	− 8.2	− 11.9	− 12.4
Canada	− 2.6	− 10.7	− 3.1
Switzerland — worldwide business	− 6.4	− 7.7	− 11.7

Source: *Sigma* (September, 1985)

insurance protection. In many markets they have sought authorizations in order to be able to do so while in others they have operated through international insurance brokers. Secondly, Japanese insurance companies did try to expand into international reinsurance business. Although they were successful in writing considerable volumes of reinsurance business they were unsuccessful in being able to write it profitably. In a short period of time considerable amounts of money were lost and as a result they have reduced their exposure in this area.

The lack of Japanese interest in international insurance can be explained by a number of reasons the most important of which are:

— The Japanese domestic market has been very buoyant and so insurance companies have not needed to look to foreign markets for expansion.
— The Japanese insurance industry has faced little by way of a challenge from overseas. Although no quota system is said to be in operation it is perhaps remarkable that the foreign penetration of the non-life market has been restricted to under 3%.
— Japanese insurance companies are particularly strong in life insurance which is considerably less international in character than non-life. To date foreign involvement in the Japanese life market has been extremely modest and, at a lower level, even than the non-life market.

It may well be that the situation will change in future. If liberalization of services becomes a reality in Japan, Japanese insurance companies could be faced with significant competition from overseas insurers. If successful, foreign insurance could make inroads into the market and it could cause some of the major Japanese insurance companies to look to international business as a good way of seeking future growth. They have excellent links throughout the world and the Japanese have been remarkably successful in the exports of goods. There is no reason to believe they will be any less successful as far as trade in services is concerned. Indeed they have a very strong capital base with the backing of an extremely large and profitable domestic insurance market.

Another major factor affecting the insurance industry over the last few decades has been the increasing growth and importance of major international insurance brokers. They play a leading role in arranging insurance cover for industry not only in national markets but also internationally by putting together global insurance programmes for multi-nationals. They also have an important role to play in captives, risk management and self insurance.

With the growth of international reinsurance, brokers have also assumed a vital role in the world reinsurance networks that have been established.

A considerable concentration has taken place amongst insurance brokers in the last few years. US brokers have been particularly active in acquisitions and have taken over a number of leading UK brokers or alternatively forged strong links. Four of the five largest insurance brokers in the world are from the United States. They are each extremely large companies in their own right with the largest having a revenue well in excess of US$1,000 million.

In discussing the international insurance market it would be unthinkable not to make particular mention of Lloyd's. The total premium income of Lloyd's is only around 1% of the world total but its relative importance is considerably higher for international insurance. Lloyd's is situated exclusively in London. It is an international market for all classes of insurance with the exception of long-term life and financial guarantee business.

Around 75% of Lloyd's business emanates from overseas with the US being by far their most important market (approximately one third of Lloyd's premium income arises from risks situated in the US).

Lloyd's has not been immune to the international competitive pressures of the last few years. It has also had to cope with additional factors which have specifically affected US business — an increase in regulation and additional competition from the creation of insurance exchanges. The first such exchange was formed in 1978 in New York with encouragement from the New York Insurance Commissioner. The prime aim was to develop as a serious competitor to Lloyd's and to encourage business to remain in the US. It was associated with increased regulation of insurance which had the effect of discouraging business leaving New York.

The New York Exchange was modelled on Lloyd's with a similar system of underwriting syndicates. It has been successful but it is very limited in size when compared to Lloyd's. In 1985 the premium income of the New York Exchange was only just over 5% of that of Lloyd's. It would undoubtedly have been larger were it not for the fact that it has developed during a period of intense competition and unprofitability of non-life insurance. Other exchanges have been established in Chicago and Miami in the last few years.

Lloyd's has faced up to the new challenges. The capacity of the market has increased considerably and Lloyd's has started to take a much closer interest in European markets and expanding links with the rapidly expanding economies in the far east. Careful attention has, in parcticular, been given to developing strong ties for reinsurance business with Japan and China. It remains to be seen whether Lloyd's will be able to successfully continue its unique role. The confidence to do so was certainly there as is evidenced by their move in May 1986 into their new futuristic building in Lime Street.

A final important component of the international market is the provision of reinsurance. Spreading the risk is of considerable importance in non-life insurance and to a lesser extent in life business. In excess of 90% of all reinsurance premiums worldwide relate to non-life insurance business.

In 1984 reinsurance premiums were estimated at in excess of US$40,000 million. Over the last two decades reinsurance premiums as a percentage of total non-life premiums have steadily increased although there has been stability for the last few years at around 15–16%.

A number of reasons explain the growth in importance of reinsurance:

— Traditionally reinsurance has been less regulated both domestically and internationally. This has enabled reinsurance companies to expand in a number of markets which have introduced restrictions on direct business.

— Captive insurance companies have come to rely on reinsurance protection for their very large risks and exposures. The growth in captives has in turn helped expand the size of the reinsurance market.

— The natural growth of non-life business and, in particular, the every increasing size of risks and technological developments have caused insurers to turn to reinsurance companies for additional protection. Many of the new companies entering international business have been able to do so by effecting special reinsurance arrangements. In addition there has been a tendency for domestic insurance companies to expand internationally by way of reinsurance rather than by direct operations.

From the foregoing it is hardly surprising that the insurance industry has taken a very close interest in the discussions on liberalization of trade in services. It is a very international industry and hence will be greatly affected by whatever is eventually decided in discussions in international fora such as the OECD, UNCTAD and GATT.

3. Liberalization of Trade in Insurance

In the last few years more work has probably been undertaken on insurance than any other industry on a liberalization of trade in services. Insurance has been seen as a natural "pilot" exercise. There has been close insurance involvement in various academic studies and in the work of the ICC, OECD, UNCTAD, GATT and other bodies. Certainly the internationalism of the industry is a major factor for this but there are other reasons which have tended to focus attention on the industry:

(i) A number of prominent individuals involved in insurance have taken a close interest in the subject. The involvement goes back over the last decade and comprises UK and US insurance company representatives and trade association officials. They have been following developments very closely and co-operating in exchanging information and views.

(ii) Insurance is a major component of services as a whole and its importance is likely to expand in the future with the increasing integration of financial services. The pace of change has quickened dramatically in the last year or two, so has the realization that a liberal environment is crucial in order not to restrain artificially future growth.

(iii) Discussions on the creation of a single common market in insurance in the EEC has also focused attention. The discussions have a long way to go but they have already made considerable progress. There are agreed directives in force providing freedom of reinsurance, freedom for intermediaries and freedom of establishment for life and non-life business. On the negative side, however, Member States have yet to agree on the much more difficult task of creating a genuinely free market in insurance. By this is meant permitting insurers to transact business in another Member State without being established there i.e. across frontiers. It is a very major step but it is disappointing that despite the fact that active discussions have been going on in Brussels for the last decade progress has been extremely slow. Continuous attempts are being made to break the deadlock but fundamental differences remain. There are legitimate fears and differences in interpretation of the Treaty of Rome and the level of supervision and consumer protection required. So far, however, the main difficulty has been that politically the time has not been right for progress in this area.

The situation may not last very much longer. The Commission have taken a number of countries to court concerning the transaction of business across frontiers and implementation of one of the insurance directives (the Coinsurance Directive).

The Opinions in the court cases were given at the end of March 1986. They are not binding on the court but are normally followed by it to a large extent. The judgements will appear later in 1986 but it is worthwhile noting some of the main points to emerge from the Opinions:

— An establishment requirement is prima facie a restriction of freedom of services (transaction of business across frontiers). Such a requirement on the grounds of public policy can only be justified in exceptional circumstances.
— Restrictions on the provision of services must be justified in the general interest, proportional to the aim sought to be achieved and must take account of conditions satisfied by the provider in the country where he is established.
— It is against the Treaty of Rome for a country to prevent its nationals from using an intermediary to place insurance outside that country. This deprives the insurance company of the assistance of a local broker and may also prevent the insured obtaining more favourable terms and conditions.

When the judgements are given they should point the way forward to final agreement on the Non-life Service Directive. They may also indicate the likely direction on life freedom of services where the Commission's White Paper envisages full implementation by 1992 at the latest.

(iv) The work of the OECD Insurance Committee has increased in importance over the last year or two. The Committee was formally reinstated and has been undertaking much useful work on international insurance operations. In 1984 it published a comprehensive survey of barriers under the title *International Trade In Services Insurance*. Since then an examination has been started of OECD member countries' positions under the revised liberalization obligations of the Invisibles Code. Member countries have been asked to re-state their outstanding reservations to the Code. It is proposed that once the accuracy of these reservations has been checked work will begin on the detailed consideration of the reasons underlining these reservations. The ultimate aim is to negotiate the removal of the reservations and the corresponding restrictions as part of the general progress towards increased liberalization. It is expected that it will be a lengthy process but nevertheless one which could be important in the medium to long term.

Taking just the developments in the EEC and OECD alone they do show the practical importance of discussion on liberalization of insurance. There is a natural link between the two as over half the OECD members are Community countries. Progress in the OECD could be on a considerably shorter time scale than in the GATT and could be more fundamental, especially as 95% of world insurance premium income is involved. Governments will need to be careful to ensure that action in one forum does not, however, prejudice progress in another.

There are many ways in which progress on liberalization of services could have an important impact on the insurance industry. The degree will depend on individual markets and it is for them to study the implications and to make their views known. Of importance for some countries is the fact that they may have a comparative competitive advantage in certain markets in which they operate. Thus the opening up of markets could reduce profits if it results in more intense competition, rate cutting and higher underwriting losses. Many insurers and brokers have also become adept at finding ways round barriers or adjusting to them. If barriers are removed a comparative advantage may be lost.

Even discussion could have an impact. For example, a decision to create and publish a comprehensive listing of all barriers known throughout the world, or an analysis of ways in which barriers have an impact on business or have been overcome in practice. Such material could be of considerable interest to a country thinking of creating new barriers. It could be of use to companies wishing to transact business overseas as a ready guide to the restrictions and ways round them.

Many developing countries fear their own domestic industries would be swamped if restrictions were reduced or removed. Their main concerns can be summarized as:

(a)   It is maintained that foreign insurers make excessively high profits on their business in developing countries.

(b)   The outflow of currency can be reduced by the maintenance or introduction of restrictions, i.e. the purchase of foreign insurance or reinsurance is seen as a drain on the balance of payments of developing countries.

(c)   Consumers protection and public policy considerations are expressed by maintaining that it is much more difficult to control a foreign insurer operating in the market than a domestically owned and controlled company.

(d)   It is suggested that foreign insurance companies are more likely to invest abroad the savings accumulated in the form of insurance funds. If true, it is argued, this denies the domestic capital market of funds and makes it more difficult for industry to raise funds for investment at a reasonable rate of interest. It would hamper the growth of domestic capital market leaving it exposed to further foreign penetration.

(e)   Foreign involvement in the market, it is maintained, inhibits the acquisition of insurance expertise by residents of developing countries. It is said there is a tendency for foreign insurers not to impart their knowledge but instead to try and ensure that they are a necessary component of markets because of technological advantages.

Many other fears could be expressed, but the essential need is for all the points of concern to be very carefully studied if liberalization negotiations are to be successful. Answers must be found which satisfy all concerned and in many cases counter arguments can be successfully advanced.

Looking at it another way, however, it is possible to suggest there would be very appreciable benefits to the world economy from a reduction of barriers. Many markets have been artificially restricted by barriers being erected which it could be argued have been to the detriment of the economies concerned, their industries and their consumers. Examples can be cited of industrial concerns being forced into self insurance, dual insurances, placement of risks in complex, expensive ways to either comply with or overcome regulations and so on. It is essential to be clear as to whom it is intended restrictions should benefit. Often the answer is difficult.

A number of studies over the past year or two have concluded that countries have actually disadvantaged themselves as a result of placing barriers on service industries and insurance in particular. In a 1980 UNCTAD report attention was drawn to the "relatively high insurance costs in developing countries, compared with those in developed countries". The report also commented that "high premium rates discouraged the public from covering their risk by insurance, particularly in the absence of sufficient awareness of the benefits of insurance". Dr. Brian Hindley has been undertaking work in this area. In a booklet *Economic Analysis and Insurance Policy in the Third World*, published by the Trade Policy Research Centre, he raised doubts about the insurance policies being pursued by developing countries. He concluded "the arguments typically adduced for governmental intervention in the insurance industries of the developing countries (beyond fiduciary regulation) are not compelling when viewed from the standpoint of rational economic policy or genuine national interest". In a separate chapter on reinsurance he questioned many of the basic assumptions behind restrictive policies.

Another interesting example has been the efforts taking place in Sri Lanka to privatize the insurance market. In 1961 the Government assumed the role of monopoly for life assurance in Sri Lanka. It was followed by the nationalization of general insurance business in 1964. Prior to the nationalization there were over fifty insurance companies, both local and foreign, competing for business in the market. Over the years dissatisfaction with the Government monopoly has been voiced. In the last year or two a concerted effort has been made by industry in Sri Lanka to privatize the insurance market. The efforts have been led by the Chamber of Commerce which has submitted a detailed memorandum to the Government, extracts of which have been published in the press.

The reports quote from the memorandum as follows:

"The motives which prompted the Government in 1964 to nationalize insurance were (a) the need to curb the outflow of foreign exchange being remitted by way of profits by foreign companies; also to minimise the outgo of reinsurance premia abroad, (b) to provide what was thought to be better security to policyholders by reason of the Government backing, (c) to carry the message of insurance to the rural sector and to encourage more people to save through life insurance, with the laudable objective of thus harnessing funds for developments."

However, the Memorandum went on to explain why these objectives had not been fulfilled. It stated:

"The Government's monopoly over insurance has created new problems. The service provided as compared to the pre-nationalization era has shown a steep and continuing deterioration. Corruption has set in, and the insured have taken second place, a situation which was not unexpected in a monopoly climate.

A better more comprehensive, competitively priced and more efficiently organised insurance scheme will become effective once the monopoly in insurance is replaced by competition amongst a modest number of private insurers operating alongside the state insurance organisations.

Delays in settlement of claims without adequate justification have become commonplace, causing considerable loss and inconvenience to those members of the population who have had the misfortune to suffer a loss recoverable under insurance".

The Government in Sri Lanka appears to have been satisfied with the Chamber's arguments. Steps are in hand to privatize the market which it is thought will show marked expansion and improved efficiency.

The potential of liberalization in such markets and in the world as a whole could be enormous. An increase in international trade in services could stimulate economic growth and be of benefit to all countries. The removal of certain barriers may also have a multiplier effect. For example, if restrictions on transport insurance disappeared there could be a consequent stimulus to trade in goods from an easing of insurance requirements.

In reflecting on the practical importance of international discussions on liberalization it is also necessary to consider the consequences if the process does not proceed. As far as the insurance industry is concerned the signs are that barriers will increase. There will be a fragmentation of markets, higher local retentions and a reduction in the importance of the international insurance market. Some countries are already adopting new restrictions and there is a danger of this process accelerating. A most worrying aspect is that new barriers have been created both by developed and developing countries. Numerous examples could be quoted including barriers that have been erected by the United States only fairly recently.

It is all too easy for countries to find plausible explanations why new barriers are required or existing restrictions amended to be made more effective. The problems associated with trade in goods have led most countries to look elsewhere for ways of improving their balance of payments. Outflows of currency for insurance and reinsurance have clearly been identified by some countries as an area where apparent saving can be made by imposing restrictions on placing insurance abroad and introducing regulatory obstacles to a free movement of reserves. Should insurers just ignore the trend, seeing it as inevitable, or should attempts be made to combat such policies by seeking global alternatives such as discussions on liberalization of services? An increase in protectionlism would be to the detriment of all: insurers, their customers and economies. In time it could make the functioning of the international insurance industry extremely difficult. The ever increasing size of risks, technological developments, natural catastrophes and so on require the co-operation of insurers and reinsurers throughout the world. This will clearly be difficult if domestic markets become more protectionist and insular.

As with many issues involving the insurance industry it would be comforting to agree that there should be no further discussion or action on barriers to insurance or other services for, say, the next 10 years. The status quo would be maintained. This would, however, be to ignore the realities of the situation both as regards specific insurance matters and for other areas which have a bearing on insurance.

Mention has already been made of the inevitability of the EEC discussions. A policy of marking time is not possible for many reasons. Among these are the political initiatives over the last few years which have a momentum all of their own, the EEC Commission's need to continue negotiations as a requirement of the Treaty of Rome, the judgements expected later this year in the European court cases on insurance and most importantly the fact that freedom of services is advantageous to people and bodies other than insurance companies and brokers i.e. notably the consumers.

Insurance is, of course, only one of the service sectors involved in the overall discussions in GATT and other bodies. It seems certain now that these discussions will proceed regardless of whether or not the insurance industry makes a contribution. However, there are strong reasons to support the view that the insurance industry has as much to gain as any other sector and possibly considerably more to lose if discussions proceed with adverse consequences. It must be better for the insurance industry to be actively involved in such discussion guiding them in a way which meets the industry's requirements on a sound, commercial basis.

As more information is generally available on insurance than many other sectors, the absence of insurers from negotiations could result in the industry being selected for special study. Alternatively, insurance could be traded off against other sectors. There might be pressure to proceed on a sector-by-sector basis with trade offs and reciprocity.

Careful study is required of the correct policies to be pursued. It is important that there should be full discussion and as far as insurance is concerned full co-operation and involvement between markets. In an ideal world it would be comforting to put forward a policy advocating a phased approach to greater liberalization. This could be based on the prevention of new restrictions, equality of treatment for companies established under existing regulations and finally the creation of new business possibilities resulting from the removals of barriers. However this may not be possible under the GATT process where discussions will be on a multi-lateral and a multi-sector basis. It will probably be necessary to agree that new restrictions can be imposed by countries, but only as a last resort. Possibly the criteria should be national interest but even with this notion it is necessary to be cautious. Some countries could determine that even the most insensitive subjects fall within national interest.

From the work undertaken by and on behalf of the insurance industry it does seem that the industry should be able to associate itself with the overall policies which have been advanced in favour of greater liberalization of trade in services. Similar policies have been advanced by the US, EEC and several other interested parties such as private sector service groupings. A key factor which has emerged to date is that greater liberalization must be based on attempting to stimulate world trade so that all countries share in an expansion of the world economy. It would be quite wrong and pointless to be advocating just a reallocation of existing business especially in favour of developed countries. Legitimate fears will need to be recognized as it is such a sensitive and important subject. For example, it is only right that infant service industries should be allowed a measure of protection. However, as research is beginning to indicate much of the protection that has perhaps been afforded them in the past it has been to the detriment of the countries concerned. Possibly the time is right to investigate and implement new policies aimed at stimulating growth from which all can benefit.

4. Concluding Comments

Over the next few years the world insurance industry will have to face many problems. Reference has been made to the bad underwriting results, over capacity, the challenge of new risks and other factors. The industry has had to face up to increased regulation particularly as regards consumer protection and this is likely to continue. It will also have to contend with economic problems which face all sectors.

Against this background, however, liberalization of insurance should be seen as an opportunity by both developed and developing countries. It is essential for the insurance industry to follow developments closely and to organize itself for international negotiations. The temptation is to put aside such matters as being too far in the future. This would be a grave mistake. The pace is quickening and decisions are likely over the next year which could have a fundamental effect on the operation of the insurance industry towards the end of this century.

5. Bibliography

1. *Sigma*, monthly publication of the Swiss Re (UK).
2. *International Trade in Services: Insurance*. Published by the Organisation for Economic Co-operation and Development (1983).
3. *Economic Analysis and Insurance Policy in the Third World* by Dr. Brian Hindley. Published by the Trade Policy Research Centre (1982), London.
4. *Trade in Services: the UK's National Examination*. Published by the Department of Trade and Industry (1984).
5. *Liberalisation of Trade in Services: UK Objectives and Priorities — Response from the UK Insurance Industry*. Memorandum from the Association of British Insurers, British Insurance Brokers' Association and Lloyd's (1985).
6. *Liberalisation of Trade in Services — the UK Private Sector's Response to the Department of Trade and Industry Consultative Document*, a private assessment investment paper prepared by the Liberalisation of Trade in Services Committee of the British Invisible Exports Council (two reports published in 1983 and 1984).
7. *Barriers to Trade in Insurance* by Professor Robert L. Carter and Dr. Gerard M. Dickinson, published by the Trade Policy Research Centre (1979 with second edition to be published in 1986).
8. *Beyond Industrialisation — Ascendancy of the Global Service Economy* by Mr. Ronald K. Shelp, published by Praeger (1981).
9. *Has the Calvalry Arrived? a Report on Trade Liberalisation and Economic Recovery* by a study group under the chairmanship of Mr. Brian Scott, published by the Trade Policy Research Centre (1984), London.
10. "Liberalisation of Trade in Insurance — Current EEC and GATT Developments" talk given by Tony Baker at a British Invisible Exports Council Seminar in Lisbon (1985). "Towards a Freer Insurance Market" by Tony Baker (Insurance Week 8.3.85).

12. *Trade in services* by Suman Kumar Modwel, K. N. Mehrotra and Sushil Kumar, published by the Indian Institute of Foreign Trade (1984).
13. "Exchange of Information Pursuant to the Ministerial Decision on Services — Communications from Individual Countries to the GATT" individual country studies submitted to the GATT (1984–1986).
14. "Private Sector Perceptions of Community Interests in the Liberalisation of Trade in Services" report prepared for the Commission of the European Communities, directorate general for external relations by Sema-Metra (1984).

9

Tourism Services

CHRISTINE RICHTER*

Introduction

On average, contemporary man in the industrialized countries will have a lifespan of 640,000 hours of which 60,000 hours will be spent at work and 280,000 hours devoted to leisure and tourism. The trend to shortening daily, weekly, annual working hours and thus to reducing the proportion of the worker's lifespan actually devoted to work will further widen the gap by the year 2000 and will make leisure and tourism the most important sector of the world's economy.

In view of the dimensions that this service activity has already attained, an attempt will be made to give an overview of what might now be called the "science of tourism", to show the importance that tourism has acquired and also to delineate the constraints and problems with which it is faced. In the few pages available, no article such as this can hope to treat the subject matter exhaustively; nevertheless, it does offer the possibility of giving an introductory treatment of tourism, leaving certain aspects for more detailed consideration at a later date.

1. The Definition of Tourism

The first difficulty encountered in a study of tourism is to provide an adequate definition.

1.1. Tourism in International Statistics

According to the World Tourism Organization (WTO), the term

---

*International Consultant, GIRAL S. A., GENEVA. This article has been prepared with the help of the resources of the library at the CENTRE DES HAUTES ETUDES TOURISTI-QUES (CHET), Aix-en-Provence, France, which holds some 28,000 publications on the subject of tourism.

"visitor" may be broken down into two categories, namely:

— tourists: any person visiting a country other than that in which he has his usual place of residence for any reason other than following an occupation remunerated from within the country visited, and remaining at least 24 hours;

— excursionist or transit passengers: any person staying in the country less than 24 hours.

This definition applies only to international tourism, but can also be extended to national tourism without any major difficulties. Though WTO makes considerable efforts to ensure that all countries concerned use this definition, in practice, there is some lack of homogeneity in the statistics prepared in different parts of the world. Some countries draw up their statistics on the basis of international visitor arrivals, others on the basis of international tourist border arrivals or hotel registrations. European tourist administrations publish figures on national tourist flows (internal and external) — but on a basis which varies significantly from one country to another. For example, given below are the number of nights that a person, in various European countries, has to stay away from home, in order to be considered as a "tourist":

* AUSTRIA	3 nights and more
	4 nights and more
* BELGIUM, GREAT BRITAIN, IRELAND, NETHERLANDS, SWITZERLAND	4 nights and more
* FRANCE	4 times 24 hours and more
* ITALY	4 journeys and more
* SWEDEN	5 journeys and more
* WEST GERMANY	5 days and more

As a result, international comparisons are very difficult to make with any reliability unless such parameters are taken into consideration.

For a definition of tourist receipts and expenditures please refer to Chapter 4.41.

1.2. A Tentative Definition of "Tourism"

The various aspects of tourism and their multiple interactions with the environment are, in our opinion, best illustrated by a multidisciplinary approach based on systems theory. There is no way that tourism can be understood unless viewed within its global socio-economic context. Professor Kaspar's* approach is to first place tourism it is economic, social, ecological, political and technological context and then to break it down into the following subsystems:

— the subject of tourism (namely means the tourist);
— the object of tourism (comprising the tourist locations, tourist undertaking and the organization of tourism).

Each component of the system has developed its own definition of tourism; for example:

• for the tourist, tourism is a complex of different services (transportation, accommodation, entertainment, etc.), that the object of tourism supplies. Tourism is therefore a consumer activity motivated by a need;
• for the object of tourism (the country, the tourist undertaking, etc.) tourism is work, and a source of profit or of development;
• for the economist, tourism is, by its nature, an economic activity — in view of the specific and non-specific goods and services it produces for the tourist to consume.
Tourism, being international, also has an impact on the balance of payments and may, moreover, influence development in the countries or regions in which it takes place.

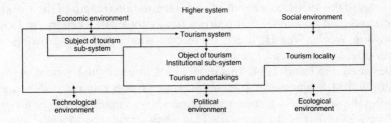

Fig. 1

---

*C. Kaspar: Le tourisme, objet d'une étude scientifique, Revue du Tourisme, No. 4, 1976, Bern.

The interactions between tourism and the social environment are numerous, and, from the sociological point of view, tourism can be seen as a phenomenon of migration, human relations, social status, etc.

We encounter the political dimension of tourism in the tourism policy practiced by the State, which may employ a variety of measures to impede, encourage, channel or plan tourism. In this context, tourism can, for example, also be looked at as an invasion in disguise.

The ecological environment is often a reason for tourism and determines certain types of demand. As with all the facets of tourism, the impact may be positive or negative.

From what has been said above, we might adopt Professor Kaspar's definition and describe tourism as the total combination of the relationships and phenomena deriving from people travelling to and staying at places which are neither their usual place of residence nor the usual place of work. Such a definition has the advantage of covering all the aspects of tourism.

1.3. Characteristics of Tourism

The main characteristics of tourism are large volume, rapid growth and qualitative change.

In 1984, international tourist arrivals reached a figure of close to 300 million; to this must be added the national tourist flows, estimated at a figure of about 1,500 million. In 1984 too, international tourist receipts amounted to some US$100 billion, i.e. about 5% by value of total world exports; however, no overall data are available for domestic tourist expenditure. These figures make international tourism the second largest single item in world trade preceded only by oil and petroleum products.

It was in the 1930s, as a result of social legislation (length of the working week and paid holidays), that tourism finally took off. Then in the 1950s, following World War II, it got its second wind, gradually growing and expanding to become a basic need.

Between 1950 and 1984, the number of international tourist arrivals multiplied 11.8 times over (i.e. an average growth rate of +7.5% p.a.). During the same period, receipts multiplied by as much as 47.6 times over (i.e. on average + 12% p.a.). This shows that the growth rate of international tourism between 1950 and 1984 was considerably higher than that for gross world product over the same period. The reasons for this rapid growth in international tourism are to be found in the following factors among others: increased productivity and incomes, industrialization, urbanization, mobility, progress in transport technology and new attitudes to leisure in general and tourism in particular.

In parallel with this trend, there has been a significant improvement in the quality of the tourist product. Furthermore, we have witnessed the birth of new forms of tourism and the growing "maturity" of the tourist him/herself.

2. Tourism Demand

2.1 Demand Factors

Economically speaking, tourism demand comprises the totality of the tourist goods and services that tourists want to or have actually consumed at any given moment and in any given country. It is expressed by such rates as:

$$\frac{\text{number of persons departing} \times 100}{\text{total population.}} = \text{net departure rate}$$

$$\frac{\text{number of trips} \times 1000}{\text{total population}} = \text{gross departure rate}$$

$$\frac{\text{net departure rate}}{\text{gross departure rate}} = \text{departure frequency}$$

which quantify a population's propensity to travel (see Table 1). However, this demand is dependent on a number of factors and has certain specific characteristics which will be analysed rapidly below.

TABLE 1. *Net and gross departure rates for a number of European countries in 1983*

Country	Net rate	Gross rate
Germany	54.4	66.5
Spain	47.0	65.3
France	58.3	107.2
Great Britain	58.0	111.4
Netherlands	58.7	81.9
Austria (1981)	39.5	51.8
Belgium (1982)	47.9	63.9
Denmark (1980)	56.0	86.7
Finland (1982)	61.0	104.8
Italy (1982)	42.8	47.5
Norway (1982)	74.0	...
Portugal (1982)	41.0	47.6
Sweden (1981)	83.3	...
Switzerland (1982)	76.0	163.6

Source: R. Baretje: Taux de départ et destinations des vacanes des Européens 1972–1983, Les Cahiers du Tourisme, CHET, Aix-en-Provence, France.

Income is, without any doubt, the most important of these factors, and there is a threshold in income levels as far as tourist consumption is concerned. This threshold will vary in time and in space. Tourist demand is highly sensitive to income increases, and research has indicated an elasticity of around 1.5.*

2.2 The Main Characteristics of Demand

Tourist demand:

— derives mainly from the advanced economy countries and, over the past 20 years, the main international tourist flows have originated primarily (about 60%) in Western Europe and North America;
— is, as has already been emphasized, constantly growing and is tending to become a global phenomenon;
— is heterogeneous, since people travel for a multitude of reasons and the variety of products on offer is becoming increasingly complex;
— is concentrated in time — even though there is considerable concern to encourage people to stagger their holidays and major efforts have been made in this direction, tourism continues to be a seasonal activity;
— is concentrated in space nationally, regionally and internationally since Europe is still the destination of 70% of all international tourists.

This concentration may be attributed to climatic, social, or economic factors or the pattern of school holidays. It frequently results in over-capacity, under-utilization, profitability problems amongst tourist firms, and either infrastructure designed to meet high-season demand with the consequent financial wastage or services which are overloaded at peak periods. The outcome for the tourist may be less-reposing holidays, soaring prices or even a halt on capacity growth (e.g. as has been the case with the camping sites on the Mediterranean coast).

2.3. The Major Tourist Flow Regions

Analysis of WTO statistics gives a valuable insight into the origin and destination of international tourists.

The major international tourist flows come mainly from the regions of:

— Western Europe;
— North America; and more recently
— Japan.

---

*cf. in particular; R. Baretje: La demande touristique, thèse de Doctorat, Aix-en-Provence, 1968.

As much as one-third of all international tourist arrivals are generated by only four countries: West Germany, USA, France and the UK.

The two main generating areas also happen to be the two major receiving areas, where tourist arrivals are concentrated. In fact, Europe and North America were at the receiving end of 80% of all international tourist arrivals in 1983.

Although certain other areas have developed their tourism, their share of the market has increased only marginally. Except in 1982, the economic crisis in most of the industrialized countries has had little effect on the international tourist demand and Table 2 (see p. 220) shows that arrivals rose from 200 million in 1975 to 300 million in 1984, i.e. an average annual increase of 4.7%.

Since 1982, Europe and North America have become somewhat less important to the advantage of other regions such as East Asian and Pacific countries. Between 1975 and 1984, Asia and Australia tripled their share of international tourists and increased their market share from 4.6% in 1975 to 9.7% in 1984. On the other hand, Africa's share increased only slightly and has remained stable since 1982 at about 2.5%. The same applies to the Middle East, with a share that has remained stable at 2.1% since 1981.

Thus, the picture commonly painted of hordes of tourists descending on the "exotic" and developing countries is not borne out by these statistics, and the imbalance that exists between the industrialized and the developing countries is at least, as marked in the field of tourism, if not more so.

3. Tourist Supply

Economically, supply may be defined as the quantity of goods and services offered at any given price on the market. Tourist supply, therefore, comprises all the goods and services supplied by the tourist object to the tourist within the tourist system — i.e. "the holiday" as such.

3.1. Characteristics of the Tourist Product

Economists put tourism in the tertiary, service sector. Yet tourism is a composite product, a combination of both material goods (hotels, swimming pools, etc.) and immaterial (climate, personnel) goods and/or services. It would therefore be more accurate to put tourism into the mixed-service sector.

The main characteristics of tourist services are as follows:

— they cannot be stored;
— they are dependent on the client's presence (the product can not be shipped) hence the role played by transport;

TABLE 2. International tourists arrivals by region
1975–1984

Region	1975 mio.	1975 %	1977 mio.	1977 %	1979 mio.	1979 %	1981 mio.	1981 %	1982 mio.	1982 %	1983 mio.	1983 %	1984 (1) mio.	1984 (1) %
Africa	4.3	2.1	4.5	1.8	5.3	2.0	6.2	2.1	7.0	2.5	7.0	2.4	7.5	2.5
North America	29.4	14.2	31.3	12.8	} 49.3	18.3	57.3	19.7	33.5	12.0	} 52.3	17.8	53.0	17.7
Latin America & Carrib.	12.2	5.9	13.0	5.7										
Asia & Australasia	9.6	4.6	12.2	5.0	15.8	5.8	19.0	6.6	17.9	6.4	27.5	9.3	29.0	9.7
Europe	148.0	71.5	178.3	73.3	196.0	72.6	202.0	69.5	195.9	70.0	200.7	68.3	204.0	68.0
Middle East	3.4	1.7	3.5	1.4	3.6	1.3	6.0	2.1	5.6	2.0	6.2	2.2	6.5	2.1
Total	206.9	100.0	243.6	100.0	270.0	100.0	290.5	100.0	279.9	100.0	293.7	100.0	300.0	100.0

Note: (1) Estimation
Source: WTO

—they are produced and consumed simultaneously and at the same location;
—their consumption also leads to their destruction — the only residual value that remains is the experience, the memory, etc.;
—they cannot be reproduced exactly;
— the sub-products are complementary.

The tourist product has two distinct components:

—tourism resources — natural or man-made;
—infra- and superstructure required to exploit tourism resources (hotels, transport facilities, auxiliary equipment, etc.).

3.2 The Components of Supply

3.2.1 Tourist resources

P. Defert* defines a tourist resource as any natural factor, any human activity or any product of human activity that may stimulate a visit.

These resources are the basis for the development of tourism — although initially they had no link with tourism, and it is these resources which determine the degree of attraction a resort or a region will exert and its tourist potential and appeal.

Tourist resources may be either:

—natural, such as climate, topography, landscape, flora, fauna, beaches, lakes, rivers, etc.; or
—man-made, such as historic monuments or any other man-made structure, museums, human activities and even just the presence of man: civilizations and populations, customs, languages, folklore, culture, festivals, sport, etc.

Every resort, region or country needs to draw up an inventory of its resources so as to be able to formulate a tourist policy that exploits these riches without however, having a detrimental or destructive effect on them in the long term.

3.2.2 Transport

A prime aspect of tourism is the travel it entails; without travel there would be no tourism, which puts it in contrast with leisure activities carried out at home.

---

*Les ressources et les activités touristiques. Les Cahiers du Tourisme, CHET, Aix-en-Provence, 1972.

There is no doubting that the development that has taken place in transport facilities has made a major contribution to tourism as we know it and has allowed us to travel to far-away destinations. The share of the total tourist product accounted for by transport varies depending on the type of product and the travel destination.

Transport is a dominant component of the economy as can be seen from the following figures:

— in the OECD countries, transport absorbs about 5% of total investments, and it accounts for about 10% of energy consumption;
— in 1984, the 152 member countries of the International Civil Aviation Organisation carried 832 million passengers.

Although the transporters realize that tourism accounts for only a part of this traffic, they have nevertheless recognized the importance of this segment of the market and are wooing these customers with more insistence and imagination.

Four main forms of transport can be distinguished, and are used to differing degrees by tourists:

— rail transport;
— air transport;
— sea transport;
— road transport.

Of these, it is air transport that has had the major influence on international tourism over the last two decades and has made accessible certain far-off destinations. Growth in air traffic has been affected by two factors in particular: the introduction of large-capacity aircraft and the increase in "charter" traffic which is, however, now stagnant or even decreasing.

The WTO reports that it is in air transport that the share of international tourist travel has risen most rapidly in recent years: 160 million passengers in 1960; 383 million passengers in 1970; 735 million passengers in 1980; and 832 million passengers in 1984.

Competition has forced the scheduled carriers to bring their prices closer into line with those charged by the charterers; this trend has been even more marked following the deregulation of North Atlantic traffic.

In spite of this constant trend, however, the private car is still the main means of tourist transport with its prime advantage being the freedom and flexibility it offers. At the same time, car rental is experiencing regular growth — a feature which is closely linked with growth in air traffic — since, as WTO states, 70% of rental firms' receipts are taken at their airport counters.

TABLE 3. *International tourist arrivals by means of Transport- 1983 — OECD region (%)*

Country visited	air	sea	rail	road
Greece (1)	66.6	20.9	2.3	10.2
Ireland (2)	8.6	9.6	0.8	81.0
Italy (1)	10.4	2.2	12.2	75.0
Portugal (1)	15.2	2.4	1.0	81.4
Spain (1)	28.3	3.5	5.9	62.3
Turkey (3)	33.4	27.3	4.7	34.6
Canada (1982) (4)	23.3	1.7		75.0
Australia (5)	99.4	0.6		
Japan (1982) (6)	97.5	2.5		
Yugoslavia (1)	5.1	3.1	5.1	86.7

(1) visitors arrivals
(2) visitors arrivals, including those from
    Northern Ireland
(3) travellers arrivals
(4) tourist arrivals, road includes those by rail,
    bus, car and others
(5) visitors arrivals of 1 year stay maximum
(6) visitors arrivals including Japanese coming
    back from abroad
Source: OECD

Ships, trains and buses are less widely used by tourists, even though efforts are being made to attract these customers back.

3.2.3 Accommodation

The range of different forms of tourist accommodation is considerable, as can be seen from Table 4 (see p. 224).

The hotel trade usually accounts for a relatively large share of overall accommodation capacity, especially in countries which are just launching out into tourism. WTO estimates that the hotel trade has a worldwide capacity of 20 million beds, around 54% of which are located in Europe, 36% in America, 7% in Asia (South and East) and the Pacific region, 2% in Africa and 1% in the Middle East.

At present, capacity is constantly expanding in response to customer base growth.

Whereas prior to 1980, it was supply that determined the types of tourism, a major change is now underway, and from now on it will mainly be demand which shapes supply in both accommodation and accommodation facilities.

TABLE 4. *Types of tourist accommodation*

		Fixed	Mobile
A	Private	— parents and friends homes — second homes — co-ownership	— pleasure boats, yachts — mobile homes
B	Commercial	— furnished apartments — guest houses	— house boats (rental) — boats
	Not-for-profit or social tourism	— farm guest houses	— farm camping — off-site camping
C	Commercial	— hotels (various types) — residential hotels — commercial holiday villages — condominiums	— cruises — camping — caravaning
	Not-for-profit or social tourism	— social-type holiday villages — children's camps — family holiday homes — youth hostels — huts and stop-overs	— camps

A = Individual
B = Open to public
C = Group

There are, however, a number of obstacles in the way of further growth in accommodation supply, such as:

— capacity under-utilization and low profitability due to the seasonal nature of demand in many regions;

— unsuitability (quantitative and/or qualitative) of accommodation to the customer's needs;

— staffing problems (shortage of skilled employees, inadequate training, poor service) and labour costs.

Given below are some data* on the breakdown of national holiday-makers by type of accommodation, in 1980: (in %)

Country	Hotels and similar	Flat rental	Secondary residence	Parents/ friends	Camping/ caravaning	Other
France	13.9	11.6	9.3	42.7	13.8	8.7
W. Germany	49.2	10.2	11.3	12.2	10.1	7.0
Switzerland	31.0	24.0	9.0	22.0	7.0	7.0

It may be said, in general, that the more international tourists travel, the more they use hostels.

3.2.4. Supplementary facilities

Attracting the tourist, lodging and feeding him are now no longer enough. The visitor wants to enjoy all the tourist resources there are and to be involved in a variety of activities as well. This entails provision of leisure facilities and the development of available resources. Leisure facilities and equipment can be divided up into those linked with sports, nature, cultural activities and those which form the focus for entertainment. Tourists are increasingly less satisfied with passive holidays. Entertainment is now a key factor in the tourist supply.

Club activity holidays (Club Méditerranée, Robinson Club, etc.) push the entertainment aspect to the full by offering a selection of activities ranging from the welcome party through group meditation to computer and pottery courses, for example.

3.3 Commercial Organization of Tourism

There are three types of commercial undertaking involved in the organization of tourism: tour operators, travel agencies and official tourism organizations.

The tour operator puts together complete holiday packages which he prepares on a speculative basis even before any demand appears. He sells these packages either directly through his own sales offices or indirectly through tied or independent travel agencies. The tour operator needs to have a thorough knowledge of the market and be able to foresee probable trends. These are essential skills in a trade in which the risks are high, the

---

*See R. Baretje: Les vacances des Européens, les Cahiers du Tourisme, CHET, Aix-en-Provence, 1981

competition tough profit margins meagre and bankruptcies frequent, especially among the small tour operators.

The importance of tour operators (or the number of packaged-tours purchased) varies significantly from one country to another. In Western Europe, it is the West German, Swiss, British and Scandinavians who most use the service of the tour operator, whereas this influence is limited or even marginal in the other countries of Western Europe.

Another feature of this sector is the high degree of horizontal or vertical integration — attributable to factors which are economic, financial or specific to the tourist industry.

The integration is horizontal when it brings together units producing the same goods or service (e.g. in West Germany two tour operators have 60% of the market). Vertical integration is used to describe the combination of firms at different levels of the production process which are complementary to each other (e.g. Air France with its Meridien hotel chain, Sotair the tour operator (better known under the name of Jetour) or Viajes Melia S. A. of Spain which covers activities such as shipping and forwarding, travel agencies, hotels and the Club Melia (credit card and preferential tariffs).

Travel agencies are commercial firms that act as intermediaries between the customer and the tour and leisure service supplier. Their income comes from a percentage on sales. A travel agency may also, at the same time, be a tour operator. However, in such a case, the travel agency organizes a holiday package at the client's request and in line with his requirements whereas the tour operator prepares the travel package in advance.

There are some 25,000 travel agencies throughout the world, and the majority of the are to be found in North America and Western Europe.

The official tourism agencies include all the international, national, regional, local, private, semi-private or public institutions which help promote tourism development. They can be classified as follows:

— tourist offices which represent a resort, a region or a country;
— organizations which represent a profession in the tourist trade (e.g. PATA, IATA, IHA, national hotel federations, travel agency associations, etc.);
— international or national consulting organizations (e.g. WTO, ICAO, OECD, AIEST, etc.).

WTO occupies a "special" place amongst these organizations. It was set up in 1975 to succeed the old UIOOT and has its headquarters in Madrid. Its membership comprises the national tourist organizations in more than 100 countries. Its main objective is to promote and develop tourism in order to contribute to economic growth, international understanding, peace, wealth, and the universal respect and observation of human rights and liberties. The WTO devotes particular attention to the interests of developing countries in the field of tourism.

4. Economic Impact of Tourism

Tourism has become a major economic activity, and a powerful factor for economic development, with an importance that varies depending on the country's tourist potential and its economic strength in other sectors. However, no matter how high the tourist potential of a country, it does not mean that tourism is necessarily the right answer for that country's economic development and growth.

It is necessary for each country to make an in-depth assessment of the costs to the national economy in terms of investment and foreign-currency expenditure for the necessary imports.

Given below are a number of factors that should be considered in assessing the contribution that tourism can make to the national economy internally and externally — on the basis of a general outline of the economic system of tourism. The economic system of international tourism is being studied in detail by Professor R. Baretje and the economists of CHET*. Professor Baretje's outline and description are given in Appendix†.

In particular, the economic impact of tourism may have a significant effect on various key aspects of the economy:

— tourism accounts for a large part of consumption in numerous countries;
— tourism generates productive activities directly or indirectly;
— tourism creates jobs;
— tourism is an important factor of infrastructure development;
— it has an effect on a country's international trade by increasing the surplus in the balance of payments travel account.

4.1 Tourism and Consumption

Tourism has an increasingly important place in overall consumption — and has been little affected by adverse economic conditions and external factors such as inflation, rising unemployment and doubts about continued prosperity. Certain economists even consider it an essential need and a part of people's life-style; nowadays, travel for pleasure is less likely to be dispensed with or postponed than is the purchase of durable consumer goods.

---

*Including the author of the article
†R. Baretje: les Cahiers du Tourisme/CHET/Aix-en-Provence '78

The share of annual disposable income spent on tourism is constantly rising, and it has been tourism in particular which has benefited from an overall shift in demand from material consumer goods to services (see Table 5).

It should be stressed that the figures given for tourist expenditure relate solely to international tourism. If one adds the amounts spent on domestic tourism, the percentages will increase significantly in industrialized countries to about 10% or more of private end consumption, this includes the expenditure on transport and that related to holidaymaking proper (clothing, insurance, real estate investment, etc.). This last figure is the one that corresponds more to the reality than those given in Table 5.

TABLE 5. *Share of international tourist expenditure in private consumption*

	1981	1982	1983
Austria	7.5	7.1	7.5
Benelux	4.6	4.0	4.0
Denmark	4.0	4.3	3.9
Finland	2.2	2.3	2.3
France	1.6	1.5	1.3
Germany	4.4	4.3	4.1
Greece	1.5	1.5	1.6
Iceland	3.8	4.4	4.7
Ireland	0.5	0.5	
Italy	0.8	0.8	0.8
Netherlands	1.8	1.7	1.6
Norway	6.0	6.5	6.4
Portugal	1.5	1.6	1.6
Spain	0.8	0.8	0.8
Sweden	3.7	3.5	3.4
Switzerland	4.5	4.6	4.6
Turkey	0.2	0.4	0.3
United Kingdom	2.2	2.2	2.2
EUROPE	2.6	2.5	2.5
Canada	2.5	2.4	2.7
USA	0.6	0.6	0.6
NORTH AMERICA	0.8	0.8	0.8
Australia	1.9	1.9	1.8
New Zealand	3.6	3.4	3.2
Japan	0.7	0.7	0.6
AUSTRALASIA-JAPAN	0.9	0.9	0.8
OECD	1.5	1.5	1.4
Yugoslavia			

Source: OECD — Balance of Payments Division.
Main Economic Indicators

4.2 Tourism and National Production

Tourism makes a contribution to national production. Money spent by tourists (both national and international) provides income (wages, interest, dividends, etc.) for the employees and employers in the tourist sector. International tourist receipts (excluding international tourist transport) are an important element in gross domestic product. Among the OECD countries, the figures for 1983 ranged between 0.10% (Japan) and 7.8% (Austria) (see Table 6). However, total expenditure by international tourists cannot be considered the net contribution of the tourism sector to

TABLE 6. *Share of international tourist receipts in gross domestic product*

	1970	1981	1982	1983
Austria	6.9	8.6	8.4	7.8
Benelux	...	1.7	1.9	2.1
Denmark	2.0	2.2	2.3	2.3
Finland	...	1.4	1.1	1.0
France	0.8	1.3	1.3	1.4
Germany	0.7	0.9	0.8	0.8
Greece	1.9	5.1	4.0	3.4
Iceland	...	0.7	1.0	1.2
Iceland	...	0.3	0.3	
Italy	1.6	2.1	2.4	2.6
Netherlands	1.5	0.5	0.5	0.4
Norway	...	1.4	1.3	1.2
Portugal	...	4.3	3.8	4.1
Spain	4.5	3.6	3.9	4.3
Sweden	...	0.8	1.0	1.2
Switzerland	3.5	4.2	4.1	4.2
Turkey	...	0.7	0.7	0.8
United Kingdom	0.8	1.2	1.1	1.2
EUROPE		1.7	1.7	1.8
Canada	...	1.1	1.0	1.0
USA	0.2	0.4	0.4	0.3
NORTH AMERICA	...	0.5	0.5	0.4
Australia	...	0.7	0.7	0.7
New Zealand	...	1.0	0.9	1.0
Japan	...	0.1	0.1	0.1
AUSTRALASIA-JAPAN	...	0.2	0.2	0.2
OECD	...	0.9	0.9	0.9
Yugoslavia	...			

Source: OECD. Balance of Payments Division. Main Economic Indicators; the figures given for 1970 are the author's own findings

the domestic product. It is first necessary to deduct the following items from gross receipts:

— the cost of the imported goods and services that are included under tourist goods and services;
— the import content of products sold to the tourism sector by other branches of the economy, e.g. consumer goods, capital goods, etc.

Unfortunately, in view of the difficulties involved, such a procedure implies considerable research due to:

— the amalgam of the different activities that go to make up the tourism sector (accommodation, transport, distribution, etc.);
— the fact that certain sectors sell only a part of their final production to tourists (e.g. transport: what proportion?);
— the interrelations with other branches of the economy (e.g. building industry) which supply intermediate products.

Consequently, only few countries have a really clear picture of the exact contribution of the tourism sector to the national economy. However, France's "Compte Satellite du Tourisme Français"* is an interesting experiment.

It should not be forgotten, however, that tourism also produces, alongside its direct effects (income distributed to production factors), certain indirect effects i.e. creation of other income as a result of expenditure on the purchase of local goods and services for personal consumption by those involved in the tourist sector, commonly known as the multiplier effect†.

4.3 Tourism and Employment

It is widely accepted that, since the tourist sector is highly labour intensive, it generates employment. However, the investment costs of a job in the tourist sector may be just as high as those for another branch of the economy — whilst having a lower economic value. Precise knowledge of these two parameters (costs and economic value) will make it possible to help in guiding development choices. This is particularly important in the case of developing countries faced with a choice between tourism or another branch of industry.

---

*t.f.: Regards sur l'économie du tourisme, Tourisme Français: Regards sur l'Economie du Tourisme, No. 24, 1979.
†For more information on this point, see T. Var, J. Quayson and J. Liu: Tourism multipliers revisited. Les Cahiers du Tourisme, CHET, Aix-en-Provence, 1982. See also the bibliography published on the multiplier effect in: Collection "Etudes", Vols, 175 and 224, Les Cahiers du Tourisme, CHET, Aix-en-Provence.

Tourism may create three types of jobs:

— direct jobs: jobs in tourism itself (accommodation, catering, tourism organization, etc.) — according to the WTO, the hotel trade accounts for 75% of the direct jobs;
— indirect jobs: jobs in sectors which may or may not be tourism sector suppliers (e.g. banks, insurance, etc.);
— induced jobs: jobs deriving from the activities made necessary by the grouping in a given area of persons living directly from tourism (e.g. health services, education, etc.).

4.4 Tourism and Balance of Payments

The balance of payments is an accouting document which surveys all economic transactions that have taken place over the period of a year between a given economy and the rest of the world. However, as far as international tourism is concerned, recorded income and expenditure give only a partial — and usually inaccurate — picture of the size of foreign-currency earnings. We will briefly review the recording method (IMF method) and will then present a new method — the Foreign Tourism Account — which brings together all the expenditure (income) occurring before, during and sometimes even, after a tourist's stay abroad.

4.4.1 On the basis of internatioanl statistics

The importance of tourism in international trade can be seen from the figures in Table 7.

In the same way as for the flow of international tourist arrivals, Western Europe and North America account for the lion's share of international tourist receipts.

A prime objective in basing a country's economic development on international tourism — especially for the developing countries — is to earn foreign currency to purchase the capital goods and other goods

TABLE 7. *International tourism receipts and world exports (billions US$)*

Year	World exports	International tourism receipts	International tourism receipts/international trade
1960	128.8	6.8	5.3
1970	312.2	18.2	5.8
1980	1990.0	97.0	4.8
1981	1970.0	97.7	5.0
1982	1840.0	93.6	5.1
1983	...	(97.4)	
1984	...	(100.8)	

Source: WTO, GATT

TABLE 8. *Breakdown of international tourism receipts by region, 1980–1982*
(US$ billions)

Region	1972	%	1980	%	1981	%	1982	%	1983	%	1984	%
Africa	0.7	2.7	2.0	2.1	2.0	2.1	2.0	2.2	2.1	2.1	2.1	2.1
North America	6.4	24.5	12.3	12.7	14.7	15.0	13.5	14.4	} 24.6	25.3	25.7	25.5
Latin America and Caribbean			9.6	9.8	10.5	10.8	9.2	9.8				
East Asia and Pacific	1.4	5.4	7.2	7.4	8.5	8.7	8.9	9.5	9.8	10.1	10.6	10.5
South Asia	0.2	0.8	1.0	1.0	1.2	1.2	1.3	1.4	1.6	1.6	1.6	1.6
Middle East	0.4	1.5	3.2	3.2	3.5	3.6	3.3	3.5	3.5	3.6	3.7	3.6
Europe	17.0	65.1	61.7	63.6	57.3	58.6	55.4	59.2	55.8	57.3	57.2	56.7
Total	26.1	100.0	97.0	100.0	97.7	100.0	93.6	100.0	97.4	100.0	100.9	100.0

Source: OMT

required for general economic growth; in this respect, tourism can be considered as an export activity (for the ingoing country) and an import activity (for the outgoing country). For example, some 20% of Spain's total exports are accounted for by international tourism. The figure is smaller for other OECD countries with a strongly tourism-based economy. On the other hand, international tourist expenditure accounts for a large share of imports of goods and services made by West Germany, Austria and Switzerland, in view of the high number of people from these countries who take holidays abroad (see Table 9 and 10, p. 234).

4.4.2 Conventional treatment of tourism in the balance of payments (IMF)

In the balance of payments procedure recommended by the IMF, only direct international tourism receipts and expenditures are recorded separately under the item "Travel"; all the other international tourism receipts and expenditures are included under other balance of payment items.

The IMF's definition of the "Travel" item includes all receipts for goods and services provided to foreigners visiting the reporting country, including transportation within that country (credit): and all payments for goods and services provided by foreigners to the reporting country's residents travelling abroad (debit). It also covers receipts and expenditures on the account of tourists, business travellers, students, patients undergoing medical treatment, military personnel on leave, and travelling government officials.

In this way, the "travel" account refers only to the *direct* receipts and expenditures of tourists, even though these represent only a part of the receipts and expenditures resulting from international tourism.

Two methods are used to calculate/estimate international tourist receipts and expenditures:
— the bank recording method: all banks and official exchange offices have to report to the central/state bank the detail of operations concerning the purchase/sale of foreign currencies for tourism purposes. Most countries use this method;
— the census method: travel receipts and payments are estimated by applying an average per-diem expenditure to the number of days spent by residents abroad or by foreigners in the reporting country. The per-diem expenditure is based on surveys made among travel agents, banks, hotels, shops, etc. Great Britain, for example, uses this method.

4.4.3 A trial tourism-specific balance of payments ("Compte extérieur du tourisme")

The conventional approach to the balance of payments tourism gives only a partial picture of the monetary flows generated by international tourism and does not show the exact contribution of tourism to the balance

TABLE 9. Share of international tourist receipts in exports of goods and services

	1981	1982	1983
Austria	18.7	18.3	16.9
Benelux	1.8	1.9	2.2
Denmark	5.4	5.9	5.8
Finland	4.0	3.5	3.2
France	4.3	4.6	5.0
Germany	2.7	2.5	2.6
Greece	20.5	19.4	16.4
Iceland	1.8	2.4	2.4
Ireland	5.1	5.1	
Italy	7.7	8.6	9.4
Netherlands	1.8	1.8	1.8
Norway	2.7	2.7	2.5
Portugal	16.3	14.8	13.3
Spain	19.7	20.5	20.9
Sweden	2.6	2.9	3.0
Switzerland	9.4	8.6	9.1
Turkey	5.9	4.8	5.3
United Kingdom	3.8	3.8	4.0
EUROPE	5.2	5.3	5.5
Canada	3.7	3.7	3.6
USA	3.4	3.5	3.4
NORTH AMERICA	3.5	3.6	3.5
Australia	4.3	4.3	4.4
New Zealand	3.6	3.3	3.4
Japan	0.4	0.4	0.5
AUSTRALASIA-JAPAN	0.9	1.0	1.0
OECD	4.2	4.3	4.4
Yugoslavia			

TABLE 10. Share of international tourist expenditure in imports of goods and services

	1981	1982	1983
Austria	8.0	8.9	9.4
Benelux	3.1	2.5	2.7
Denmark	5.2	5.5	5.2
Finland	3.3	3.7	3.8
France	3.4	3.2	2.9
Germany	8.1	8.7	8.0
Greece	2.8	3.3	3.4
Iceland	5.1	5.6	5.8
Ireland	3.9	3.9	
Italy	1.5	1.7	1.9
Netherlands	4.2	4.1	4.2
Norway	6.2	6.8	7.1
Portugal	2.1	2.1	2.3
Spain	2.5	2.5	2.4
Sweden	5.6	5.0	4.6
Switzerland	6.9	6.8	7.0
Turkey	0.9	1.4	1.1
United Kingdom	4.7	4.7	4.6
EUROPE	4.8	4.7	4.7
Canada	4.5	5.0	5.7
USA	3.2	3.5	3.8
NORTH AMERICA	3.4	3.8	4.2
Australia	5.5	5.6	5.7
New Zealand	6.4	5.6	5.3
Japan	2.5	2.4	2.8
AUSTRALASIA-JAPAN	3.1	3.1	3.3
OECD	4.2	4.3	4.4
Yugoslavia			

of payments as a whole. To remedy this shortcoming, it has proved necessary to draw up a proper tourism income and expenditure account which groups together all the items currently included under other headings in the conventional balance of payments. Its bottom line will show whether there has been a net inflow or net outflow of foreign exchange.

The "Foreign Tourism Account" (see Table 11) differs in substance and presentation from the "Travel" item is the conventional balance of payments in that it includes:

— imports and exports of capital and consumer goods, required for or derived from the tourist industry, and which were previously included under the "Merchandise" item;
— international tourism transport receipts and expenditure on transport (previously included under the "Transport" item);
— tourist investment abroad or from abroad (previously included under the heading "Capital");

TABLE 11. *Model tourism income and expenditure account*

Expenditure		Receipts	
Items	Amounts	Items	Amounts
— Tourist expenditure (expenditure by nationals abroad)		— Tourist receipts (expenditure by foreign tourists)	
— Import of goods (mainly foodstuffs and capital goods)		— Exports (goods, consumer durables, handicrafts, etc.)	
— Transport (share of international hauls paid to foreign carriers)		— Transport (share of international hauls paid by foreign carriers)	
— Tourist investments abroad		— Tourist investments abroad	
— Interest payment on foreign investments and capital repayments		— Revenue from tourist investments made abroad	
— Vocational training abroad		— Vocational training of from abroad	
— Repatriation of income paid to foreign tourist-industry workers		— Repatriation of income of national tourist-industry workers resident abroad	
— Publicity		— Publicity	
— Miscellaneous services, etc.		— Miscellaneous services, etc	
TOTAL EXPENDITURES CREDIT BALANCE SURPLUS		TOTAL RECEIPTS DEBIT BALANCE DEFICIT	

—interest payments on investments and capital repayments (in both directions for foreigners within the country and for nationals abroad) previously included under the heading "Capital" or "Income from investments";

—training of employees abroad or training of foreigners within the country, previously included under the heading "Transfers without counterpart";

—repatriation of income paid to foreigners working in the national tourism industry, or repatriation of income paid to nationals working abroad in the tourism industry, previously included under the heading "Transfers without counterpart";

—publicity and other services, etc., previously included under the heading "Other goods, services or incomes".

Even though the design of this model presents no theoretical problems, its widespread practical application is a long-drawnout affair*.

It entails very close collaboration between all the various administrations, branches, enterprises, etc. concerned — which, in the author's experience, is the major obstacle — the collection and analysis of a multitude of statistics, and in-depth research to develop reliable estimates to fill the gaps in the available data.

The Tunisian "Foreign Tourism Account" has shown that this new approach may produce results significantly different from those obtained with conventional methods. An industrialized country, with a conventional "Travel" account which shows a net outflow of foreign currency, may find that a "Foreign Tourism Account", once drawn up, shows that there is, in fact, "a net inflow". On the other hand, a developing country, whose "Travel" item in a conventional balance of payments presentation is positive, may find that a large part of its foreign currency earnings are

TABLE 12. *International tourist receipts and expenditure, Tunisia 1977 (millions of dinars)*

Item/Source	Central Bank of Tunisia	Tunisian Foreign Tourism Account
Receipts	135.0	128.5
Expenditure	16.9	40.5
Total	118.1	88.3

Source: Author's thesis entitled: Le Compte Extétieur du Tourisme de la Tunisie — Tourisme et échanges internationaux dan les pays en voie de devéloppement, CHET, Aix-en-Provence, 1981.

*France and Tunisia have already been drawing up a tourist-specific balance of payments based on this model for several years now. That for Tunisia was prepared by the author. CHET is currently preparing similar exercises for Mexico and Morocco.

spent on purchasing goods and services abroad to keep this sector operating.

The value of the Foreign Tourism Account is, however not limited to its accounting aspect, and the lessons that can be learned from it. The Foreign Tourism Account can also be an effective management tool for drawing up and directing national tourism policy.

5. Social Impact of Tourism

Tourism is not an industry which should be judged solely or even mainly on its economic impact. Tourism's social, as opposed to its financial benefits, were studied comparatively little in the early 70s although there has since been an increase in this area. Yet the social function of tourism is a vital one. The mushrooming of repetitive and monotonous jobs could have had very serious consequences indeed for the physical and mental health of the workforce. The fact that this has not been so is due largely to the worldwide development of leisure time and the possibility of using it.

The efficiency with which tourism dissipates social tensions depends not only on the degrees of participation in tourism but also on other factors, notably the quality of the product. The latter has been influenced significantly by the phenomenon of "mass tourism". This, as its name implies, consists of the large-scale movement of travellers and the development of a standardized product. Of all the factors that have influenced the development of mass tourism, only few are "tourism" factors; however, the advent of mass tourism has brought with it negative effects, for example, the overloading of attractions, facilities and networks, leading to a degradation of the tourism product (cf. "La Cote d'Azur Assassinée", "La Montagne Colonisée").

On the other hand, no other human activity depends so directly on the maintenance and care of a nation's heritage as tourism. With rising tourism demand, governments have to face up to the choice between extending public access and availability of sites, and conservation and protection of the overall environment against over-development. Careful management is necessary if over-development of regions of natural beauty is to be avoided*. Saturation of the main destination areas will require a policy of diversification and redistribution of tourist flows.

6. Barriers to Tourism

Despite the fact that organizations such as WTO, OECD and OAS are striving to reduce obstacles to travel, international tourism seems to have

---

*The result may be that certain countries close their borders to mass-tourism by forbiding charter flights (as India has done) or by applying higher prices (as, for example, Seychelles).

become increasingly enmeshed in a network of barriers to travel in nearly every country.

A study was recently undertaken by the Tourism Committee of OECD to enumerate all the barriers which exist within the OECD region. In spite of the important place of international tourism in the service area, it was found that this is the only economic activity where major obstacles prevent the customer from using the services offered by the tourism industry as a whole. These barriers affect national tourists as well as international tourists and can therefore rarely be qualified as discriminatory. The types of barriers encountered within the OECD region are as follows:

— obstacles to tourist travel;
— tourist allowance;
— entry exemption;
— visas;
— special taxes on international travel;
— imports/exports of national currency;
— use of private cars, driving licences and insurance;
— obstacles for firms in the tourism sector (e.g. employment);
— obstacles related to transport, especially air transport.

These obstacles constitute non-tariff barriers and interfere with the freedom of movement. Since tourism is now the most important service activity, it should no longer be considered as a privilege but a right; and this right has, in fact, been recognized by the Universal Declaration of Human Rights and reaffirmed in the Declarations of Manila (1980) and Acapulco (1982) on the occasion of the World Tourism Conferences there.

A milestone was made in accelerating the elimination or progressive reduction of barriers to international tourism when, in July 1985, the OECD Tourism Committee adopted a new instrument in international tourism policy by which member countries agreed to set up procedures to identify obstacles to travel and to take corrective steps to eliminate them.

Conclusions

Tourism is a phenomenon of our leisure society, and every country in the world will in due course be either actively or passively exposed to its effects.

However, its expansion may result in serious problems at various levels — be they economic, financial, cultural, social or ecological. The ensuing concentration of demand in time and space — with all its concomitant constraints — entails the need for a rigorous policy for the control of this same time and space in the face of what is a — more or less — peaceful

TABLE 13. *Travel documents required to visit Member countries*
Position at 1st January 1985

Tourists from	Australia	Austria	Belgium	Canada	Denmark	Finland	France	Germany	Greece	Iceland	Ireland	Italy	Japan	Luxembourg	Netherlands	New Zealand	Norway	Portugal	Spain	Sweden	Switzerland	Turkey	United Kingdom	United States	Yugoslavia
Australia*													V			O			V					V	V
Austria‡			IP		—	—	IP	IP	IP			IP		O	IP	V	—	IP	IP	—	IP	IP	—	V	IP
Belgium	V	IP			—	—	IP	IP	IP	—	—	IP		—	IP		—	—	—	—	IP	IP	—	V	I
Canada*	V													—	V					O			—	O	—
Denmark*	V		—		O	—		—		O	—	—		IP	V		O	IP		O	IP		—	V	V
Finland†	V	IP	IP		—		IP	IP	IP	—	—	IP		IP	IP		—	IP	IP	—	IP		—	V	—
France	V	—	—		—	—		—	—	—	—	—		—	V		—	—	—	—	—	—	—	V	—
Germany	V	—	IP		O	—	IP		IP	—	—	IP		IP	IP		O	IP	—	O	IP	—	—	V	—
Greece	V	—	—		—	O	IP	IP		—	—	—		IP	V		—	—	—	—	IP	—	—	V	V
Iceland	V	—	—		O	O	—	—	—		—	—		—	—		O	—	—	O	—	O	—	V	—
Ireland*	V	—	V		—	—	—	—	—	—		—		—	—		—	—	—	—	—	—	O	V	—
Italy	V	—	—		—	—	IP	IP	IP	—	—			IP	IP		—	IP	IP	—	IP	—	—	V	V
Japan*	V																							V	—
Luxembourg	V	—	IP		—	—	IP	IP	IP	—	—	—			IP		—	—	—	—	IP	IP	—	V	—
Netherlands*	V	—	IP		—	—	IP	IP	IP	—	—	—		—			—	—	—	—	IP	IP	—	V	—
New Zealand*	V																			V				V	V
Norway*	V	—	—		O	O	—	—	—	O	—	—		—	—			O	—	O	—	V	—	V	—
Portugal	V		—		—	—	IP	IP	IP	—	—	IP		—	IP	V	—		—	—	IP	IP	—	V	—
Spain	V	—	IP		—	—	IP	IP	IP	—	—	IP		IP	IP	V	—	IP		—	IP	IP	—	V	V
Sweden*	V	—	IP		O	O	—	—	—	O	—	—		—	—		O	—	—		—	V	—	V	—
Switzerland‡	V	—	IP		—	—	IP	IP	IP	—	—	IP		IP	IP		—	IP	IP	—		V	—	V	—
Turkey	V	—	IP		—	—	—	—	—	—	—	IP		IP	IP	V	—	—	—	—	—		—	V	—
United Kingdom*	V	—	IP		O	O	—	—	—	O	O	—		—	—	V	O	—	IP	V	V	—		V	—
United States*	V	—	V	O	—	—	V	V	V	V	V	V	V	V	V	V	V	V	V	V	V	V	—		V
Yugoslavia	V	—	I	—	V	—	—	—	—	—	—	V	—	—	—	V	—	—	V	—	—	—	—	V	

I   Agreements under which identity cards (national cards or special tourist cards) are accepted.
IP Agreements under which passports having expired for less than five years or identity cards are accepted.
O   Agreements under which control of identity documents is abolished.
—   Valid passport is required.
V   Visa and valid passport required for visits of any length.
* Countries where no identity cards exist.
†   Nationals from Austria and Switzerland are required to produce a visitors' card in addition to their identity card.
‡   Finnish nationals travelling outside the Nordic countries must be in possession of a valid passport.

TABLE 14. *Currency restrictions imposed on residents of Member countries when travelling abroad*
Position at 1st January 1985

Country	Credit cards	Allowances in foreign currency or travellers' cheques[1]	Additional allowance *per journey* in domestic currency
Australia	UL	Unlimited. Amounts in excess of A$ 50 000 per person *per journey* require the completion of a declaration form for taxation screening purposes.	$A 5 000 in notes or coins.
Austria	UL	The equivalent of Sch 26 000 *per journey* is granted automatically[2].	Sch 15 000.
Belgium	UL	Unlimited.	Unlimited.
Canada	UL	Unlimited.	Unlimited.
Denmark	UL	Unlimited.	DKr 25 000.
Finland	UL	The equivalent of Fmk 10 000 *per journey* in foreign and/or national currency[3].	
France	UL	The equivalent of FF 5 000 per person and *per journey*. For business purposes, a supplementary allowance of the equivalent of FF 1 000 per person and per day is granted automatically[2].	
Germany	UL	Unlimited.	Unlimited.
Greece		The equivalent of $250 per trip. For business educational or other purposes, higher allowances are granted upon request. For hospitalisation, unlimited amounts are granted. Use of credit cards by Greek nationals limited to the equivalent of $300 per year[4]	Dr 3 000.
Iceland		The equivalent of $1 350 per person and *per journey*. Amount reduced if the person is taking part in an organised tour or has paid for accommodation and other expenses through a travel agency in Iceland. The allowance for children is half the authorised amounts. Credit cards use limited to $1 350.	1Kr 2 100 in notes of 1Kr 100.
Ireland	UL	The equivalent of Ir£500 *per journey* is granted automatically[2].	Ir£ 100.
Italy	UL	The equivalent of L I 600 000 *per person*[5,10].	L 400 000.

TABLE 14. *Currency restrictions imposed on residents of Member countries when travelling abroad* — Continued

Country	Credit cards	Allowances in foreign currency or travellers' cheques[1]	Additional allowance *per journey* in domestic currency
Japan	UL	Unlimited.	Y 5 000 000.
Luxembourg	UL	Unlimited.	Unlimited.
Netherlands	UL	Unlimited.	Unlimited.
New Zealand	UL	Unlimited.	Unlimited.
Norway		The equivalent of NKr 10 000 *per journey*[2].	NKr 2 000.
Portugal		*Per person and per journey:* Esc 70 000 for persons over 18 years: Esc 50 000 for persons from 12 to 18 years or independent: Esc. 30 000 for persons under 12 years. Authorisation required for all amounts exceeding the above limits for travel undertaken for educational, family, business or health reasons.	Esc 5 000[6].
Spain	UL	The equivalent per person *per journey* of Ptas 80 000 for private travel and the equivalent of Ptas 200 000 for business travel. Travel allowances for education or health are freely granted within the limits of expenses incurred[7].	Ptas 20 000.
Sweden	UL	Unlimited. Amounts in excess of the equivalent of SKr 6 000 *per journey* require justification of use.	SKr 6 000.
Switzerland	UL	Unlimited.	Unlimited.
Turkey		The equivalent of $1 000 per person and *per journey* for travellers over 18 years, and of $500 for travellers under 18 years. Business travellers may take up to the equivalent of $2 000 per trip, subject to bank approval.	LT 450 000 ($1 000).
United Kingdom	UL	Unlimited.	Unlimited.

TABLE 14. *Currency restrictions imposed on residents of Member countries when travelling abroad* — Continued

Country	Credit cards	Allowances in foreign currency or travellers' cheques[1]	Additional allowance *per journey* in domestic currency
United States	UL	Unlimited[8].	Unlimited.
Yugoslavia		Unlimited provided the currency has been derived from a foreign currency bank account.	Din 2 500[9].

UL. No limits on the use of credit cards for the payment of tourism services.

[1] When the allowance is limited, travel tickets (return and circular) can generally be paid for in national currency without reducing the travel allowance.
[2] Additional amounts are granted on request, subject to verification of the bona fide of the transaction.
[3] Additional amounts are granted for business travel on special request.
[4] For travel to EEC countries, up to the equivalent of 720 European units of account.
[5] This allowance may be used within the following framework:
 a) foreign banknotes up to a total countervalue of L 1 000 000.
 b) travellers cheques and various other means of payment up to the remaining balance of the allowance.
 No limits are placed on business, health or study journeys.
[6] For nationals over 18 years old and bearers of a passport.
[7] Additional amounts are granted up to Ptas 320 000 for four private journeys or more per year and up to Ptas 1 400 000 for seven business journeys or more per year.
[8] Amounts in excess of $5 000 must be reported to United States customs.
[9] On first exit and Din 500 for subsequent occasions in the same year.
[10] Justification for use of over L 5 000 000 per year may be requested up to five years after the year in question.

invasion by the nomads of our modern era. It cannot be denied that, over the last thirty or so years, tourism has done much to bring peoples of different nations together; nevertheless, at the same time and under the pretext of the needs of tourism, there has been widespread destruction of natural, sociological, cultural, etc. values.

In view of the complexity of the problems that tourism poses — both nationally and internationally, no study has yet been carried out that gives a clear, interdisciplinary and global picture of the diverse aspects of the tourist industry in both the source and host countries. The science of tourism — in spite of the tremendous growth in the literature — is still too often specialized, sectoral and segmented.

TABLE 15. *Limitations imposed on foreign tourists concerning importation and exportation of the currency of the country visited*
Position at 1st January 1985

Country visited	Authorised importation	Authorised exportation
Australia	Unlimited	AS5 000
Austria	Unlimited	Sch 15 000
Belgium	Unlimited	Unlimited
Canada	Unlimited	Unlimited
Denmark	Unlimited	DKr 50 000[3]
Finland	Unlimited	Fmk 10 000[1]
France	Unlimited	F 5 000
Germany	Unlimited	Unlimited
Greece	Dr 3 000	Dr 3 000
Iceland	IKr 2 100[1]	IKr 2 100[1]
Ireland	Unlimited	Ir£ 100
Italy	L 400 000	L 400 000
Japan	Unlimited	Y 5 000 000
Luxembourg	Unlimited	Unlimited
Netherlands	Unlimited	Unlimited
New Zealand	Unlimited	Unlimited
Norway	Unlimited	NKr 2 000
Portugal	Esc 5 000	Esc 20 000[3]
Spain	Ptas 200 000	Ptas 20 000
Sweden	Unlimited	Unlimited[4]
Switzerland	Unlimited	Unlimited
Turkey	Unlimited	LT 450 000[5]
United Kingdom	Unlimited	Unlimited
United States	Unlimited	Unlimited
Yugoslavia	Din 2 500[2]	Din 2 500[2]

[1] Restricted to denomination of IKr 100.
[2] Restricted to denominations of Din 100 or less. Maximum of Din 2 500 on first visit and of Din 500 on subsequent visits in the same year.
[3] A higher amount if traveller can prove that the amount does not exceed the sum imported in national or foreign currency.
[4] Amounts in excess of the equivalent of SKr 6 000 require justification of their purchase abroad.
[5] LT to the equivalent of $ 1 000.

Bibliography

1. R. Baretje, La demande touristique. *Thèse de Doctorat,* Aix-en-Provence, 1968
2. R. Baretje, Les vacances des Européens. *Les Cahiers du Tourisme,* CHET, Aix-en-Provence, 1982
3. R. Baretje, Le Compte Extérieur du Tourisme, *Les Cahiers du Tourisme,* CHET, Aix-en-Provence, 1978
4. CHET: Collection *Essais,* Vols. 175 and 224, CHET, Aix-en-Provence
5. CHET, Le tourisme et la Balance des Paiements, Le Compte Extérieur du Tourisme de la France. Rapport réalisé pour le Commissariat Général au Plan, Aix-en-Provence, 1977
6. B. Coignat, *La Montagne Colonisée.* Editions CERT, Paris 1973
7. P. Pefert, Les ressources et les activités touristiques, *Les Cahiers du Tourisme,* Centre des Hautes Etudes Touristiques (CHET), Aix-en-Provence, 1972
8. Direction du Tourisme Française, "Regard sur l'Economie du Tourisme", No. 24, 4ème trimestre, 1979
9. C. Kaspar, Le tourisme, objet d'une étude scientifique, dans *Revue du Tourisme,* No. 4/1976, Bern
10. Office Mondial du Tourisme (OMT), *Etude Economique du Tourisme Mondial,* Edition 1980–1984, Madrid
11. OMT, *Statistiques du Tourisme Mondial,* Publication annuelle, Madrid
12. OECD, *Politique du Tourisme et Tourisme International dans les pays membres de l'OCDE,* Publication annuelle, Paris 1982–1985
13. OCDE, Rapport du Comité de Tourisme sur les obstacles aux activités touristiques internationales dans la zone de l'OCDE, OCDE, Paris 1984 (draft report)
14. R. Richard and C. Bartoli, *La Côte d'Azur Assassinée,* Editions Roudil, Paris 1971
15. C. Richter, Le Compte Extérieur du Tourisme de la Tunisie — Tourisme et échanges internationaux dans les pays en voie de développement, *Thèse,* CHET, Aix-en-Provence, 1981
16. T. Var, J. Quayson and J. Liu. Tourism Multiplier Revisited, *Les Cahiers du Tourisme,* CHET, Aix-en-Provence, 1982

Abbreviations

AIEST	Association Internationale des Experts Scientifiques du Tourisme
CHET	Centre des Hautes Etudes Touristiques
COTAL	Confederation of Latin-American Tourist Organizations
FURAV	Fédération Universelle des Associations d'Agents de Voyage
IATA	International Air Transport Association
ICAO	International Civil Aviation Organization
IHA	International Hotel Association
OECD	Organization for Economic Co-operation and Development
OMT	Office Mondial du Tourisme
PATA	Pacific Tourism Association
TO	Tour operator
UIOOT	Association Internationale des Organismes Officiels de Tourisme (subsequently became WTO)
WTO	World Tourism Organization

10

About Trade in Tourism Services

GEZA FEKETEKUTY*

An alternative approach one may take to the analysis of trade in tourism services is to examine the barriers faced by commercial enterprises seeking to supply tourism services internationally. The purpose of such an analysis would be to establish the basis for international discussions or negotiations aimed at the removal of government policy measures which restrict international competition in tourism services.

Tourism services can be defined narrowly as services offered primary to leisure travellers, or more broadly as the full range of services offered to leisure and business travellers. A workable definition might cover the following producers of services: hotels, travel agencies, tour operators, transportation (particularly air, ship or bus charters and support services offered to tourists at transportation terminals), financial services (particularly credit cards and travellers checks) travel insurance and telecom services (particularly access to airline reservation systems).

Under the usual definition of international trade, trade of tourism services takes place when residents of country sell tourism services to residents of another country. Three alternative scenarios are possible: (1) The supplier of tourism services sells services in his own country to foreign travellers (2) The supplier of tourism services sells services in the home country of the traveller (3) The supplier of tourism services sells services in another country to travellers from third countries. A fourth scenario would not be considered trade under the usual theoretical definitions of trade, but in practice would need to be considered trade. Under this fourth scenario the supplier of tourism services sells services in another country to residents of his own country. Indeed, this fourth scenario is probably one of the most common forms of trade.[†]

---

*Office of the United States Trade Representative, Washington
†Statisticians for balance of payments purposes would not want to treat transactions under the fourth scenario as trade, unless there was a local component to the transaction. This is because trade is defined as sales by residents of one country to residents of another country. Sales abroad to citizens of one's own country are excluded. However, statisticians have no way of segregating sales abroad to foreigners from sales abroad to residents of the home country. Transactions under the fourth scenario would therefore result in both exports of tourism services by suppliers, and an equal import of tourism services by consumers.

245

Barriers to tourism services can be analysed in terms of the four scenarios outlined above. Moreover, each of the four scenarios can be analysed in terms of impediments faced by either the suppliers of tourism services or by the consumers of tourism services. Analysis along these lines can provide useful insights into individual market segments in tourism, the impact of government policies on the competition between domestic and foreign suppliers of tourism services and the commercial policy issues raised in the context of each scenario. The resulting conceptual framework can provide a useful basis for evaluating the potential scope for trade-oriented negotiations in tourism.

Under the first scenario, the consumer of tourism services (the foreign tourist) travels to the home market of the supplier of tourism services. Since the supplier is in his own country, he is unlikely to face discriminatory domestic barriers in supplying the services to the visiting traveller. However, the supplier of tourism services could face regulations in the home country of the traveller, which impede the marketing (presale) of the services involved before the trip was started. Since travellers usually buy many of the services they will need during the trip in advance, any regulations that impede the marketing or presale of services in a foreign market constitute barriers to trade in tourism services. American travel operators, for example, have complained that various regulations inhibit their ability to sell tour packages in Japan to prospective travellers to Hawaii, thus leaving much of this lucrative trade in their own home market to their Japanese competitors.

Another category of trade barriers to tourism under the first scenario involves restrictions imposed by the home government on foreign travel by its citizens. Such restrictions can be in the form of foreign exchange restrictions, a tax on foreign travel, or outright restrictions on leaving the country. Most of these restrictions are usually not imposed to protect the domestic tourism industry, but they nevertheless constitute major barriers to trade in tourism services. It also follows that it is difficult to negotiate a reduction of these barriers purely in terms of their impact on the tourism industry, but that pressure from foreign tourist industries and their governments can influence governments in liberalizing restraints. Such pressures helped persuade the French government a few years ago to relax the foreign exchange restrictions that had been imposed on French citizens travelling abroad.

Under the second senario, suppliers of tourism services seek to make their services available in the home country of the traveller. Any government regulation which limits the ability of foreign suppliers to perform or market services in the home market of the traveller can be viewed as a trade barrier. It is often argued that the local performance of services in a foreign market should not be considered trade, since services performed locally are not truly imported. On the other hand, many services performed locally depend on extensive service inputs supplied by the exporting country. While a traveller abroad may buy a traveller check from a local bank clerk, the sale of that traveller check depends on a global network of support services which are in effect imported from abroad. The traded component of tourism services thus is frequently not the services supplied directly to the traveller abroad, but the indirect services inputs used by those who interface with the foreign traveller. Government regulations which impede the ability of foreign suppliers to make available tourism services through local distributors therefore should be considered full fledged barriers subject to trade negotiations.

In the third scenario, where suppliers of tourism services sell services abroad to tourists from third countries, the range of trade barriers is likely to cover those found in both scenarios one and two. One could also extend the third scenario into a global model, where tourism services companies compete on a global basis for the international travel business with (global networks). A global model could prove most useful if one were to consider the development of a broad multilateral sectoral agreement for trade in tourism services. Under various approaches being considered for multilateral negotiations on trade in services in the GATT, the most likely course will involve the development of a general code for trade in services in the first stage of the negotiations, and the negotiation of agreements covering individual services sectors in the second stage. Tourism is a prime candidate for a sectoral agreement in the early stages of the negotiations because a wide range of both developed and developing countries would benefit from such an agreement.

Trade barriers to tourism services can be analysed in terms of the original motivation or rationale of the government regulations involved. In some cases, the original intent of measures identified as barriers may have been to protect domestic suppliers of tourism services, in other cases the measures involved may have been designed to achieve other policy goals. Thus foreign exchange restrictions are usually imposed to deal with balance of payments problems. Limitations on foreign travel are imposed to achieve political objectives. The establishment of a public monopoly to the exclusion of either domestic or foreign competition is usually justified by the need to achieve efficient economies of scale or the need to provide a public good on the basis of a uniform standard. The prohibition of services performed by non-licensed professionals is designed to assure consumers competent service. Onerous requirements placed on foreign insurance companies are justified by the need to protect policy holders against losses by fly-by-night insurance companies.

An analysis of motivations can shed light on the difficulty one is likely to experience in seeking to remove the barriers involved. Where the original intent was to achieve a non-commercial policy goal, one can raise the question whether that goal remains valid, and if so, whether alternative measures that are less distortive of trade in tourism services might not be preferable. Of course, whatever the original intent of the measure, regulations that inhibit competition by foreign suppliers of tourism services could have created a domestic constituency for the continued maintenance of such measures. A further analysis might therefore need to be undertaken to examine the extent to which domestic tourism services have developed a vested interest in measures that were designed to achieve non-protectionist policy objectives, but have the side-effect of impeding foreign competition in tourism services. Trade barriers which are primarily designed to protect domestic tourism should be negotiable as other trade barriers.

An analysis of barriers to trade in services can also be organized in terms of the different types of barriers encountered. Various types of barriers are usually associated with particular policy instruments, and an understanding of those instruments can help shed light on how their restrictive effect might be reduced or eliminated.

The Office of the US Trade Representative a few years ago asked its services industries to identify some of the more common barriers they face in foreign markets. The barriers identified by the tourism industry at the time are enumerated in the appendix. On the basis of that initial input, and subsequent discussion with the industry, it appears that the most typical barriers are limitations on foreign travel agents and tour operators to establish representative offices, limitations on foreign transportation charters, foreign exchange restrictions, the use of public monopoly power to keep out foreign competition, limitation placed on the ability of foreign suppliers to provide credit card, traveller check or ATM services, and limitations on access to airline reservation systems.

A commercially-oriented approach to trade in tourism services is demonstrated by an agreement recently negotiated between the United States and Israel on tourism services. In 1985, a Free Trade Area between the United States and Israel were negotiated. Parallel discussion on services between the two countries resulted in a non-legally binding document, The U.S.-Israel Declaration on Trade in Services*, whose objective was to remove trade barriers between the two nations and to assure that no further services trade barriers would be imposed. While the services agreement takes the form of best effort commitment, the agreement also provided for a sectoral review of services for the purpose of considering how the Declaration could be transformed into a legally binding agreement.

---

*(to be referred to hereafter as the "Services Declaration")

Because of the importance of tourism to Israel, and because the sector appeared relatively trouble free, the two sides agreed to begin their sectoral review with the tourism services. A procedure was developed whereby the basic principles of the Services Declaration — open market access, national treatment, fair play by monopolies, and transparency — were applied to the tourism sector, with a view to removing trade problems encountered by tourism firms in their foreign operations. The resulting document, which came to be known as "Annotations to the Declaration on Trade in Services for Travel and Tourism," (to be referred to hereafter as "Annotated Declaration") was based on extensive consultations among USG agencies and the private sector to assure that the industry's trade concerns were addressed in the application of the services trade principles. This paper in turn provided the basis for consultations between the US and Israel in the fall of 1985 in Jerusalem.

The Annotated Declaration covers travel agencies, tour operators, hotels, transportation charters, travel insurance, tourists and financial services such as credit cards, traveller checks, and automated teller machines and related communication networks such as airline reservation systems.

The Annotated Declaration adopted as its starting point the position that the tourism market is reversible — it extends to firms wanting to offer their services in foreign markets and to cases where the market (i.e., the tourist) comes from abroad to the domestic market. The focus of the document is clearly on the supplier of tourism services, and the ability of suppliers to offer tourism services in foreign markets or to market services provided at home to foreign tourists.

From this perspective, the principle of market access, for example, may be interpreted to mean the ability of a tourism enterprise of one country which, having complied with regulations of the other Party, to promote and sell its services in the other Party; it may also mean avoidance of burdensome exit formalities (such as foreign currency restrictions and exit visas) which impede outbound travel by residents or impede the ability of a resident to make purchases while travelling abroad.

In focusing on the business activities of the tourism firm, the national treatment principle may in turn be interpreted to include the tourism enterprise's reliance on telecommunications to carry out its international operations. Such activities, for example, could include a firm's ability to send and receive data via international telecommunications; connect with specified telecommunication networks in the host country, such as hotel, car rental and air transport reservation system; and send processed and unprocessed data to the tourism enterprise and receive processed and unprocessed data from the tourism enterprise located in the other country.

While the Services Declaration between the US and Israel is essentially a trade document, it extends to those activities where the physical presence of a foreign firm in the host country is required in order for trade to take place. Examples of such situations, which the document calls "commercial presence," could be interpreted to apply to these situations where a firm is required to maintain an administrative office in the other nation to maintain the relationship of the parent company administration with its designated agents in the host country. It could also extend to situations where a firm needs to send its representative to the host country to accompany a tourist group, subject to visa and licensing requirements of the other nation.

Problems encountered by tourism firms in competing with tourism activities offered by foreign airlines which are national monopolies may be included in the section of the Services Declaration that deals with fair play by public monopolies. For example, — when national airlines which are public monopolies enter into travel-related activities, they shall nonetheless buy and sell these tourism-related activities in accordance with the other principles of the Declaration — i.e., open market access and national treatment.

The principle of transparency as applied to tourism activities is intended to apply to situations where the two parties agree to make public their national domestic laws and regulations which govern or affect the operations and activities of enterprises which supply tourism services, as for example, laws which affect employment practices of tourism enterprise of the partner country. Transparency would also apply to proposed national laws and regulations which may restrict travel to the country of destination (such as a travel advisory) or restrict movement of the outbound tourist to the supplier country (exit visas or currency controls).

Appendix: Selected Problems Encountered by US Service Industries in Trade in Services

Tourism

Country	Details
Austria	Currency restrictions apply to residents travelling abroad, discouraging or inhibiting tourism to some degree.
Belgium	Travel agencies operated by non-EC or associated foreign companies are required to have a permanent establishment in Belgium.
Canada	10% Federal sales tax applied to tourism promotion literature imported for free distribution.

Appendix — Continued

Country	Details
Finland	Operation of travel agencies is limited to Finnish nationals and subject to extensive requirements.
Finland	Currency restrictions apply to residents travelling abroad, discouraging or inhibiting tourism to some degree.
France	Limitations on access to airline reservations systems. See "Transportation Air" section for details of problem.
Greece	Currency restrictions apply to residents travelling abroad, discouraging or inhibiting tourism to some degree.
Greece	Non-national airlines are subject to discriminatory ground handling practices. See "Transportation Air" section for details of problem.
Iceland	Currency restrictions apply to residents travelling abroad, discouraging or inhibiting tourism to some degree.
India	Radio, TV, or other commercials on tourism are subject to local production requirements or discriminatory treatment. See "Advertising" section for details of problem.
Ireland	Currency restrictions apply to residents travelling abroad, discouraging or inhibiting tourism to some degree.
Italy	Currency restrictions apply to residents travelling abroad, discouraging or inhibiting tourism to some degree.
New Zealand	Currency restrictions apply to residents travelling abroad, discouraging or inhibiting tourism to some degree.
Norway	Currency restrictions apply to residents travelling abroad, discouraging or inhibiting tourism to some degree.
Portugal	Currency restrictions apply to residents travelling abroad, discouraging or inhibiting tourism to some degree.
Spain	Currency restrictions apply to residents travelling abroad, discouraging or inhibiting tourism to some degree.
Sweden	Special licenses are required for foreign non-permanent residents to operate travel agencies, as well as any other business.
Sweden	Currency restrictions apply to residents travelling abroad, discouraging or inhibiting tourism to some degree.
Turkey	Currency restrictions apply to residents travelling abroad, discouraging or inhibiting tourism to some degree.

USTR Computer Group

Statistics, Measurement Problems and Informations

11

Improving Services Trade Data

BERNARD ASCHER and OBIE G. WHICHARD*

1. Introduction

Technological advancements in transportation, communication, and computerization have permitted more timely and efficient production, delivery, and consumption of services on a worldwide scale. The development of statistics to measure and monitor these activities generally lags far behind their advent, both nationally and internationally.

With business opportunities growing and international trade in services receiving greater attention as a policy issue, the need for accurate, complete, and internationally comparable statistics covering this trade is becoming increasingly evident. As trade negotiations draw near, the need will become even more striking. During the course of any negotiations, participating countries inevitably will be seeking information to answer the key questions that will arise:

— What is the overall magnitude and importance of trade in services?

— What are the effects of barriers to trade in services?

— What are the areas of reciprocal advantage in which mutual agreement to reduce barriers might be expected?

— What are the approximate values of trade liberalization packages offered or received during the negotiating process?

— What is the probable impact of liberalizing services trade and, especially, what economic benefits can be expected to flow from more open services markets?

Obviously, these questions cannot be adequately addressed in the absence of a strong statistical base. Although the existing base is deficient

*Office of the US Trade Representative and Bureau of Economic Analysis, US Department of Commerce, respectively. The views expressed in this article are those of the authors, and not those of the agencies with which they are affiliated.

255

in many respects, and may never match that which exists for merchandise trade, a process of data improvement is underway in the United States and elsewhere that, if continued, should markedly increase the adequacy of statistics on services trade. This article discusses some of the problems involved in improving the data, as well as some of the progress that has been made in resolving them. The remainder of the article consists of five parts, dealing with (1) definitional and conceptual issues; (2) data limitations; (3) efforts underway to improve US data; (4) available US data; and (5) the need for international comparability. Although the focus is on US efforts, with which the authors have been involved, other countries and international organizations as well are also devoting attention to data improvement.

2. Defining Services Trade

Defining services trade involves two tasks—defining "services" and defining "trade". Each task can be handled easily in the abstract, but it nevertheless may be quite difficult to quantify and classify particular transactions. The two tasks are discussed in turn below.

Defining Services

Obviously, defining services entails answering a number of difficult questions. Yet, the definition is of fundamental importance in trade negotiations. Since the definition of services and its interpretation will determine the scope of negotiations, the definition itself can be expected to be subject to negotiation. It should be emphasized that, although definitional problems may seem formidable when simply presented in a long list, as is done below, they need not impede pragmatic efforts at data improvement, as is illustrated in the summary of United States data improvement efforts later in the article.

While there is a core group of activities that virtually everyone would consider as "services", opinions vary on the precise scope of coverage, characteristics of activities or outputs, and types of transactions to be included. For example, some definitions include, while others exclude, such activities as transportation, communication, public utilities, construction, and wholesale and retail trade, which may be classified separate and apart from "services."* Some definitions stress such characteristics as

---

*In the United States, official statistics are generally classified according to, or on a basis closely related to, a system known as the Standard Industrial Classification. This system contains a somewhat narrowly defined "services" division (see note to Table 2). as well as several other divisions that, in a dichotomy of all industries into goods-producing and services-producing categories, would, at least in some instances, be considered as services-producing. These include the groups mentioned in the text.

tangibility, visibility, portability, and storability to mark the dividing line between goods and services. Some include factor income (i.e., income from the services of factors of production, such as land, labour, and capital), along with the nonfactor income derived from the performance of services. One frequently used definition describes services simply as economic activities other than agriculture, mining, and manufacturing. While this definition does not conflict with the one used in this paper, it lacks specific reference to what is included in the term.

For purposes of outlining data needs, a broad definition of services can be used. As used here, services are economic outputs, generally other than tangible goods, including (but not limited to) accounting, advertising, banking and other finance, communication, data processing and information services, education, employment, engineering and construction, franchising, health care, insurance, leasing, lodging, management consulting, motion pictures, public relations, transportation, tourism, law, and other business, professional, and technical services. This definition includes some services or industries whose output has elements of tangibility, visibility, portability, and storability. However, in focusing on outputs, it implicitly restricts itself to nonfactor services, as is the general custom in analysing trade in services. Factor services (services for which factor income is paid, such as investment income and earnings of workers temporarily resident abroad) would normally not be included as trade in services, although they may be of interest for some purposes.* Similarly, fees and royalties for the sale or use of intangible assets are also of interest, but do not correspond to services trade in the sense of the sale of currently performed services. Conceptually, they resemble factor incomes in that they represent payments for existing intangible assets. Many policy issues,

---

*For example, the interest income banks earn on foreign loans would need to be examined as a part of an analysis of the international operations of banks. However, the interest flows do not measure the value of services performed in the same sense that the foreign revenues of, say, an accounting firm would measure the value of services it provided to foreigners. Inclusion of factor income as trade in services has been said by Sapir [8, p. 78] to represent a confusion between "services" and "invisibles." (The latter include essentially everything except merchandise trade in the current account of the balance of payments.) The OECD Secretariat has observed that the borderline between factor and nonfactor services "is controversial and that some items shown in certain national presentations combine elements of both categories" [7, p. 1]; accordingly, it included factor income in its review of services data availability in member countries. The *1986 U.S. Industrial Outlook* presents two totals of US international services transactions, one including and one excluding investment income [US Department of Commerce, International Trade Administration, [13]]. A recent US Government policy statement has indicated that "categories under the "services" heading of the balance-of-payments accounts that cover [the returns to] capital and labour would not be included in a framework [of negotiating principles] since these represent factors of production in both goods and services. As in the case of goods, a services trade agreement would pertain to the final output of a sector" ["Annual Report of the President of the United States on the Trade Agreements Program," [1], p. 153].

such as those involving intellectual property rights or the transfer of technology, would require such data. Thus, the data are clearly needed, but probably should be viewed separately from those covering receipts and payments for services performed.

Even with an agreed definition, numerous problems could arise in attempting to classify particular outputs as goods or services. Several of them are discussed below. It should be noted first, however, that it is possible to overstate the importance of the particular industries or activities to be counted as services. It may be more important simply to insure that all outputs are covered by the statistical reporting system in order that (a) trade can be measured in the aggregate, and (b) data on trade of individual industries, whether they are considered primarily as goods-producing or services-producing, are available.

The delineation of boundaries between individual services sectors is complicated by the nature of some service activities which include or overlap activities of other sectors. Conceivably, for example, "telecommunication" services could encompass, not only the transmission and reception of video, voice, and data, but also the material that is broadcast (news, information, entertainment, data processing) and the activities that provide the means of communication (launching of satellites, laying of undersea cables). This multiplicity of activities creates problems in determining to which industry the value of a particular service should be ascribed.

Other examples of multiple services include franchising and tourism. Franchising, although an industry in itself, is essentially a package of marketing and management techniques, applicable to many industry sectors—soft drink bottling, auto dealership and rentals, fast-food restaurants, exercise clubs, and hotels. For some firms, franchising may be the primary activity, whereas for others, the actual type of business operated under the franchise may constitute the primary activity. Tourism encompasses the output of several individual industries—lodging, meals, transportation, travel, insurance, and entertainment.

Some services may be performed as a secondary activity by companies classified primarily in other service-producing or goods-producing industries. Educational services, for example, may be performed by schools and other entities engaged in the provision of such services and therefore classified in the educational services "industry". They may also be performed commercially as a secondary activity by such diverse entities as insurance companies, financial advisors, management consultants, data processing companies, accountants, tax preparers, and even manufacturers, who may offer instructional services related to the use, maintenance, or repair of their own products. Banks and industrial companies may sell data processing and information services. Engineering and construction companies may contract for the erection of a finished structure (a "construction" activity) or simply for the design of a particular project (an "architecture and engineering" activity). Retailers and wholesalers sell and distribute merchandise, but also may sell marketing services to other firms. For example, mass merchandisers are increasingly using the strength of their worldwide organizations, their knowledge, experience, and buying power to procure goods for retailers or buyers in other countries.

In the above examples, the statistics collected ideally should isolate the value of service activities from the value of goods. In some cases, industries such as construction, wholesaling, and retailing are eliminated from consideration as services because they are regarded merely as part of the process of delivering goods to international markets. Their service functions, however, are often separable from the goods and often are sold as such. Although isolating the value of such services is not always possible, to exclude these industries entirely from a data system for international trade in services would result in an underestimation of the role that services play in international commercial affairs.

Goods and services are often sold jointly, without the goods and services components of the sale being valued separately. For example, airline caterers sell not just the food for passengers, but the planning and preparation of a compact, well balanced, packaged meal, delivered at the proper time to the aircraft. Computing or telecommunications equipment may be sold as a package including such services as installation, maintenance, repair, and training. In such a case, it may not be feasible to separate the goods components of the sale from the services component, since the two components may be combined even in the records of the firms selling the goods and services. Yet, the availability of after-sale service and support may be an important consideration of the buyer in making the purchase. Many manufacturers and retailers sell service contracts, which are valued separately, but usually durable goods are warranted for a short period of time, and the estimated cost of servicing products under warranty is implicitly included in the price of the goods. Ideally, information on both types of service—the separately priced contract and the cost of meeting obligations under warranties—should be available.

Segregation of goods from services is particularly difficult when tangible outputs (goods) serve as media for the delivery of intangible outputs (services). For example, artistic or theatrical performances may be delivered through the media of phonographic records or motion picture film. A consultant's assessment or advice may be transmitted to a client through a printed report. Books represent information or entertainment in tangible form. Computer users purchase specialized, pre-programmed software encoded on diskettes or other media to simplify and speed their own work. Videotape can be used for a variety of purposes to provide information or entertainment. The development of reproduction and recording technologies has increased the potential for delivery of services in these tangible forms.

Purchases by those temporarily visiting another country—tourists and students, in particular—also present problems. These individuals may purchase both goods and services during their stay. For purposes of balance of payments statistics, however, estimates of such purchases are recorded entirely in the travel account, where they tend to be viewed as services and not goods. Although this treatment is in accordance with the recommendations of the IMF *Manual*[5], and may be done partly for reasons of practicality, the end result is that the official data for travel and tourism services tend to overstate services transactions and to understate merchandise trade.

Service activity may be understated to the extent that services are performed both by and for the same company. These services generally will not be identified as such, since data tend to be recorded on the basis of sales to outside purchasers. For example, when a goods-producing company has its own accounting department, the services it performs will not be included in the accounting industry's data, but if the company contracts with specialized outside firms to meet its accounting needs, the services will be included. In the case of multinational firms, the problem is heightened by the international aspects of the business. Services performed in the home office for the subsidiary or affiliate would not be counted as an international transaction unless there were an explicit charge or allocation, and even then the nature of the services performed generally would not be available in official statistics.

Defining Trade

According to balance of payments conventions, international trade occurs when goods or services are sold or otherwise exchanged between residents of different countries.* In the case of merchandise trade, goods move physically from the exporting country to the importing country. For services, the balance of payments conventions are the same, but the transactions are more varied, and cannot be characterized solely by simple analogy to the country-to-country movement of merchandise. For example, the transactions include:

    1. Cross-border transactions, including the transmission of voice, video, data or other information and the transportation of goods and passengers from one country to another;

---

*Conceptually, a change in ownership is required. In practice, statistics on merchandise trade usually record the physical movement of goods.

2. Contractual arrangements conferring rights to use intellectual property, technology, or other intangible assets (e.g., patents, trademarks, franchises, copyrights, and film, broadcast and recording rights);

3. Travel of individual consumers to another country (e.g., expenditures of non-resident tourists, students, and medical patients); and

4. Travel of individual producers to another country (e.g., services provided to foreign clients by business consultants, engineers, attorneys, etc.).

In addition to these diverse transactions between residents of different countries, it is important to consider services sold abroad through foreign affiliates.* Affiliates are considered residents of the country where they are located, not of the country of their owners. Their sales within that country are transactions between residents of the same country and, therefore, are not included in balance of payments accounts. They are nevertheless of interest for commercial policy purposes and, as illustrated later using US data, are an important channel for selling services abroad. In some cases, this is because of the nature of the service. For example, routine maintenance and repair of equipment installed in a foreign country is unlikely to be done by entities not residing in that country. In fact, local availability of after-sale service may be a stipulated requirement in contracts for the sale of sophisticated equipment to be exported from the country of manufacture. In other cases, the sale of services by nonresidents may be restricted.

Inasmuch as a significant portion of affiliate sales may be to the country of the parent or to third countries, it is necessary to itemize these sales separately, possibly with further disaggregation showing, for each destination, sales within the multinational company apart from sales to unaffiliated parties. As discussed later, this approach is being taken in current US surveys. (Table 2 illustrates the variety of data available.)

Other methods of accounting for the services activity of foreign affiliates have been suggested. Shelp [9, p. 12] has suggested counting the investment income attributable to service-industry affiliates (although he also recognized the importance of data on affiliate sales [9, p. 64]). While this would represent a large component of the value added attributable to factors of production owned by residents of the investing country, it would

---

*As noted earlier, these transactions do not involve the current performance of a service, and perhaps should be viewed separately from those that do. This is facilitated by the convention of providing separate "fee and royalty" categories for such transactions in balance of payments accounts (see, e.g., Table 1).

Table 1. *Selected US Current Account Services Transactions, 1970–85*

[Millions of dollars]

	1970	1975	1980	1981	1982	1983	1984	1985
Exports:								
Total	9,625	18,796	37,040	41,724	41,652	41,796	43,786	45,878
Total, excluding fees and royalties	7,294	14,496	29,995	34,440	34,519	33,941	35,671	36,566
Travel	2,331	4,697	10,588	12,913	12,393	11,408	11,386	11,655
Passenger fares	544	1,039	2,591	3,111	3,174	3,037	3,023	2,993
Other transportation	3,125	5,840	11,618	12,560	12,317	12,639	13,799	14,342
Fees and royalties	2,331	4,300	7,085	7,284	7,133	7,855	8,115	8,512
Other private services	1,294	2,920	5,158	5,856	6,635	6,857	7,463	7,576
Imports:								
Total	9,090	16,412	29,428	32,093	32,594	35,397	41,460	44,905
Total, excluding fees and royalties	8,865	15,939	28,703	31,442	32,405	35,169	40,944	44,698
Travel	3,980	6,417	10,397	11,479	12,394	13,997	16,008	17,043
Passenger fares	1,215	2,263	3,607	4,487	4,772	5,484	6,508	7,385
Other transportation	2,843	5,708	11,790	12,474	11,710	12,324	14,666	16,383
Fees and royalties	225	473	725	651	189	228	516	287
Other private services	827	1,551	2,909	3,002	3,529	3,364	3,762	3,967

Source: US Department of Commerce, Bureau of Economic Analysis

not be comparable to the sales measures used to measure services provided directly to foreigners from that country, and would not provide a measure of services performed. (Indeed, income might even be negative during a time when the level of services performed by affiliates was high.)

Lederer *et al.*[6], have approached the problem in a different way, proposing that an ownership-based system of balance of payments accounts be compiled to supplement the conventional residence-based accounts. In those accounts, the residence of the *owners* of transactors, rather than the residence of the transactors themselves, would be used to identify international transactions. Because transactors could not reasonably be expected to trace the ownership of those with whom they transact, such a system probably could not, as its proponents acknowledge, be implemented in its pure form.

Aside from the United States, few, if any, countries are likely to conduct formal surveys to collect data on sales by foreign affiliates. Thus, a gap in

Table 2. *Sales of Goods and Services by US Parents and Foreign Affiliates, 1982–83*

[Billions of dollars, or percent]

	1982			1983			Services as a percentage of total	
	Total	Goods	Services	Total	Goods	Services	1982	1983
US Parents:								
All nonbank parents of nonbank affiliates	2,348	1,815	533	2,403	1,850	552	22.7	23.0
To US persons	2,068	1,551	516	N.A.	N.A.	536	25.0	N.A.
To foreign persons	280	264	17	N.A.	N.A.	16	6.1	N.A.
To foreign affiliates	109	106	3	N.A.	N.A.	4	3.1	N.A.
To unaffiliated foreigners	171	158	14	N.A.	N.A.	12	8.0	N.A.
Foreign affiliates:								
All nonbank affiliates of nonbank parents	936	N.A.	N.A.	902	N.A.	N.A.	N.A.	N.A.
Majority-owned affiliates	730	664	66	714	646	68	9.1	9.5
To affiliated persons	160	N.A.	N.A.	170	153	17	N.A.	9.9
To unaffiliated persons	570	N.A.	N.A.	544	493	51	N.A.	9.4
To US persons	77	69	7	81	72	9	9.7	10.6
to US parents	64	N.A.	N.A.	68	61	7	N.A.	10.2
To unaffiliated US persons	13	N.A.	N.A.	13	11	2	N.A.	12.4
To foreign persons	653	595	59	633	574	59	9.0	9.4
To other foreign affiliates	96	N.A.	N.A.	102	92	10	N.A.	9.7
To unaffiliated foreigners	557	N.A.	N.A.	531	482	49	N.A.	9.3

Table 2. Sales of Goods and Services by US Parents and Foreign Affiliates, 1982–83 - Continued

[Billions of dollars, or percent]

	1982			1983			Services as a percentage of total	
	Total	Goods	Services	Total	Goods	Services	1982	1983
Local sales	478	427	51	461	410	51	10.8	11.1
To other foreign affiliates	28	N.A	N.A.	31	25	6	N.A	19.5
To unaffiliated foreigners	450	N.A.	N.A.	430	385	45	N.A.	10.5
Sales to other countries	175	168	7	172	164	8	4.2	4.8
To other foreign affiliates	68	N.A.	N.A.	71	68	4	N.A.	5.4
To unaffiliated foreigners	107	N.A.	N.A.	101	97	4	N.A.	4.4
Minority-owned affiliates	206	N.A.	N.A.	188	N.A.	N.A.	N.A.	N.A.

N.A. Not available.   Source: US Department of Commerce, Bureau of Economic Analysis

Note: In this table, "services" include industries in the services division of the Standard Industrial Classification (SIC) (see below); finance except banking, insurance, and real estate; agricultural services; mining services; various petroleum services; and transportation, communication, and public utilities. The services division of the SIC includes hotels and lodging places; various business services; motion pictures, including television tape and film; engineering, architecture, and surveying services; health services; and miscellaneous services. It includes several industries that are in other divisions, but would be considered services if all industries had to be classified as either goods producing or services producing. The exclusion of banking from finance reflects the exclusion of banks from the data set, not a judgement that banking is not a service.

information on this important aspect of international service business is likely to remain unless other ways are found to develop the needed information for major trading countries.

3. Data Limitations

Obviously, data needs cannot be met simply by virtue of having resolved definitional and conceptual problems such as those discussed above. In addition, the data must actually be available in the form required. At present, this is not always the case. Existing data systems have been designed primarily to meet the needs of macroeconomic-oriented balance of payments analysis. For this purpose, the data generally do not need to be as comprehensive and detailed as for the purpose of supporting trade liberalization efforts or addressing other trade-in-services policy issues. Four problem areas, relating to the classification, aggregation, coverage, and recording of data, are discussed below.

Classification

For most trade policy purposes, data classified on the basis of the type of service performed are needed. Sometimes, data are classified, instead, on the basis of the type of enterprise that sold or purchased the service. Typically, such data are, in the absence of alternatives, used as a proxy for data classified by type of service performed. Thus, for example, the sales of a computer manufacturer would be shown under computer manufacturing, and the fact that the manufacturer also was engaged in service activities such as maintenance, repair, data processing, programming, consulting, and training would go unnoticed.

The potential for misrepresentation when enterprise (company) statistics are used as if they were classified by activity (or establishment) varies with the degree of specialization of the enterprises involved. Data on US parent companies and their foreign affiliates, which are classified on an enterprise basis, can be used as an illustration. Foreign affiliates tend to be highly specialised, and, judging from sales data collected for industry coding purposes, it seems generally satisfactory to treat data on them as if the classification were by type of good or service sold. US parent companies, on the other hand, are much less specialized, and it generally is not safe to use their industry classification as a proxy for the type of good or service sold.*

---

*The difference in specialization partly reflects consolidation practices. For reporting purposes, affiliates generally are not permitted to be consolidated across industry lines, and consolidation across country lines is uniformly prohibited. US parents, on the other hand, report as fully consolidated domestic enterprises, and large, diversified enterprises account for much of the value.

Aggregation

Data on merchandise trade are much more detailed than those on trade in services. In US data, for instance, while there are more than 10,000 product categories for merchandise trade, there are only six line items for services in the current account of the balance of payments, and only about 40 industry codes are used for services in direct investment survey data.[†]

To some extent, the large number of categories available for merchandise trade reflects the method of collecting data. The data are obtained from customs documents which require, for tariff and administrative purposes as well as for statistical purposes, reporting in fine product detail. For trade in services, data are generally collected in surveys.[*] The surveys are often completed at company headquarters by comptrollers, rather than by individual units within companies, and it would be quite burdensome for them to assemble information on services trade in nearly the same detail as that available for merchandise trade. Also, the level of detail that can be published may be limited by the requirement to protect the confidentiality of data of individual firms.

Coverage

Coverage problems in services trade data may be of two types. The first occurs when services transactions that conceptually should be covered by the statistical reporting system are, in fact, not covered and have not been estimated. The second occurs when universe estimates have been made based on inadequate samples.

In the United States, coverage problems have perhaps been greatest in the area of "other private services" (see Table 1), a category that, in principle, covers both sales to, and purchases from, unaffiliated foreigners of a wide variety of services. In practice, however, little information has been available on purchases, and the available information on sales has tended to be restricted to a few types of services, particularly architecture, engineering, construction and related technical services. Services not currently reported include advertising; data base and other information services; performing arts, sports, and other live performance or events; management, consulting, and public relations services; accounting and legal services; various other business and professional services; and certain

---

[†]Although some subdivision of the six line items is possible, the degree of available detail remains quite limited in comparison with merchandise trade data.
[*]Many countries rely upon central bank statistics, such as those on requests for foreign exchange, as the primary source of information on service trade. This method, like the survey method used in the United States and a few other countries, does not seem capable of producing detail comparable to that obtainable from customs documents.

expenditures or disbursements by US persons to carry out activities abroad, or by foreign persons to carry out activities in the United States. Current data improvement efforts, described later, are attempting to reduce these coverage gaps.

Inadequate coverage of "other private services," or an equivalent category, is a deficiency shared by many countries. Statistics on these transactions usually cannot be collected as a byproduct of a regulatory program, as can those on merchandise trade, and the transactions may not have been thought large enough to warrant the use of widespread surveys or extensive efforts to develop other sources of information. With the evident growth in the transactions that *are* covered, and the increasing interest in liberalizing services trade, a stronger case can now be made for efforts to improve coverage.

Coverage is a special problem in service businesses where entry and exit are relatively easy and where technology is changing rapidly. Many of the firms in such businesses are new and small, and thus are difficult to identify for purposes of conducting statistical surveys. Firms that have become extinct cannot be surveyed on their past transactions.

A similar problem applies to entertainment and sports, where often a new company is formed to organize or manage a single event or tour, after which it is dissolved. Although large sums may be involved, collection of statistics on such international business is hampered by the difficulty in identifying the entities to be surveyed.

Improving coverage of purchases of services also can be expected to be a problem as countries attempt to improve their statistics. For obvious reasons, companies need to maintain fairly detailed information on their sales and would ordinarily be able to develop the sales information needed for statistical purposes, even though the existing information may not be kept in exactly the form required. They usually do not require such detailed information on purchases of services, and may simply record them in their books on an aggregated basis under the category of "selling, general, and administrative" expenses. Also, purchases of services from foreigners may occur at irregular intervals and, for some companies, may be uncommon. In commenting upon US data improvement efforts, some of the companies that would be required to supply the data have complained that it would be burdensome to conduct extensive searches of records for purchases that they expect, but cannot verify a priori, to be small.

Recording

"Recording problems" is used here to refer to a variety of phenomena related to the way transactions are entered into economic accounts.

Generally, the problems stem either from practical considerations (e.g., data availability) or from the fact that a method of recording that may have been selected with a view to the needs of one purpose, such as balance of payments analysis, may not yield the information needed for another type of analysis, such as a broader analysis of the international aspects of services activities.

One type of recording problem is what may be called "commingled recording," which refers to situations in which related transactions cannot be separately identified because they have been commingled with other transactions. An example of commingled recording exists in the area of business travel expenses, which are usually commingled with expenses for personal travel, thus precluding the isolation of the expenses and their association with other transactions, services or otherwise, with which they may have been associated. In this example, the problem is for all practical purposes intractable, and it is presented more to indicate the limitations of data than to suggest an area in need of improvement. (Travel may combine business and pleasure, and it may be impossible to associate a given trip with its ultimate result.)

Another problem is "net recording," which refers to a situation in which debit and credit entries associated with particular transactions, or types of transactions, have been netted against one another and recorded as a single amount, rather than being recorded separately. Information on the individual debit and credit entries is thus lost.

In US data, net recording methods, where used, are being replaced as opportunities arise. Two instances where this has been done are in fee and royalty payments between parents and affiliates and in data on foreign contract operations of US firms. For fees and royalties, sample data on receipts and payments related to a given type of investment—US abroad or foreign in the United States—had been netted before being expanded to universe estimates, thus precluding the examination of receipts and payments separately. The estimation procedure has recently been changed to permit receipts and payments to be estimated separately. For contract operations, for which information has been available only on net US receipts, after deduction of foreign expenses and associated US exports, information has recently begun to be collected on the gross amounts— gross receipts, foreign expenses, and associated exports—needed to derive the net amount recorded in the balance of payments accounts.

A final class of recording problems encompasses cases in which a need to examine transactions between residents of the same country may exist. Transportation and advertising can be used to illustrate why such transactions would sometimes be of interest.

In recording transportation transactions in the balance of payments, two related conventions are generally followed. One is that the importer is assumed to pay the freight, irrespective of whether it is actually paid by the importer or the exporter.* The other is that only domestic carriers' receipts for transporting exports are recorded as exports of transportation services, and only domestic payments to foreign carriers for transportation of imports are recorded as imports of transportation services. Under these conventions, the receipts of a country's carriers from the transportation of that country's imports are not international transactions and are not recorded in the transportation accounts of the balance of payments. (Such transactions are, by the conventions, between domestic entities—the carriers and the importers.) However, information on such transactions may be needed to complete the picture of the international shipping business provided by balance of payments accounts, to permit a more thorough evaluation of the competitiveness of domestic shipping companies in the transportation of both imports and exports, and to facilitate the assessment of barriers to trade in transportation services.*

The case of advertising illustrates a problem of data collection, as well as a recording problem. The advertising agency responsible for a given campaign may perform a variety of services, ranging from preparing copy and hiring actors and models to contracting for media space and time. Although a large portion of the client's funds ultimately is used to pay for these outside services, the funds would typically pass through the agency, rather than being disbursed directly by the client. What, then, is the appropriate measure of advertising services, and who should report the data? In planning a proposed benchmark survey of services transactions with unaffiliated foreign residents (discussed later), it became obvious that, whatever the answer to the first question, the data would have to be reported by the advertising agencies alone, and not by media suppliers and

---

*For this convention to yield logically consistent results the imported goods themselves obviously must be recorded exclusive of transportation charges, even in cases where the importer actually pays a price that includes freight. The convention obviates the need to determine on a case-by-case basis who was responsible for paying the transportation charges or who held title to the goods when they were shipped. It is in accordance with reality in the sense that, ultimately, the cost of freight *is* borne by the importer.

†The IMF recommendation that the conventions be followed reflects practical considerations (data availability), prevailing practices, and a judgement that the additional information is "generally regarded as of only secondary interest *in a balance of payments context*" [emphasis added] [⁵, p. 88]. However, the IMF *Manual* does outline specifications for two alternative methods, which would provide such information, of recording transportation transactions. In general, they involve grossing up the transactions to include all those related to the international transportation of goods, and then providing offsetting entries for those assumed to be between residents of the same country. In view of the need to maintain continuity of time series and comparability among countries, a more practical alternative for meeting data needs in the short term may simply be to develop information on the latter transactions wherever possible, to be used as an adjunct to the information found in balance of payments accounts. In the US, limited sample data have been collected on both US carriers' revenue on US imports and foreign carriers' revenue on US exports, but universe estimates of such revenues have never been developed.

others who received funds channelled through the agencies. It was the agencies, and not the media suppliers, who would have had direct dealings with foreign advertisers, and the media suppliers thus might be unable to separately identify sales to foreigners.* The answer to the first question, regarding the choice of a measure of advertising services, was that two measures would be collected—gross billings and gross income of advertising agencies. The former includes all charges to clients, while the latter includes only those not representing charges for media space and time. Then it would be possible to measure the charges by the agencies for their own (and certain outside) services separately from charges for media space and time. An advertising industry association was consulted to determine that both measures would be reported.†

4. What the United States is Doing to Improve Services Data

The inadequacies of services trade data have been recognized within the US Government for some time. Several years ago, the Government commissioned two studies by private consulting groups to determine what improvements were needed. These groups examined existing data and gaps in US information on international trade in services.

One study identified official and unofficial data on US international services transactions for 16 selected service industries with an important stake in trade (Economic Consulting Services, Inc.[4]). Based on that data, the consultants attempted to estimate independently the value of US companies' foreign-source revenues for 1980. The estimates suggested that the official data substantially understated the extent of services trade. While the estimates were limited to data for only one year and were not comparable conceptually to official US statistics, they demonstrated the

---

*A related problem is determining if the work is being done for a resident affiliate of a foreign company, in which case the transaction is domestic, or directly for a foreign company. In some cases, the affiliate of a foreign company may be acting merely as a local point of contact, with the work being done for the account of the foreign parent. In other cases, the work might be done for the account of the affiliate. Determining the nature of the transaction, for whose account the work was done, and the proper method of reporting may be difficult even for the advertising agency (or other seller of services) dealing directly with the client or its representative.

†The existence of the two measures—income and billings— presents a certain ambiguity as to who had the international transaction. Was it only the advertising agency, or was it also the media suppliers? The ambiguity arises because, although the billings measure represents funds received by the agency from a foreigner, only the income measure represents funds carried through the income statement of the agency. Thus, the funds that are merely channelled through the agency (after deduction of commissions) in going from the foreign client to the domestic media suppliers are, at least from the viewpoint of the agency, more like a deposit received by a bank than like a cost of producing advertising services.

need for more comprehensive data to fully reflect US international trade in services.

The second study examined many of the conceptual problems in defining trade in services and developed a series of specific proposals for obtaining the needed data through Government surveys (Lederer *et al.*[6]). Some of the proposals dealt with ways in which balance-of-payments type data could be made more useful for non-balance-of-payments purposes and could be combined with other types of data to analyse the international services business of a country.

Studies were also conducted within the US Government. The Commerce Department's Bureau of Economic Analysis, which collects much of the US data on trade and investment in services and compiles the US balance of payments accounts, published an article analysing long-term trends in US international services transactions and presenting related data in more detail than usually published (DiLullo[3]), and a staff paper describing and evaluating available data and making suggestions for improvement (Whichard[16]). A national study on trade in services prepared by the US Government for submission to GATT also included an analysis of data needs (US Government[14], Appendix II).

These studies helped lay the groundwork for further efforts to develop more comprehensive and detailed data. As a first step in this effort, a US Government interagency task force was established in 1982 to review the existing statistics and to examine the specific needs of data users. Other functions of the task force are to: (1) help plan the development of a comprehensive data collection and reporting system, including improvements in existing data; (2) co-ordinate the work of the various US agencies with an interest in the data; (3) co-ordinate with the private sector to develop needed information and to assess the feasibility, cost, and burden of collecting the data; (4) identify technical, legal, administrative and financial problems arising from the data improvement program; and (5) recommend ways of resolving these problems.

A private sector counterpart also was established by the US Chamber of Commerce to work with the Government task force by co-ordinating the views of individual companies in various service industries on data needs and the means of obtaining the data without undue cost and burden. As noted later, other private business groups have been involved in the development and evaluation of specific data collection proposals.

Until recently, attempts to improve services data were hampered by the absence of a requirement for mandatory reporting on Government surveys of services transactions. Authority for mandatory reporting was enacted in October 1984, as a part of the Trade and Tariff Act of 1984. That act amended the International Investment Survey Act of 1976, which had provided for mandatory reporting on investment surveys. The amended

Act, which has been redesignated as the International Investment and Trade in Services Survey Act, authorizes the collection of data on trade in services, as well as investment transactions, on a mandatory basis. Mandatory reporting will result in higher response rates on surveys of services transactions, and will permit more accurate and detailed estimates of those transactions to be made.

Steps Taken

As outlined below, several steps have already been taken to improve existing data. In addition, a new survey is being planned to help fill the gap in coverage of services transactions with unaffiliated foreign persons.

Benchmark survey of US direct investment abroad.—The 1982 benchmark survey (census) of US direct investment abroad provided one of the first opportunities to respond to the demand for improved statistics on services.* Several improvements were made in the survey itself, and estimating procedures used to derive universe estimates from sample data collected in nonbenchmark years were changed to permit production of certain estimates on a gross basis that, in the past, had been available only on a net basis. The new procedures, which use the foreign affiliate rather than the published country-industry cell as the unit of estimation, also allow more flexibility in generating country or industry detail not normally published. With the new procedures, the detail that can be made available is limited only by the industry coding system and legal confidentiality requirements. The results of the survey were summarized in the December 1985 issue of the *Survey of Current Business*; some of the highlights appear later in this article in the section dealing with data availability.

In the survey itself, three types of improvements were made. First, several services industry codes for use in classifying US parents and foreign affiliates were added. Second, sales were disaggregated to show services separately from goods (see Table 2 and the accompanying discussion). Finally, questions on services transactions between parents and affiliates were redesigned to obtain more complete information.

Annual sample survey of US direct investment abroad. A new annual sample survey of US direct investment abroad was instituted in 1984 to provide data on operations in years in which a benchmark survey was not

---

*For statistical purposes, US direct investment abroad is defined as the ownership or control by a US investor of 10% or more of the voting securities of a business enterprise in another country (or the equivalent interest in an unincorporated business enterprise). Foreign direct investment in the United States is defined analogously. Although a 10% interest is used as the criterion for direct investment, the sales data shown later in the article cover only majority-owned affiliates, which perhaps are of greatest interest for policy purposes.

taken. (Benchmark surveys are usually conducted every 5 years.) This survey contained most of the improvements related to services that had been instituted in the 1982 benchmark survey (with an additional cross-classification of sales of services by affiliation of customer). Results of the first annual survey, covering 1983, were published in December 1985 (US Department of Commerce, Bureau of Economic Analysis[12]). The results are summarized in the January 1986 issue of the *Survey of Current Business*; some of the highlights appear later in this article, in the section dealing with data availability.

Survey of foreign contract operations. Beginning in 1983, the Commerce Department's annual survey of foreign contract operations of US technical and other services firms, which covers sales of services to unaffiliated parties, was expanded to permit recording the transaction on a gross basis. In addition to data previously collected on net US receipts (which met the needs of the balance of payments accounts), information is now requested on gross income or operating revenue, merchandise exports included in gross income, and foreign outlays and expenses.

Tourism and travel in-flight surveys. In the fourth quarter of 1982, the US Travel and Tourism Administration of the US Department of Commerce instituted an in-flight survey of non-US citizens departing from the United States. Collection of information from US citizens departing from the United States began in January 1983. These surveys provide estimates of total expenditures, disaggregated by type of purchase, such as lodging, transportation, meals, entertainment, and gifts. Almost all of the resulting information is sold on a subscription basis, mainly to businesses and to tourism promotion agencies of State, local and foreign governments. The data on expenditures in the United States by foreign residents will be used in compiling the balance of payments, and the expenditures abroad by US residents are being evaluated for use at a later date.

Census Bureau Surveys. In the 1982 Census of Service Industries, information was developed on sales to non-residents by four US service industries: (1) computer and data processing services; (2) management, consulting, and public relations services; (3) equipment rental and leasing services; and (4) engineering, architectural, and surveying services.

Respondents in these industries were asked if they had sales to non-residents and, if so, to estimate their share in total sales. More than 6,000 establishments reported that they had such transactions and supplied the estimated percentages. The results of the census are outlined later in this article, in the section on data availability.

The census results are currently being evaluated. Consideration is being given to continuing these questions for the four subject industries in the next census, covering 1987, and, possibly, adding them to questionnaires for additional service industries.

Further Improvements

The Bureau of Economic Analysis has proposed to conduct a benchmark survey to obtain comprehensive information on selected service transactions between US persons and unaffiliated foreign persons. This survey, which would be the first of its type conducted in the US, would obtain data on sales and purchases of a variety of services, from both goods-producing and services-producing US companies. It would cover services that are now covered by BEA through sample surveys, as well as services that are essentially outside the scope of those surveys. The results would be used both to meet the needs of trade policy and to fill gaps in the balance of payments accounts.

The experience of BEA and the user Government agencies in attempting to secure approval of this survey illustrates a major problem in data improvement efforts, namely, that of obtaining the support of the businesses that must supply the data. In the United States, proposals by Government agencies to collect data must be approved by the Office of Management and Budget (OMB) under an act known as the Paperwork Reduction Act. In the face of strong opposition to the survey from businesses, in 1985 OMB rejected the proposed survey as being excessively burdensome. Much of the opposition came from businesses that are primarily engaged in the production of goods, but sell services as a secondary activity. These companies felt that they would bear a large share of the burden of responding to the survey but, as good producers, would receive few of the benefits from efforts to liberalize services trade. Because of the demonstrated need for data improvement, as well as the legal requirement for the survey, which is mandated by the International Investment and Trade in Services Survey Act, efforts are being made to revise the survey forms. Business groups, including the Business Advisory Council on Federal Reports and the Financial Executives Institute, are now being consulted with a view to developing a less burdensome survey that will gain OMB approval, while still providing useful information for trade policy needs and for improving the balance of payments account.

Even if the above survey is approved, much work will remain particularly in the areas of financial and transportation services. Current surveys of the financial sector tend to focus on capital transactions, which in turn are used in the estimation of receipts and payments of factor income. Little information is available, however, on the nonfactor service income of banks and other financial institutions. In transportation, the need is for development of universe estimates of transactions that, while involving the transport of goods among countries, are excluded from balance of payments accounts because they are between residents of the same countries. In addition, renewed attention needs to be devoted to services purchased by foreign students, medical patients, and other visitors. Obviously, these and other data improvements cannot be made all at once, but rather will require review, planning, and action over a protracted period. They will also require close consultation and co-operation with businesses and others who must supply the data.

5. Available US Data

Tables 1 and 2 summarize available US data on trade in services. Table 1 shows, for 1970–85, private services transactions as recorded in the current account of the US balance of payments, while Table 2 shows, for 1982–83, sales of services by US parent companies and their foreign affiliates. Table 3 shows data on sales of services to nonresidents in the four industries for which questions had been added to the 1982 Census of Services Industries conducted by the US Bureau of the Census.

In addition to these data developed by US Government statistical agencies, estimates of the services transactions of selected industries have also been developed from time to time by others in and out of government. For example, the study by Economic Consulting Services, Inc., cited earlier, estimated using a variety of sources of information, the "international commercial stake" of the United States in 16 selected services industries art approximately $60 billion in 1980 [4, p. xviii]. A study by the US International Trade Commission estimated, based on its own survey, the "foreign revenue generated by 14 US services industries operating overseas" to be about $90 billion in that same year [15, p. 2]. Both figures include some sale by foreign affiliates, as well as direct exports from the United States. Although these measures are not conceptually identical to

Table 3. *Sales of Services to Nonresidents of the US, Selected Service Industries, 1982*

[Millions of dollars]

Computer and data processing	317
Management, consulting, and public relations	504
Equipment rental and leasing	210
Engineering, architectural, and surveying services	1,433
Total	2,464

Source: US Department of Commerce, Bureau of the Census

Note: The figures in this table were derived by multiplying receipts of establishments reporting sales to nonresidents by the reported percentage of receipts accounted for by such sales.

those found in official US statistics, both studies have been taken to suggest that the official statistics understate the actual value of US services exports.

Balance of Payments Data

In Table 1, five categories of private service transactions are shown as recorded in the US balance of payments accounts—travel, passenger fares, "other" transportation, fees and royalties, and "other private services." Income on investment is not shown.* Although, in view of the coverage and recording problems noted earlier, these statistics should be used and interpreted with care, it is clear that both US exports and US imports of services have grown substantially over the period in question. The total of exports for the five categories grew from $9.6 billion in 1970 to $45.1 billion in 1985.† For imports, the growth was from $9.1 billion in 1970 to $44.9 billion in 1985. Although the United States had an export surplus on these transactions in each year, the surplus was quite small—only $0.2 billion—at the end of the period. At that time, surpluses in "fees and royalties" and "other private services" were roughly offset by deficits on travel, passenger fares, and "other transportation".

Throughout the period, the transaction recorded under travel and "other transportation" were by far the largest for both exports and imports. It should be noted, however, that two of the remaining categories, fees and royalties and "other private services," suffer from less than complete coverage and include some data that are recorded on a net basis. If the universe of transactions was completely covered by the statistical reporting system, and all transactions were recorded on a gross basis, the travel and transportation categories probably would not occupy so dominant a position in services trade as is indicated by the table, although they still might be the largest. Although not shown here, additional country detail is available.

Foreign Affiliate Sales Data

Table 2 shows data on sales of goods and services by nonbank US parent

---

*With the exclusion of investment income, the table is essentially restricted to private nonfactor services. However, the "other private services" category does contain relatively minor amounts related to US workers employed abroad and foreign workers employed in the United States. Also, as noted elsewhere, the fees and royalties category has some elements in common with factor income.

†The table also strikes totals for categories other than fees and royalties, in recognition of the characteristics this item shares in common with factor income. These totals are somewhat smaller than, but move in a manner similar to, those for the total of all five categories.

companies and their majority-owned nonbank foreign affiliates.* Although total sales of services were much larger for US parents than for their majority-owned foreign affiliates ($552 billion compared to $68 billion in 1983), sales of services abroad by the affiliates were much larger than sales made directly by the parents to foreign persons ($59 billion compared to $16 billion). Thus, for US companies that have foreign affiliates (this group would include virtually all of the largest US companies), a very strong tendency to deliver services abroad through affiliates is evident, perhaps reflecting the need for a local presence discussed earlier. Of the $16 billion in direct sales abroad by US parent companies, $4 billion was to foreign affiliates and $12 billion was to unaffiliated foreign persons. The sales abroad by foreign affiliates were also largely to unaffiliated persons ($49 billion out of $59 billion); however, their sales to US persons were largely accounted for by sales to their parents [$7 billion out of $9 billion].[16]

Of the $68 billion of sales of services by affiliates in 1983, about one-third ($24 billion), was by affiliates in financial services other than banking, including insurance ($13 billion). Another large amount ($11 billion) was by those in petroleum, including oil and gas field services ($7 billion). Affiliates in the manufacturing sector sold over $5 billion of services, mainly affiliates in computer and other machinery manufacturing ($4 billion). Affiliates in business services had sales of services of $8 billion, of which $815 million were accounted for by those in computer and data processing services.

Most sales of services by affiliates originated in developed countries ($42 billion, about 60% of the total), with affiliates in European countries accounting for $25 billion; Canada $12 billion; Australia, $3 billion; and Japan, $2 billion. Most of the sales by affiliates in developing countries ($19 billion) originated in Latin America ($13 billion).

Growth in sales in 1983 was greater for services than for goods. For parents, the rate of increase was 3.6% for services and 1.9% for goods;

---

*Sales of minority-owned affiliates are also available in the aggregate, but not disaggregated between goods and services. The data in the table are from the 1982 benchmark survey and 1983 sample survey of US direct investment abroad (US Department of Commerce, Bureau of Economic Analysis,[11] and [12]. The publications containing detailed survey results show the data in Table 1 disaggregated by industry of parent or affiliate and by country of affiliate. The definition of services used in the survey instructions is given in a note to the table.

In the table, and in the surveys from which the data were obtained, affiliation is defined with respect to a given multinational corporation, not with respect to the country of the parent. Thus, sales by affiliates to unaffiliated foreign persons would include sales to foreign affiliates of other US companies. Information needed to quantify such sales is unavailable, but it appears fairly common for a US parent company to arrange for another US company to provide services to its (the parent's) foreign affiliates. Often, the services would be performed by a foreign affiliate. The transactions between foreign affiliate would be "unaffiliated" transactions because the affiliates had different US parents.

however, their sales of services to foreign persons declined by 5.9%. For majority-owned foreign affiliates, sales of services grew 2.3%, compared with a 2.7% decline in sales of goods. For sales by these affiliates to foreign persons, services grew 0.7%, compared with a 3.5% decline for goods.

The figures shown in Table 1 on services exports directly from the US can be added to, and compared with, the figures shown in Table 2 on sales to foreigners by majority-owned foreign affiliates to give an idea of the total US sales of services to foreigners, whether directly or through majority-owned affiliates.* The resulting sum for 1983, the latest year for which the affiliate data are available, is $104 billion, and consists of $45 billion of direct exports from the US and $59 billion of sales abroad by majority-owned foreign affiliates. As can be seen from the above dicussion, the composition of the two types of sales is quite different. The sales included as exports in the balance of payments accounts are heavily concentrated in travel and transportation, whereas the sales of affiliates are distibuted among a variety of industries. Various other totals could be struck using these data and the more detailed estimates that underline them. (For example, fees and royalties could be included or excluded, as could transactions between affiliated parties.)

Census Survey Data

Table 3 summarizes data derived from the 1982 Census of Service Industries on sales to non-residents by four US service industries. The survey shows that these industries sold at least $2.5 billion of services to non-residents in 1982. Of the four industries, the largest volume of sales to non-residents was reported by the engineering, architectural, and surveying industry, close to 60% of the total ($1.4 billion). The management, consulting, and public relations industry reported receipts of $0.5 billion; computer and data processing, $0.2 billion; and equipment rental and leasing, $0.2 billion. Collectively, these receipts represented about 3% of total receipts reported by these service industries. They included, but did not distinguish between, receipts from both affiliated and unaffiliated parties.

These data are subject to a number of limitations. One is that they do not include separate values for individual countries involved in these transactions. Another is that they may understate the value of the

---

*There is no commonly accepted term for what is here called "US sales." It would be misleading to refer to the sum as "US exports," since most of the value added associated with affiliate sales occurs abroad, and these transactions do not enter the balance of payments accounts. Because of the fundamental difference in the impact of the two types of transactions on the selling and purchasing economies, it is probably best that the sum always be presented side by side with its two components.

transactions to the extent that establishments classified in other industries provide these services as a secondary activity. For example, sales of data processing services by establishments classified in banking or manufacturing industries are not included in these data, although many of the largest providers of data processing services are primarily engaged in other activities. Finally, the data cover only a very small number of services sectors.

6. International comparability

The United States and other countries report balance-of-payments data to the International Monetary Fund. The IMF *Balance of Payments Manual*[5] provides guidelines and definitions to facilitate international comparability of the reported data. The IMF converts data reported in local currencies into a common unit—Special Drawing Rights. Data published by the IMF, however, do not show separately the value of trade in individual service industries, and the IMF *Manual* does not provide a detailed system of classification for services.

As countries seek to develop more comprehensive and refined data on international trade in services, the need to attain international comparability of data is bound to be recognized. Comparability problems already exist because of the vast amount of economic activity covered by balance-of-payments data, the complicated nature of modern business transactions, and the multiplicity of sources of information available and methods of compilation used in different countries. Co-operation and exchange of information among countries are needed to assure the maximum international comparability of statistics. A review of data availability is currently being conducted by a working party of the Trade Committee of the Organization of Economic Co-operation and Development. This group has assembled data of member countries and prepared a paper presenting the data in such a way that the availability and comparability of the data can be more readily ascertained[7]. Other international organizations also are examining the problems involved in compiling data on services trade. (See, for example, GATT[2] and UNCTAD[10].)

7. Conclusion

No country or international organization compiles data in a manner that fully and accurately measures services trade activities and disaggregates the data to reflect the activities in finely drawn services sectors. Considerable work by individual countries and by international organizations lies ahead in developing the methodology and data collection systems and techniques for improving the services data base.

Multilateral discussion and resolution of most of the important conceptual trade issues in services can proceed on the basis of statistical information currently available. Consideration of issues in specific services sectors, however, will require more refined statistics and greater degree of international comparability. While statistics on services trade may never reach the specificity and precision available for merchandise trade, significant improvement is attainable and, with the attention being given to the issue, some improvement seems inevitable. Indeed, as previously noted, several improvements already have been made.

Efforts in the US will continue in pursuit of more comprehensive and detailed coverage of international service transactions. Among the numerous improvements needed, perhaps the most crucial are: determining, by sector, how trade in services should be measured, and developing the necessary intelligence and strategy for surveying the appropriate universe or samples of services transactions. To establish a more useful and meaningful body of data for services trade, co-operation between the Government and the private sector, which must report the data, is essential.

During the process of developing an improved body of statistical information on services trade, it is imperative that the US and other countries exchange information and ideas, so that a greater degree of international comparability can be achieved.

References

1. "Annual Report of the President of the United States on the Trade Agreements Program, 1984–85," 28th edition.
2. Contracting Parties to the General Agreement on Tariffs and Trade. *Services: Analytical Summary of Information Exchanged Among Contracting Parties*, MDF/7/Rev. 1, September 16, 1985.
3. DiLullo, Anthony J. "Service Transactions in the U.S. International Accounts, 1970–80," *Survey of Current Business*, 61 (November 1981). 29–46.
4. Economic Consulting Services, Inc. *The International Operations of U.S. Service Industries: Current Data Collection and Analysis*. Report prepared for the US Departments of State and Commerce and the Office of the US Trade Representative. 1981.
5. International Monetary Fund. *Balance of Payments Manual*. 4th ed. 1977.
6. Lederer, Evelyn Parrish; Lederer, Walther; and Sammons, Robert L. *International Services Transactions of the United States: Proposals for Improvement in Data Collection*. Report prepared for the US Departments of State and Commerce and the Office of the US Trade Representative. 1982.
7. Organisation for Economic Co-operation and Development, Working Party of the Trade Committee, "Statistics on Trade in Services: Availability and Work in Progress," TC/WP (84)54(1st rev.), June 13, 1985.
8. Sapir, André, "Trade in Services: Policy Issues for the Eighties," *Columbia Journal of World Business*, Fall 1982. 77–83.
9. Shelp, Ronald K. *Beyond Industrialization: Ascendancy of the Global Service Economy*. Praeger, New York, 1981.

10. United Nations Conference on Trade and Development. *Services and the Development Process*, TD/B/1008, Annex I, August 1, 1984.
11. US Department of Commerce. Bureau of Economic Analysis. *US Direct Investment Abroad: 1982 Benchmark Survey Data.* US Government Printing Office, Washington, D.C. 1985.
12. US Department of Commerce. *U.S. Direct Investment Abroad: Operations of U.S. Parent Companies and Their Foreign Affiliates, Preliminary 1983 Estimates*. 1985.
13. US Department of Commerce. International Trade Administration. *1986 US Industrial Outlook*, January 1986.
14. US Government. *US National Study on Trade in Services*. Prepared under the direction of the Office of the US Trade Representative. 1983.
15. US International Trade Commission. *The Relationship of Exports in Selected U.S. Service Industries to U.S. Merchandise Exports*, USITC Publication 1290, September 1982.
16. Whichard, Obie G. *US International Trade and Investment in Services: Data Needs and Availability*. US Department of Commerce, Bureau of Economic Analysis. Staff Paper 41. 1984.

12

Bibliography Related to Services

RAYMOND KROMMENACKER and JEAN REMY ROULET

Bibliography

1. Selected Articles

Atinc, A. *et al.* (1984) International Transactions in Services and Economic Development. *Trade and Development*, No. 5 pages 141–214.

Baumol, W. J. (1985) Productivity Policy and the Service Sector, in: Inman R. P., ed., *Managing the Service Economy, Prospects and Problems*. Cambridge University Press, pages 301–318.

Benz, S. (1985) Trade Liberalization and the Global Service Economy. *Journal of World Trade Law*, March-April, pages 95–120.

Bhagwati, J. N. (1984) Splintering and Disembodiment of Services and Developing Nations. *World Economy*, June, pages 133–144.

Black, F. (1985) The Future for Financial Services, in: Inman, R. P., ed., *Managing the Service Economy, Prospects and Problems*. Cambridge University Press, pages 223–230.

Brock, W. E. (1982) A Simple Plan for Negotiation on Trade in Services. *World Economy*, Vol. 5, No. 3, November, pages 229–240.

Boehme, H. (1983) Current Issues and Progress in European Shipping Policy. *World Economy*, Vol. 6, No. 3, September, pages 325–352.

Broclawski, J.-P., de Gaulle, Y. and Miermont, A. (1981) De Bons Résultats pour l'Economie Française: Les Echanges de Services. *Paris, Economie, Previsions Statistiques et Etudes Financières*, No. 49, April, pages 25–48.

Canton, I. D. (1984) Learning to Love the Service Economy. *Harvard Business Review*, May-June, pages 89–97.

Cohen, M. and Morante, T. (1981) Elimination of Non-Tariff Barriers to Trade in Services: Recommendations for Future Negotiations. *Law and Policy in International Business*, Vol. 13, No. 2, 1981, pages 495–519.

Diebold, W. Jr. and Stalson, H. (1983) Negotiating Issues in International Service Transactions, in: Cline, W. R., ed., *Trade Policy for the 1980s*. Washington D. C., Institute for International Economics.

Eken, S. (1985) Integration of Domestic and International Financial Markets: The Japanese Experience. *World Bank Staff Paper*, March, pages 499–548.

Ewing, A. F., (1985) Why Freer Trade in Services is in the interest of developing countries? *Journal of World Trade Law*, Vol. 19, No. 2, March-April, pages 147–169.

Feketekuty, G. and Aronson, J. D. (1984) Meeting the Challenges of the World Information Economy. *World Economy*, Vol. 7, No. 1, March, pages 63–86.

Feketekuty, G. and Hauser, K. (1985) The Impact of Information Technology on Trade in Services. *Transnational Data Report*, Vol. 8, No. 4, pages 220–224.

Feketekuty, G. (1986) Trade in Professional Services: A Trade Policy Perspective, in: *Barriers to International Trade in Professional Services*. University of Chicago Legal Forum, Vol. 1, Summer.

Fuchs, V. R. (1985) An Agenda for Research on the Service Sector, in: Inman, R. P., ed., *Managing the Service Economy, Prospects and Problems.* Cambridge University Press, pages 319–326.

Giarini, O. (1981) Some Considerations in the Activity of Insurance Business and Its Relevance for a General Reassessment of Economic Theory, in: *The Geneva Papers on Risk and Insurance.* Geneva, Vol. 6, No. 21, October pages 44–103.

Giarini, O. (1984) The Notion of Economic Value in Post-Industrial Society, in: *Cycles, Value and Employment.* Oxford, Pergamon Press, 43 pages.

Giarini, O. (1985) The Consequences of Complexity in Economics: the Vulnerability, Risk and Rigidity Factors in Supply, in: *The Theory and Practice of Complexity.* Tokyo, The United Nations University, pages 133–145.

Gibbs, M. (1985) Continuing the International Debate on Services. *Journal of World Trade Law*, Vol. 19, No. 3, May-June, pages 199–218.

Gramlich, E. M. (1985) Government Services, in: Inman, R. P., ed., *Managing the Service Economy, Prospects and Problems.* Cambridge University Press, pages 273–289.

Gray, P. H. (1983) A Negotiating Strategy for Trade in Services. *Journal of World Trade Law*, Vol. 17, No. 5, September–October, pages 377–388.

Hindley, B. and Smith, A. (1984) Comparative Advantage and Trade in Services. *World Economy*, Vol. 7, No. 4, December (1985) pages 369–389.

Holmstrom, B. (1985) The Provision of Services in a Market Economy in: Inman, R. P., ed., *Managing the Service Economy, Prospects and Problems.* Cambridge University Press, pages 183–213.

Jussawalla, M. (1985) Constraints on Economic Analysis of Transborder Data Flows, *Media, Culture and Society*, Vol. 7, No. 3, Sage, London, pages 297–312.

Kane, E. J. (1984) Technological and Regulatory Forces in the Developing Fusion of Financial Services Competition, in: *Journal of Finance*, Vol. 39, No. 3, July, pages 759–806.

Karunaratne, N. D. (1985) The Information Revolution, Australia and the Developing Neighbours. *Economia Internazionale*, March, Vol. 38, No. 2, pages 179–196.

Kendrick, J. W. (1985) Measurement of Output and Productivity in the Service Sector, in: Inman, R. P., ed., *Managing the Service Economy, Prospects and Problems.* Cambridge University Press, pages 111–123.

Kravis, I. B. (1985) Services in World Transactions in: Inman, R. P., ed., *Managing the Service Economy, Prospects and Problems.* Cambridge University Press, pages 135–161.

Krommenacker, R. (1979) Trade-Related Services and the GATT. *Journal of World Trade Law*, Vol. 13, No. 6, November, pages 510–522.

Krommenacker, R. (1986) Services, Their Regulatory and Policy Framework in the Light of the Emerging Integrated Services Digital Networks (ISDN), in: *Proceedings of the Pacific Telecommunications Conference*, Honolulu, January, (1986).

Krommenacker, R. (1986) Discussions on Services in GATT. *Transnational Data and Communications Report*, February, pages 15–16.

Krommenacker, R. (1986) The Impact of Information Technology on Trade Interdependence, in: *Journal of World Trade Law*, Vol. 20, No. 4, July–August, pages 381–400.

Lanvin, B. and Prieto, F. (1986) Les Services, Clé du Développement Economique? *Revue Tiers Monde*, Vol. 27, No. 105, January-March, pages 97–108.

Legris, P. and Jegon, A. (1983) La Contribution des Services à l'Equilibre Extérieur: Le Cas Français et quelques exemples étrangers. *Banque*, March, No. 426, pages 323–340.

Leveson, I. (1985) Services in the U.S. Economy, in: Inman, R. P., ed., *Managing the Service Economy, Prospects and Problems.* Cambridge University Press, pages 89–102.

Lowenfield, A. (1986) GATT Principles and an Agreement on Services, in: *Barriers to International Trade in Professional Services.* University of Chicago Legal Forum, Vol. 1, Summer.

Madec, A. (1981) Aspects Économiques et Juridiques des Flux Transfrontières des Données, *Problèmes Economiques et Sociaux*, January, pages 5–16.

Malmgren, H. B. (1985) Negotiating International Rules for Trade in Services. *World Economy*, Vol. 8, No. 1, March, pages 11–26.

Momigliano, F. and Siniscalco, O. (1983) The Growth of Service Employment: A Reappraisal. *Banca Nazionale del Lavoro, Quarterly Review*, No. 142, September.

Nusbaumer, J. (1983) Some Implications of Becoming a Services Economy, in: *Communication Regulation and International Business*, J. Rada and G. Russel Pipe, eds. Amsterdam, North-Holland, pages 23–37.

Nusbaumer, J. (1985) L'Economie des Services: Nouvelle Donne de l'Economie, in: *Le Secteur des Services: Quel Avenir pour le Luxembourg?* N. von Kunitzki, ed., Luxembourg, Institut Universitaire International, pages 13–27.

Nusbaumer, J. (1985) Services and the International Economic Agenda. *International* Geneva, Graduate Institute of International Studies, pages 100–106.

Nusbaumer, J. (1986) Services in the International Economy: Issues and Prospects. (Forthcoming, J. Rada, ed., North-Holland).

Nusbaumer, J. (1986) Services in the World Economy: the Issues, in: *Kuelgazdasag*, pages 3–10 (*Hungarian Economic Journal* — in Hungarian)

Porter, M. E. and Millar, V. E. (1985) How Information gives you Competitive Advantage. *Harvard Business Review*, July-August, No. 4, pages 149–160.

Rada, J. (1984) Advanced Technologies and Development: Are Conventional Ideas about Comparative Advantage Obsolete? Geneva, *Trade and Development*, No. 5.

Reboud, L. (1984) L'Importance Economique des Services, in: *Le Marché Commun des Services*. Grenoble, Centre Universitaire de Recherche Européenne et Internationale, 1 March, pages 3–35.

Reboud, L. (1985) Signification d'un Marché Commun dans le Domaine des Services au Regard de la Libéralisation des Echanges et du Protectionnisme, in: *Le Protectionnisme*, Lassudrie-Duchêne, B. and Reiffers, J.-L., eds. Paris, Economica, pages 335–346.

Ruyssen, O. (1985) Les Services à Marée Montante, in: Lesournes, J. and Godet, M., eds., *La Fin des Habitudes*. Paris, Seghers, pages 326–347.

Sampson, G. P. and Snape, R. H. (1985) Identifying the Issues in Trade in Services. *World Economy*, Vol. 8, No. 2, June, pages 171–182.

Sapir, A. (1982) Trade in Services: Policy Issues for the Eighties. *Columbia Journal of World Business*, Fall, pages 77–83.

Sapir, A. (1983) North-South Issues in Trade in Services. *World Economy*, Vol. 8, No. 1, March, pages 27–42.

Satterthwaite, M. A. (1985) Competitiveness and Equilibrium as a Driving Force in the Health Services Sector, in: Inman, R. P., ed., *Managing the Service Economy, Prospects and Problems,* Cambridge University Press, pages 239–267.

Schott, J. J. (1983) Protectionist Threat to Trade and Investment in Services. *World Economy*, Vol. 6, No. 2, June, pages 195–214.

Schrier, E., Nadel, E. and Rifas, B. (1984) Forces Shaping International Maritime Transport. *World Economy*, Vol. 7, No. 1, March, pages 87–102.

Schultz, S. (1984) Trade in Services: Its Treatment in International Forums and the Problems Ahead. *Intereconomics,* November-December, pages 267–273.

Self, R. (1982) The Importance of Trade in Services. *Economic Impact*, No. 2.

Semkow, B. W. (1985) Japanese Banking Law: Current Deregulation and Liberalization of Domestic and External Financial Transaction. *Law and Policy in International Business*, Vol. 17, pages 81–155.

Shapiro, I. (1986) Opportunities for U.S. Lawyers in Asia, in: *Barriers to International Trade in Professional Services*. University of Chicago Legal Forum, Vol. 1, Summer.

Stalton, H. (1985) U.S. Trade Policy and International Service Transactions, in: Inman, R. P., ed., *Managing the Service Economy, Prospects and Problems*. Cambridge University Press, pages 161–178.

Summers, R. (1985) Services in the International Economy, in: Inman, R. P., ed., *Managing the Service Economy, Prospects and Problems*. Cambridge University Press, pages 27–48.

Thomas, D. R. E. (1978) Strategy is Different in Service Business. *Harvard Business Review*, July-August, pages 158–165.

Trigano, G. (1983) Une Multinationale des Loisirs, in: Cotta, A. and Ghertman, M., eds., *Les Multinationales en Mutation*. Paris, Presses Universitaires de France, pages 133–140.

286   R. Krommenacker and J. R. Roulet

2. Selected Books and Studies

Albrecht, K. and Zemke, R. (1985) *Service America, Doing Business in the New Economy*. Homewood IL, Dow Jones Irwin.
Allen, F. (1984) *Reputation and Services*. Wharton School, University of Pennsylvania, Discussion Paper No. 3, November.
Aronson, J. D. and Cowhey, P. F. (1984) *Computer, Data Processing and Communication Services*. Ann Arbor, University of Michigan, Research Seminar in International Economics, October, 27 p.
Aronson, J. D. and Cowhey, P. F. (1984) *Trade in Services: a Case for Open Markets*. Washington D. C., American Enterprise Institute for Public Policy Research, 46 p.
Aronson, J. D. (1986) *Trade in Services, An Agenda for International Trade Negotiations*. Washington D. C., mimeograph, February, 10 p.
de Bandt, J. *et al.*, (1985) *La Productivité dans les Services*. Paris, Ministère de la recherche et de la Technologie, November, (1985).
de Bandt, J., ed. (1985) *Les Services dans les Sociétés Industrielles*, Paris, Economica.
Bannon, M. and Blair, S. (1985) *Services Activities, The Information Economy and the Role of Regional Center*. Dublin, University College, January, 173 p.
Bavishi, V. B. and Wyman, H. E. (1983) *Who Audits the World: Trends in the World Accounting Profession*. Storrs, Conn., Center for Transnational Accounting of Connecticut School of Business Administration, 1109 p.
Beca, R. (1985) *Les Flux de Données d'Accompagnement du Commerce International; Elements pour une Négotiation Internationale*. Paris, Ministère du Développement Industriel et du Commerce Extérieur, 11 p.
Boehme, H. (1978) *Restraints on Competition in World Shipping*. London, Trade Policy Research Centre, 86 p.
Brender, A., Chevallier, A. and Pisani-Ferry, J. (1980) *Etats-Unis: Croissance, crise, changement technique dans une économie tertiare*. Paris, Centre d'Etudes Prospectives et d'Informations Internationales.
Bressand, A. (1985) *Le Prochain Monde*. Paris, Seuil, 316 p.
Bressand, A. (1985) *Services in the New Worldeconomy. In search of a Conceptual Framework*. Hannover, International Symposium on the Services Sector, 12–13 May, 12 p.
Bressand, A. (1986) *Services, Corporate Strategies and GATT Negotiations: A New Challenge for Europe*. Ditchley Park Conference, 14–16 February, 21 p.
Brochand, B. and Lendrevie, J. (1983) *Le publicitor*. Paris, Dalloz, 1983, 568 p.
Bulthuis, R., van Holst, B. and de Wit, G. R. (1985) *The Service Sector and Technological Developments*. Rotterdam, The Netherlands Economics Institute Foundation, April.
Carter, R. L. and Dickinson, G. M. (1979) *Barriers to Trade in Insurance*. London Trade Policy Research Centre, 84 p.
Chamoux, J.-P. (1980) *L'Information sans Frontière*. Paris, Documentation Françaies, 179 p.
Channon, D. F. (1978) *The Service Industries: Strategy, Structure and Financial Performance*. London, MacMillan, 292 p.
Chant, J. F. (1984) *The Canadian Treatment of Foreign Banks: A Case Study in the Workings of the National Treatment Approach*. Ann Arbor, University of Michigan, Research Seminar in International Economics, October, 44 p.
Clark, M. G. (1986) *Services and the General Agreement on Tariffs and Trade*. Discussion Paper Commissioned by the International Economics Programme of the Institute for Research on Public Policy, Ottawa, January, 40 p.
Deardorff, A. V. (1984) *Comparative Advantage and International Trade and Investment in Services*. Ann Arbor, University of Michigan, Research Seminar on International Economics, 7 November, 35 p.
Dobell, R., McRae, J. J. and Desbois, M. (1986) *The Service Sector in Canadian Economy: Government Policies for Future Developments*. Halifax, Institute for Research on Public Policy.
Dwyer, D. F. Jr. (1984) *Trade Barriers to United States Motion Picture and Television Pre-Recorded Entertainment, Publishing and Advertising*. New York, CBS Inc., September, 33 p.

Eward, R. (1985) *The Deregulation of International Telecommunications.* Dedham, MA., Artech, 400 p.

Faulhaber, G. R., Noam, E. and Tasley, R., eds. (1986) *The Impact of Information Technology on the Service Sector.* Ballinger Co., 1986.

Feketekuty, G. (1984) *Negotiating Strategies for Liberalizing Trade and Investment in Services.* Ann Arbor, University of Michigan, Research Seminar on International Economics, October, 17 p.

Findlay, C. C. (1983) *Australian International Civil Aviation Policy and the ASEAN — Australia Dispute.* ASEAN-Australia Joint Research Project, Kuala Lumpur and Canberra, 61 p.

Findlay, C. C. (1985) *A Framework for Services Trade Policy Questions.* Canberra, Australia-Japan Research Centre, Research Paper No. 16, 54 p.

Fitzpatrik, J. (1985) *Technology and Economic Development: The Role of Private Services.* Dublin, Regional Studies Association, March.

Freeman, H. (1985) *Potential of the Services Sector in Job Creation.* Hannover, International Symposium on the Services Sector, 12–15 May, 32 p.

Fuchs, V. R. (1964) *Productivity Trends in the Goods and Services Sectors 1929–1961: A Preliminary Survey.* Study No. 89, New York, National Bureau of Economic Research, 42 p.

Fuchs, V. R. (1968) *The Services Economy.* New York, National Bureau of Economic Research, 280 p.

Fuchs, V. R. (1969) *Production and Productivity in the Service Industries.* New York, Columbia University Press, 395 p.

Fuchs, V. T. (1980) *Economic Growth and the Rise of Service Employment.* New York, National Bureau of Economic Research, 30 p.

Gershuny, J. and Miles, I. (1983) *The New Service Economy: The Transformation of Employment in Industrial Societies.* London, Frances Pinter, 283 p.

Giarini, O. *The Limits to Certainty-Facing Risks in the New Service Economy.* (Forthcoming)

Grey, R. de (1983) *Trade Computer Services.* Montreal, Royal Bank of Canada, Mimeograph.

Grey, R. de (1984) *Negotiating About Trade and Investment in Services.* Ann Arbor, University of Michigan, Research Seminar in International Economics, October 17 p.

Grey, R. de (1986) *A Not-So-Simple Plan for Negotiating on Trade in Services.* London, mimeograph, 20 p.

Griffiths, B. (1975) *Invisible Barriers to Invisible Trade.* London, MacMillan, 178 p.

Herman, B. and van Holst, B. (1985) *International Trade in Services: Some Theoretical and Practical Problems.* Rotterdam, Netherlands Economic Institute, September 32 p.

Hindley, G. (1982) *Economic Analysis and Insurance Policy in the Third World.* London, Trade Policy Research Centre, 62 p.

Inman, R., ed. (1986) *Managing the Service Economy: Prospects and Problems.* Cambridge, Cambridge University Press, 336 p.

Kierzkowski, H. (1984) *Services in Development Process and Theory of International Trade.* Geneva, Graduate Institute of International Studies, June, 40 p.

Kravis, I. B. (1983) *Services in the Domestic Economy and in World Transactions.* University of Pennsylvania, National Bureau of Economic Research Working Paper, No. 1124, May (1984) 39 p.

Krommenacker, R. J. (1975) *Les Nations Unies et l'Assurance-Réassurance.* Paris, Librairie Générale de Droit et de Jurisprudence, 215 p.

Krommenacker, R. J. (1984) *World-Traded Services: The Challenge for the Eighties.* Dedham, MA., Artech House, 1984, 222 p.

Langdale, J. V. (1984) *Information Services in Australia and Singapore.* ASEAN-Australia Joint Research Project, Kuala Lumpur and Canberra, 37 p.

Larrera de Morel, B. and Dubarry, J.-P. (1981) *Le Tertiaire Exposé: Situation et Perspectives des Echanges Invisibles.* Paris, Documentation Française, 109 p.

Leveson, I. (1985) *The Service Economy in Economic Development.* New York, Hudson Strategy Group Inc., 10 p.

288   R. Krommenacker and J. R. Roulet

MacDonald, S. and Mandeville, T. (1984) *Telecommunications in ASEAN and Australia.* ASEAN-Australia Joint Research Project, Kuala Lumpur and Canberra, 32 p.

Malka, B. and Prin, E. (1985) *Du Secteur Tertiaire à l'Economie des Services: Une Bibliographie Internationale de 1979 à nos Jours.* Paris, Centre National de la Recherche Scientifique, 374 p.

Martinez, L. (1985) *Communications Satellites: Power Politics in Space.* Dedham, MA., Artech, 320 p.

Nayyar, D. (1986) *International Trade in Services, Implications for Developing Countries.* New Dehli, Export-Import Bank of India, 33 p.

Nora, S. and Minc, A. (1978) *L'Informatisation de la Société.* Paris, Documentation Française, 152 p.

Nusbaumer, J. (1986) *Les Services: Nouvelle Donne de l'Economie.* Paris, Economica, 1984, 142 p. English version forthcoming: *Services, the New Deal.* Boston, Kluwer-Nijhoff.

Oulton, N. (1983) *International Trade in Services and the Comparative Advantage of EC Countries.* Ditchley Park, Trade Policy Research Centre Meeting, April, mimeograph.

Philipps, A. and Berlin, M. (1985) *Technology and Financial Services: Regulatory Problems in a Deregulatory Environment.* Wharton School, University of Pennsylvania, Discussion Paper.

Riddle, D. I. *Services-Led Growth: The Role of the Service Sector in World Development.* New York, Praeger, 290 p.

Rimmer, P. J. (1984) *Consulting Services: Supply to South-East Asia from Australia.* ASEAN-Australia Joint Research Project, Kuala Lumpur and Canberra, 92 p.

Rosenfield, S. B. (1984) *The Regulation of International Commercial Aviation.* Dobbs Ferry N. Y., Oceana Publications.

Rutkowsky, A. (1985) *Integrated Services Digital Networks.* Dedham, MA., Artech, 300 p.

Sapir, A. and Lutz, E. (1981) *Trade in Services: Economic Determinants and Development-Related Issues.* World Bank, Staff Working Paper, No. 480, 38 p.

Sapir, A. and Lutz, E. (1980) *Trade in Non-Factor Services: Past Trends and Current Issues.* World Bank. Staff Working Paper, No. 410, 137 p.

Sauvant, K. P. (1986) *The International Transactions in Services.* Westview Press, Boulder, CO., 224 p.

Sauvant, K. P. (1986) *Trade and Foreign Direct Investment in Data Services.* Westview Press, Boulder, CO., 220 p.

Saxonhouse, G. R. (1983) *Services in the Japanese Economy.* Ann Arbor, University of Michigan, Research Seminar in International Economics, Paper No. 129, December, 50 p.

Schaumburg-Mueller, H. (1983) *A Study of Trade in Services; Some Theoretical Considerations and Trends in Denmark's Trade in Services in the 1970's.* Copenhagen, School of Economics and Business Administration.

Shelp, R. K. (1981) *Beyond Industrialization.* New York, Praeger, 234 p.

Shelp, R., Stephenson, J. C., Truitt, N. S. and Wasow, B. (1984) *Service Industries and Economic Development: Case Studies in Technology.* New York, Praeger, 150 p.

Shelp, R. K. (1985) *Entrepreneurship in the Information Society.* Washington, D.C., Conference on Entrepreneurship in the American Economy, Heritage Foundation, 16 April 17 p.

Spero, J. E. (1985) *International Trade and the Information Revolution.* Cambridge, Harvard University, Center for Information Policy Research, 17 p.

Stern, R. M. (1984) *Global Dimensions and Determinants of International Trade and Investment in Services.* Ann Arbor, University of Michigan, Research Seminar in International Economics, October 43 p.

Sternlieb, G. and Hughes, J. (1985) *A Note on Information Technology, Demographics and the Retail Response.* Wharton School, University of Pennsylvania, Discussion Paper, No. 9, June.

Tanaka, K. (1986) *On the Criticism of Japan's Distribution Mechanisms.* Tokyo, Keidanren, January, 22 p.

Tisdell, C. (1984) *Tourism, the Environment, International Trade and Public Economics.* ASEAN-Australia Joint Research Project, Kuala Lumpur and Canberra, 46 p.

Tucker, K. (1979) *Structural Determinants of the Size of the Services Sector: An International Comparison.* Canberra, Working Paper No. 4, Bureau of Industry, 32 p.

Tucker, K. (1981) *Traded Services in the World Economy.* Canberra, Working Paper No. 16, Bureau of Industry, 37 p.

Tucker, K., Seow, G. and Sundberg, M. (1983) *Services in ASEAN-Australian Trade.* ASEAN-Australia Joint Project, Kuala Lumpur and Canberra, 44 p.

Tucker, K., Seow, G. and Sundberg, M. (1984) *ASEAN-Australian Trade in Tourist Services.* ASEAN-Australia Joint Research Project, Kuala Lumpur and Canberra, 60 p.

Walter, I. (1985) *Barriers to Trade in Banking and Financial Services.* London, Trade Policy Research Centre, 123 p.

Young, D. N. (1985) *Technology Impacts on the Structure of the Insurance Industry.* Wharton School, University of Pennsylvania, Discussion Paper, No. 10, June.

Research Programmes on Services underway at:

— Management Centre	Aston University Gosta Green GB- Birmingham B4 7ET
— Dept. of Regional and Urban Planning	University College Dublin Richview, Clonskeagh Dublin 14 — Ireland
— Progress	Research Programme on the Service Economy 18, chemin Rieu CH — 1208 Geneva (Switzerland)
— CUREI	Centre Universitaire de Recherche Européenne et Internationale B.P. 47 X F-38040 Grenoble Cedex
— Institut de Recherches Economiques	Université Catholique de Louvain Place Montesquieu 3, Boîte 4 B- 1348 Louvain-la-Neuve
— CEDES	Centre de Développement et d'Echange sur les Activités de Services Economie et Humanisme 14, rue Antoine Dumont F- 69372 Lyon
— Hudson Institute	Quaker Ridge Road Croton on Hudson USA- New York N.Y. 10520
— The Institute of Financial Studies	Nottingham University University Park GB- Nottingham NG7 2RD
— CEPII	Centre d'Etudes Prospectives et d'Informations Internationales 9, rue Georges Pitard F- 75015 Paris

— INSEE

Institut National de la Statistique et des
Etudes Economiques
Boulevard A. Pinard 18
F- 75675 Paris Cedex 14

— Fishman-Davidson Centre for
the Study of the Service Sector

2102 Steinberg-Dietrich/CC
Wharton School, University of Pennsylvania
3620 Locust Walk
USA- Philadelphia, PA 19104

— Institut d'Administration des
Entreprises

Universite d'Aix Marseille
F- 13540 Puyricard

— Institut fuer
Versicherungswirtschaft

Hochschule St Gallen
Kirchlistrasse 2
CH- 9010 St Gallen

National Organizations representing Service Industries

— Lotis

Liberalization of Trade in Services
British Invisible Export Council
14, Austin Friars
GB- London EC2N 2HE

— The Swedish Coalition
of Service Industries

Tjansteforbundet
Tjansteforbundet Däbelnsgatan 64
S- 11352 Stockholm

— United States Coalition
of Service Industries

133 New Hampshire Avenue, N.W.
Suite 400
US- Washington, D.C. 20036

Intergovernmental Research Programmes on Services

— FAST

Forecasting and Assessment in the Field of
Science and Technology
European Economic Community
Square de Meeûs 8
B- 1040 Brussels

Fast sponsors studies and research programmes on services from research institutions, among which: The Technical Change Centre, London; Bureau d'Information et de Prévision Economique, Paris; Science Policy Research Unit, University of Sussex, UK; Sema-Metra, Paris; Centre for Urban and Regional Development Studies, Newcastle UK; Centre for European Policy Studies, Brussels.

— ASEAN/Australia Joint
Research Project

(Association of Southeast Asian Nations)
Research School of Pacific Studies
Australian National University
GPO Box 4
Canberra AC.T 2601 — Australia

University Courses on the Service Economy

— Professor Orio Giarini
  Graduate Institute of European Studies of
  the University of Geneva
  Villa Moynier
  122, rue de Lausanne,
  CH-1202 Geneva

— Professor Dorothy Riddle
  American Graduate School of International
  Management
  Thunderbird Campus
  USA-Glendale, Arizona 85306

International Organizations Dealing with Services

General Agreement on Tariffs and Trade
GATT
Centre William Rappard
Rue de Lausanne 154
CH- Genève 21
Tel. 310231

International Air Transport Association
IATA
P.O. Box 550
Place de l'Aviation Internationale
1000 Sherbrooke St. W
Montreal PQ H3A 2R4/Canada
Tel. (514) 844 6311

Intergovernmental Bureau for Informatics
IBI
Viale Civiltà del Lavoro 23
CP 10235
I-00144 Roma
Tel. 591 60 41

International Chamber of Commerce
ICC
38, Cours Albert Ier
F-75008 Paris
Tel. 261 85 97

International Civil Aviation Organization
ICAO
PO Box 400
International Aviation Square
1000 Sherbooke St. W
Montreal PQ H3A 2R2/Canada
Tel. (514) 285 8219

International Labour Organization
ILO
4, route des Morillons
CH- 1211 Genève 22
Tel. 99 79 52

International Monetary Fund
IMF
700 19th Street NW
Washington DC 20431/USA
Tel. (202) 477 7000

International Organization for Standardization
ISO
CP 56
Rue de Varembé 1
CH- 1211 Genève 20
Tel. 34 12 40

International Telecommunication Union
ITU
Place des Nations
CH- 1211 Genève 20
Tel. 99 51 11

International Trade Centre UNCTAD/GATT
ITC
54–56 rue de Montbrillant
CH-1202 Genève
Tel. 34 6021

Latin American Economic System
SELA
Apartado 17035
Caracas 1010/Venezuela
Tel. 324911-17

Organisation for Economic Cooperation and Development
OECD
2, rue André Pascal
F- 75775 Paris Cedex 16
Tel. 524 82 00

Pacific Telecommunications Council
PTC
1110 University Avenue, Suite 303
Honolulu Hi 96826/USA
Tel. (808) 941-3789

United Nations Centre on Transnational Corporations
UNCTC
United Nations
New York NY 10017/USA
Tel. (212) 754-3104

United Nations Conference on Trade and Development
UNCTAD
Palais des Nations
CH-1211 Genève 10
Tel. 34 60 11

United Nations Economic Commission for Europe
ECE
Palais des Nations
CH- 1211 Genève 10
Tel. 34 60 11

United Nations Economic Commission for Latin America and the Caribbean
ECLAC
Casilla 179-D
Santiago de Chile
Tel. 48 50 51

World Bank Group
1818 H Street NW
Washington DC 20433/USA
Tel. (202) 477-1234

World Intellectual Property Organisation
WIPO
Ch. Colombettes 34
CH- 1202 Geneve
Tél. 99 91 11

World Tourism Organization
WTO
Calle Capitán Haya 42
E- Madrid 20
Tél. 279 28 04

Index

295